I dedicate this Book to our first Grandchild

Farrah May Hannon

Foreword

Ailbhe as I read back over our conversations I ask myself- "Did I really write this? While the initial decision to write a memoir depicting your far too short life with us was mine- the purpose being to ensure that family members who missed out on the opportunity of getting to know you personally would have some awareness of the real you. So my plan was to write a straightforward factual portrait in words depicting your personality and physique-colour of your eyes hair, your height, your likes and dislikes, hobbies friends etc. Well "the best laid schemes of mice and men—". As soon as I put pen to paper it was as if the book took on a life of its own bringing me on a journey led by a series of surprising coincidences and memories. I became secondary. All I had to do was write the words. As we meandered along Ailbhe reflecting on aspects of your life, touching the universal themes of Family, Friends, Love, Loss,-it amazed me how incidents that previously would have seemed of little relevance assumed the greatest significance. It was mainly these little things that flooded my memory and fell on to the page- proving the old cliché "Little Things do mean a lot". The book refused to conform to my planned packaging-rejecting the linéar predictable route taking on a more unique circular mode. We never did get to explore that Big Question,-the Ultimate Question and I now accept we never will Ailbhe but I hear your gentle whisper-"Don't worry Mam. All the ultimate questions are difficult questions and these difficult questions are the most interesting". Yes Ailbhe and looking for answers can take us on exciting journeys. "OSHO" in his book "The art of living and Dying" suggests "It's not the questions that are relevant it's the Question mark". I've felt you Ailbhe as the secret agent on my shoulder directing the process. One of my favourite spiritual gurus John O'Donohue spoke of the hidden presence in absence. I'm so grateful to John and the many artists-too numerous to name (who's inspirational legacies in poetry and writing are sprinkled throughout our conversations) for their

CONVERSATIONS WITH MY DEAD DAUGHTER

Maura Hannon

ORIGINAL WRITING

Disclaimer
Should any mistakes, omissions, copyright infringements be found to have occurred I will be happy to correct same in any future editions so please bring to my notice

ISBNS
Parent : 978-1-78237-329-2
epub: 978-1-78237-330-8
mobi: 978-1-78237-331-5
PDF: 978-1-78237-332-2

A cip catalogue for this book is available from the National Library.

Published by Original Writing Ltd., Dublin, 2013.
Printed by Clondalkin Group, Glasnevin, Dublin 11

spiritual sustenance on our journey. This book is intended as a testimony to your presence in our lives-Perhaps Ailbhe it is your own un-written book. I will take personal responsibility for any shortcomings. I'll bet I've been repeating myself. That will be the old teacher in me. Old habits die hard. You'll remember the mantra-"Repition clarifies". Writing this book has been a healing journey for me. I'm grateful to you Ailbhe and the spirit guides who gently ushered me along with encouraging prompts. Thanks to family and friends who too kept nudging me on giving me the confidence to triumph my inner critic with their anticipatory question "and how is your book coming along?"
To those who read this book I hope you find the journey worthwhile, try to go easy on the author-it's her first venture and remember she is merely the Ghost Writer. Should our book make any money Ailbhe your favourite charity will be a beneficiary.

Contents

Chapter One

Reflective Meanderings

A HARD COMING YOU HAD, BUT WHAT A WELCOME!

"Something unvoiced connects us – a reality unchanged by Time"

While we were sorting out your personal belongings post your sudden, untimely death Ailbhe, it was a comforting surprise to find a collection of poems you had personally compiled. I had no prior idea as to the indepth digging you had done with your pen. But then you were an Ailbhe of surprises. The sentiment expressed in the above lines quoted from one of the poems in your collection continues to resonate a consoling definite assurance for me. Now as I put pen to paper I sense your gentle hovering presence goading me on.

It is April 2nd 2010, Friday, Good Friday as it is generally called in the western world. 63 years ago my mother, your granny was about to give birth to me. Yes, to my own amazement I'll be all of 63-years-old on April 10th or 11th. I think I told you the story. As a child I always celebrated my birthday on April 11th. I was christened Mary - plain and simple - my mother was never quite accepting of this. She talked of heavy snow in April that year. My grandparents and my father took me by horse and trap to the church. When they got there, they forgot the name my mother had selected and as my father searched for the paper on which it was written, the crusty old priest carried on quickly with the ceremony announcing dogmatically, "She is being called Mary," and so it was. Ah for the good old days when people knew their place.

My mother did insist that I be called Maura and she would seldom fail to declare this on my birthday. "I had two special names selected for you," she would say, while continuously refusing to divulge her choice despite my many requests. I have a feeling that she had chosen Margaret Ann as that is what my younger sister was christened over a year later, just a guess. My baptismal cert stated April 10th as my baptismal date, but later when I had a reason to get my official birth cert, the cert stated April 11th - work out the maths! Anyhow, I have been jokingly informed that my real birth date was April 1st and to spare me the "April fool" title they added another digit which caused the confusion.

Well according to accounts, my own birth 60 plus years ago was straight forward – a home birth. Neighbouring women helped under the watchful expertise of the local handy woman, "Kate John." My brother Gene (Eugene Michael) who was two years older than me, had I believe a more difficult entry into the world but thankfully all was well and I was followed by Margaret (Margaret Annie) and then came the youngest Seán (Seán Patrick). See I'm the only one with the single name.

Anyway, fast forward 30 years and I am expecting yourself. People found it hard to believe I was pregnant as you caused such a tiny bump - good goods. Indeed, when I was walking the corridor in the hospital the days before your birth, a neighbour came up to me and congratulated me saying, "O congrats I didn't hear you had your baby, was it a boy or a girl?"

A hard coming you had of it Ailbhe. Your brother Aonghus was a tot at home. I was hospitalised for weeks before your birth. I was heartbroken for him although Granny came and looked after him so well with Dad but there was such concern about you. Your eldest brother Aoghdhán, who was born in July 1972, had died an hour after birth - breathing problems we were told - though nothing was ever explained by anyone - how history can repeat itself - we will see later on.

Back to your arrival, I spent the weeks prior to your birth in hospital. There were some concerns about your lack of weight gain. You were born on June 19th 1977, Fathers day. Dad held you in the hospital moments after your arrival. You were so very tiny, three and a half pounds! My sister Margaret arrived, hot-footed from Dublin, held you, nearly lost her life, terrified at how little of you there was, so she quickly and nervously handed you back. She told me afterwards how she was terrified your little head would topple off, but you proved to be a hardy little bundle and there was no need for an incubator.

Your safe arrival was widely longed for and welcomed by caring family, friends and good neighbours. Visitors came and came, I still have the cards. Well wishers welcoming you from Cavan, Tipperary, England, America and Africa. Some of those nurses too were so caring, went well beyond the call of duty. Do you remember Mazie? She came out to the house to visit and support us with advice after you came home. You peed on her lap as she held you. Thanks Mazie.

A hard coming you may of had of it Ailbhe, but the Céad Míle Fáilte you got on your arrival was phenomenal. I came upon this beautifully written poem by the late great poet, philosopher and writer John O'Donohue, in the book, "Benedictus"- A book of blessings where O'Donohue through words of blessing, grace and wisdom, "helps us confront the key thresholds of our human experiences." His poem entitled "The Blessing of a Child Entering the World" imbues the hope and possibility new life can unleash.

The Blessing of a Child Entering the World

As I enter my new family,
May they be delighted
At how their kindness
Comes into blossom.
Unknown to me and them,
May I be exactly the one
To restore in their forlorn places
New vitality and promise.
May the hearts of others
Hear again the music
In the lost echoes
Of their neglected wonder.
If my destiny is sheltered,
May the grace of this privilege
Reach and bless the other infants
Who were destined for torn places.
If my destiny is bleak,
May I find in myself
A secret stillness
And tranquillity
Beneath the turmoil.
May my eyes never lose sight
Of why I have come here,
That I never be claimed
By the falsity of fear
Or eat the bread of bitterness.
In everything I do, think,
Feel and say,
May I allow the light
Of the world I am leaving
To shine through and
Carry me home.

Welcome Home

Dad bought the carrycot, (we had hesitated to do much baby buying prior to your arrival Ailbhe, something to do with not counting our chickens until they are hatched I suspect) and he arrived to take us home. Granny had everything in apple-pie order when we arrived. Katie, the housekeeper helped and Mrs. McSeaín (Bessi) our good neighbour was such a great support. Aonghus took to his new baby sister like the proverbial duck to water, so protective. You slept, ate, grew, smiled and grew stronger. The kitchen had buckets of nappies. The disposable nappies had not yet reached our radar, so it was safety-pins and washable cloth nappies. Granny was as fit as a fiddle, so delighted at your arrival, upstairs, downstairs, in and out to the clothes line. The old twin tub washing machine was a Godsend, but I do regret missing out on the disposable nappies. It seemed to be the worry of the day to get sufficient nappies properly washed and dried. The disposables would have left more quality time with you, whatever about the environmental issues. We wheeled you out on the lovely sunny days, placed your pram under a big beech tree at the front of the house with your white net over it to protect you from wasps and bees. That tree was later to become home to the family swing which gave such joy to family and visiting friends.

Yes we did have a christening ceremony. Father John Murphy who had been the celebrant at our wedding ceremony and a cousin, performed a lovely baptismal service in the house here, similar to Aonghus's. Family and friends gathered in Farranseer and a good day was had by all. Your name was now official, Ailbhe Máire. Having started with the letter A for your deceased older brother Aodhghán we kept with the A- Aonghus, Ailbhe, Aidín, Assumpta. Someone once remarked to me that when the four of you would grow up to be teenagers there would be confusion about your post (A. Hannon), which A? I don't think it was ever a problem, as e-mails and texts took over. Goes to show how it's foolish to be too concerned about the future.

Granny was a regular resident in Farranseer House during your early months. You visited Derryvella, always getting pride of place in your little cot. I remember driving down to visit one Sunday, just yourself in your little carrycot and Aonghus in the back seat with you. Dad was away. You were sleeping soundly when suddenly I felt a pull on my shoulder as Aonghus stretched forward from his baby chair. I tried to get him interested in the views from the car window, the cattle and horses in the fields, telling him it was dangerous to pull me as I was driving. He persisted, so I crossly pulled the car into the side of the road and stopped. I saw he was pointing to you in your carry cot, "She is such a good baby," I said, "sleeping quietly and letting me drive safely." But he banged on the seat saying, "No, no look Mammy." I then saw that you had been vomiting and badly needed attention. It's no wonder that you referred to him later on in life as "my great big brother."

Your beautiful sister Aidín arrived in November 1980 with her head of curls. Mags felt more confident holding her as she was a stronger little bundle. Aidín's arrival marked the arrival of Mary and Arthur into our lives. Katie had retired so we needed someone to care for our now 3 A's while we were working as teachers - no career breaks or generous maternity leave in those days. We were allowed I think just a month before birth and a month after, provided one got and paid for a suitable substitute. Europe did a lot of good in forcing our government to introduce more humane and child-centred regimes. I don't know if I ever told you Ailbhe, but I expect I did. Anyhow you no doubt were made aware of it in your Women's Studies programme which you pursued later in U.C.D.

Back then, there were two pay scales in the public sector – one for women and single men and one for married men. You can guess who got the lion's share. It was only when a husband and wife both primary teachers, took a discrimination case to Europe and won, that our government had to introduce equal pay much to the delight I might add, of most men as well as women. Yes, there were the other voices -"this would break the country" back to the old Adam and Eve. I knew one man - a teacher - who just could not countenance that we women would be paid the same salary as him (even though she had the same qualifications and did exactly the same work!) When we women got our very welcome bit of back money he insisted he got it too. Kathleen, my colleague, and myself concluded that he must have convinced the powers that be that he was bisexual.

Mary and Arthur, a retired husband and wife, came from London to live in Ireland for the fishing and soon became part of the family. Aidín became the apple of their eye, she even spoke with a slight Cockney accent at times. They were well and truly established as part of the household by the time your youngest sister Assumpta arrived and in many respects they became more Irish than the Irish themselves.

Assumpta was born on August 15th - the feast of the Assumption in the Catholic Church so we decided to go for the obvious name Assumpta - sticking with the A's. Now thanks to medical advances, Assumpta had an easy passage into the world. I was able to avail of the epidural and the birth seemed so much more civilised. Unfortunately, this was not available to me when you made your way into the world Ailbhe. It certainly was not offered to me as an option. We now had our 5 A's in the family - sounds like a good Leaving Cert result.

How much of this do you remember Ailbhe? I've often regretted that your actual birth experience was not as humane as that of your younger sisters. Ireland I think had a pretty cruel mechanistic approach to childbirth and women, which was just beginning to wane when your sisters arrived. Or was your entry into this realm of consciousness as harsh for you as it was for me? Anyhow hopefully the love you got from family and friends transcended any such misery.

We in Ireland were at that time and for many successive years bombarded with propaganda as to how we valued children and family in our so-called Republic unlike other "pagan"jurisdictions. Contraception, divorce and dare I mention it abortion, were not to be openly and freely discussed, much less available.

Since you left us Ailbhe we have had the Ryan and Murphy Reports. I got the Ryan Report from the library and sat in the porch studying each volume. I read volume five twice taking notes. I think it sort of traumatised me Ailbhe. Were you here, I'm sure that we would have had a chat about it. I also recently read the book, "The Lost Child of Philomena Lee." I would like to have been able to chat to you about these findings but maybe as our conversation here progresses we will come back and reflect on it. It does seem extraordinary to me that the reality of much of what was happening on the ground in people's lives could for so long be portrayed by those in authority in the church and state in Ireland, viewed no doubt through their hierarchical, rose-tinted glasses as morally or humanely acceptable, even commendable. Mark Patrick Hederman OSB abbot of Glenstal Abbey, Co Limerick in his book, "Underground Cathedrals" (a book I think you would have likely read or perhaps even bought as a present for me) puts it succinctly and I quote, "The Roman Catholic Church in Ireland in the twentieth century tried to fulfil this role of removing from the people their freedom and responsibility for working out their own salvation, reducing them to infantilism and treating them like children." He quotes the late John McGahern - do you remember him coming to school and speaking to you? The principal knew him personally and he very generously came and gave of his time. He was on his way to take part in a fundraiser in Dublin for the Rape Crises Centre if I remember correctly. You would have been in about fifth or sixth class, he wrote "A childishness in religion and politics and art was encouraged to last a whole life long - I think it is no simplification to state that the country was being run almost exclusively for a small Catholic middle class and its church. Those who rebelled or disobeyed instructions were ostracised. However, the other voice was kept alive by novelists who undertook to supply the other half of a dialogue which was never allowed to take place."

I remember when you told granny about John McGahern's visit to the school, she was quite delighted at how much things had progressed. She told the story of when his book "The

Barracks" was banned and Catholics discouraged from reading it. A neighbour who was a cousin of McGahern's and a returned Yank (liberated by his travels no doubt) offered her a copy to read. She was curious to find out what could be so outrageous and dangerous about a mere book so she gladly accepted. As she read the story, she found that it was not far off the mark in depicting what was a reality for many in Ireland so she wondered what the alarm was about. Later however, fear set in when she listened to some clergy man's strong disapproval. She concluded that it would not be right or lucky to keep such a book in her home. She tried to convince herself otherwise, but her sleep became disrupted and she caved in and handed back her book. We were of course in those days far too pure and holy in Ireland to accept such literature. Was it Oliver Goldsmith who said, "The most ignorant nations have always been found to think most highly of themselves."

Eventually, along came Mary Robinson as our president - (for whom you canvassed) for some "a breath of air," others, "a cold blast of wind." At last we were being challenged to question some of our own traditions. I came upon the following verse and thought it had a relevance and resonance, "Tell no man something is up young Hank something vast and new as when Moses came down from the mountain, evolution is converging the glory of man is beginning to force up a little green shoot through all the crap and crud of what's called REALITY." Author unknown to me.

You Ailbhe, missed the whole experience of giving birth. I often dream of the beautiful black-haired children yourself and Kerill spoke about having (Kerill mentioned it in the poem he wrote and read at your funeral), especially when I meet your friend Clair's lovely children. Mind you, I was quite shocked when I recently visited a friend in her local maternity hospital. The wards were so crowded, babies and mums on top of each other, nurses run off their feet, too few doing so much. I had a sizeable room all to myself while I awaited your arrival and I don't remember the wards being so crowded. What about health and safety, hygiene, the danger of infection? Thankfully much of the subservient deference seems to have disappeared but it has been replaced by a limited hospital stay. This along with a crowded ward gives mum and baby so little time to rest and bond, rushed home to face the work and responsibility that goes with a new arrival, while still quite weak. So, I think it's questionable as to whether we have made real progress. Is it back to the past, depending on extended family and good neighbours as it was over 60 years ago when I made my entry into this world? Two steps forward and one step back.

The late John O'Donohue likened birth to death in "Divine Beauty." He says, "Birth coming from a safe womb to a scary new place. Death is the leaving of a known world, forced eviction from the world and from the body." He goes onto say that, "At birth the journey here creates the traveller, the invisible becomes visible. At death the return journey recreates the traveller, the visible becomes invisible again." I sincerely hope Ailbhe that you found the welcome you got on crossing over at your death as warm and comforting as the Céad Míle Fáilte of your birth.

"The cradle rocks above an abyss and common sense tells us that our existence is but a brief crack of light between two enteritis of mystery. Although the two are identical twins, man, as a rule, vies the prenatal abyss with more calm than the one he is heading for (at some forty-five hundred heartbeats an hour." From the opening paragraph of Nabokov's – Speak Memory.

I've just received my last two lessons and assignments in the post on the correspondence course I've been doing, "Recording family history." I thought the course would help me with writing my book. So I'll get down to working on them and aiming at having the course completed for my birthday. To date the comments from my tutor have been encouraging, "Two great assignments" – "well done." You have demonstrated excellent understanding of the lessons." "Well done," I hear you say. Well done indeed, mission accomplished. My last assignment, it's ready for posting and it's just April 10th. I'll post it on Monday.

Do you remember sitting here in the computer room, on this chair working on your college assignments? "Genius at work, smell the rubber burning," you had written over the door. You never seemed stressed by deadlines or work to be done, took it all in your stride, so wise. "I'll come first, last or somewhere between first and last," you would say when at school. We'd been speaking of books and birth, well guess what? I came across a book you used for one of your assignments. It has markings (showing relevant sections) in your handwriting. I remember you giving it to me with a second book that Aonghus had brought back from India and suggesting that I read both. Strange to say both books turned up the other day. I started reading and just could not put it down, one is called 'Unveiling India' by Aness Jung and the other is entitled 'May you be the mother of a Hundred Sons' by Elizabeth Bumiller. The first is such a poignant ode to the struggle of the women of India to break free from the ties of tradition, caste, religion and ritual. You had highlighted the following sentence, "The whole birth experience for these women not to mention the social exclusion they faced if they failed to give birth (preferably to sons) I found disturbing." I expect you did too Ailbhe. "The Banjara women who wandered through villages and broke stones on the high road would just spread out their wide mirror skirt and deliver babies.....children died as naturally as they were born. When a child came they rejoiced without ceremony and when it died there was no mourning. To celebrate a joy or dwell on a pain takes time, money and food?! Perhaps not terribly far removed from the experiences of some Irish women in the not so distant past.

I remember an elderly midwife telling me how she went around on her bicycle to houses in her catchment area to assist at home births – then the norm, she could be called out at any time day or night. She said she had often prayed following the delivery of a baby in an already over-crowded, poor family that her visit would end the need for her service in that particular house. No question of contraception in holy Ireland then. How she often detected a sombre relief on the part of parents when she delivered a dead baby, relief at not having that extra mouth to feed. But then there was the added scare that their gorgeous little offspring (if it died unbaptised) would be denied entry to heaven and so destined for Limbo for eternity. I'm sure glad you escaped that type of suppression and barbaric belief system. I wish that I had read the book while you were with us, so that I could have discussed it with you.

Speaking of India, it's a pity Ailbhe you never had the opportunity to meet up with your cousin on dads' side. She was born in London and graduated from Oxford as a lawyer, no doubt on the crest of a prestigious lucrative career. But she turned her back on it all and has spent all her working life living and working in India for the poor, fighting legal battles in the courts with the many multinational companies in an effort to get a humane deal for the native poor workers. Aonghus marvelled at how he saw her work ceaselessly from dawn to dusk when he visited her and her husband, full of admiration he was. She has lived with the native poor, very frugal no luxuries and she even speaks with an Indian accent! Motivated solely by humanitarian principles, she professes no religious leanings at all, but then is not the true testament of all religions. Humanity at its best.

She would have found as John O Donohue said in verse four of the poem I've already quoted, "The Blessing of a child entering the World" that her "destiny was 'sheltered'" and she is sure "using the grace of this privilege to reach and bless others who are destined for torn places." Hopefully as verse five suggests, "those whose destiny is bleak may find in themselves a secret stillness and tranquility beneath the turmoil." Indeed the stories of the lives of many of the women recorded in your book 'Unveiling India', the accounts of their dignified, patient courage in challenging the vested interests whose greed for wealth and control would keep them forever shackled, is a glorious testament to all those who dedicate their time to working with the marginalised of society enabling them to seek liberation, justice and equality in an often times hostile and dangerous environment. I can well imagine Ailbhe, how your kind heart bled for these poor women as you read of their desperate circumstances as many sought to escape from the restricting influences of Purdah, often risking death. I find the statement "risking death" strange, as if death was the most outrageous outcome. Perhaps death was a release.

You've had the experience Ailbhe. It's not an experience any of us have had. We do not know what it is like from the other side, as no one has come back to explain what actually happens. Shakespeare in Hamlet refers to death as the "undiscovered country." Since I was with you at your death, I can tell you now Ailbhe, I no longer fear death. Yes dying can be scary alright but actual death for me, no. I do believe there are much worse things than death, such as pain and long suffering, but I do sometimes wonder if you were scared Ailbhe. Should we have talked more about death? Would that have helped you? I spoke recently about a book on death that I was reading to a nurse who works with the terminally ill. She said she would not like to think of death at all as it would be far too sad for her to contemplate her wonderful life being written off by it. I felt so sad for you. That's how it was for you. Your great young life snatched from you. I can but hope you had the internal insight to deal with any great sense of loss you felt.

I've just watched a documentary on the Magdalen laundries, where not a hundred years ago, the Irish state, and Catholic Church colluded in the incarceration of poor Irish girls, treating them like slaves, no pay, no freedom and now they have to fight tooth and nail to have their voices heard. No politician or church representative was available to appear on the programme. I remember passing a convent with you in the car. You were quite young. You said that the people who lived in that house must have been rich. Well it's no wonder so many of them have these fine places, the money they made on the backs of these poor girls. Where was their nice clean Christian conscience or rather where was their humanity?

Mary Rafferty's "The Darkest Corner No Escape" was staged in the Abbey. It was based on the Ryan report, (an investigation into the care of children in religious run institutions in Ireland). I was tempted to go and see it but having read the report I felt it would be too emotionally upsetting. Yes, as I already told you, I took out all five volumes of that report from the library and sat in the front porch reading and taking notes. During the hearings and indeed often in debate I hear leaders, of the clergy and others argue that the church authorities' response to allegations of abuse needs to be set in the context of the time rather than assessed from a late 20th or early 21st century context. Surely as human beings we know that in any era some things are always utterly wrong and child abuse is one of them. Yes, the Ryan report truly gutted me Ailbhe. We were so lucky as children to have escaped those places. I thought if my mother or father had become ill, hit very hard times or had died. we could have ended up in one of those hell holes. I'd opt for death any day. "So why were you so surprised at the stories in 'Unveiling India'?" I hear you ask. We sure have our own unveiling to do.

Do you remember Sister as we called her? She was grannies only sister who entered the convent (now sounds strange) as a young girl and became a nun. She spent most of her life in convents in America. She visited us on occasions. We were all very fond of her and she of us. She took a great interest in you, the family and the extended family and she prayed for all and helped in any way she could. When she entered the convent to become a nun she was not allowed home for years. When her father died she was on a retreat in the convent and was not told about the death until the retreat ended. She was not allowed home for the funeral. My mother told me how she missed having a sister around especially when she was having her children. She appreciated the prayers and the help sister gave, but their life experiences were so different that she always felt a gulf between them. Her own mother (my granny) (your great-granny) would advise her continuously to mind her health for the sake of her children. She would warn her, "I'm getting old, your sister is a nun and God help any child that would be left dependent on the likes of them?!" I've often wondered as did my mother how she came to that conclusion. It seemed quite out of step with the thinking of the time. My mother was so angry when the child abuse scandals started to emerge, she instructed me to refuse to give money to any catholic organisation until they sold all they possessed and shared it all out among those abused children, now adults of course. "Can't those religious and clerics live on the old age pension as many of us do?" she said or, "you'll not have to look too far to find a deserving person yourself to give help to."

I have the feeling that you would not be that shocked at the abuse revelations. You always expressed suspicion of institutions, particularly religious institutions. You believed that the protection of the ego and image of the institution would always take precedence over serving the needs of those for whom they were established. So you belived that, "no religious order should be in charge of any of these caring institutions - let them come in and serve but never hand over control to them." You felt that their obedience and first duty would always be to their superiors whose authority they were convinced, came from God. How did you conclude this at such a young age Ailbhe? Mark Patrick Hederman, the abbot of Glenstal abbey addresses the dangers inherent in the Catholic Churche's elevation and promotion of "poverty, chastity obedience" in his book "Underground Cathedrals." What kind of monstrous God were we been presented with by these self appointed conduits of Christianity? They were and still are to a large extent projecting their own crippled sick selves on to a screen they call God. I am so glad that you avoided the fear and guilt that blighted the lives of so many. The hell fire bellowing and sermons on sex, divorce, contraception and abortion bemused rather than frightened you. I suppose we your parents can take a bow here - a modest one, in that I think we provided a pretty liberal atmosphere where opinions were thrashed out and freely discussed. My mother would often quote Thomas Davis, "Educate that you may be free." I always emphasised the importance of doing your own thinking or as John O'Donohue said,"Never give your thinking over to anyone or anything outside yourself."

Then your study of psychoanalysis I expect ignited an awareness and enlightenment for you, but the depth and wisdom you had reached in a mere 26 years still astonishes me. I hope I'm not portraying you as a solemn old head on young shoulders, Ailbhe. Nothing could be further from reality. You were so young, fun-loving, gregarious, yet always caring, principled and discerning. I remember having a conversation with mum's sister (the nun) when you were a baby about some scandals in the Catholic Church, mild scandals compared to what has since emerged. I voiced my disquiet at how I felt the Vatican had covered up in an effort as I saw it, to protect its image - she nervously hushed me up, stressing that we should never allow such knowledge into the public arena as to do so would give rise to a greater scandal - that of damaging the credibility of our church and weakening people's faith. She would refer to Catholic priests as "God's holy anointed." Since you left us Ailbhe we continue to reap the awful legacy of such thinking. I was impressed to find you had written in bold capitals on one of your diary pages the old cliché ,"For evil to triumph it's enough that good people stay silent."

I tend to look back more in sorrow at sister's life than anything else. Oh yes, she would claim fulfilment and certainly there was no pressure on her from her parents to follow this path - quite the contrary. But there was such fear and extreme conformity in how she lived, safe I suppose and sheltered from much of the rough and tumble of normal life, but at what price? For such a highly-intelligent, educated, strong women the confinement and circumscribed nature of her life must have given rise to feelings of twartedness and frustration. It was more the way she, fundamentally a caring, open-minded, enquiring person would revert into this cocoon of fearful submission to what she called, "wiser minds than mine" when questions arose that were uncomfortable for her. That saddened me. She did welcome what she saw as the liberating influences of Vatican II. But there was always this non-negotiable undercurrent belief that her primary duty was to preserve the good name of the Catholic Church at whatever cost. Much more awareness of this mentality and its consequences have become evident from the various actions, inaction and cover ups that keep emerging as to how the various abuse allegations were handled, by the powers that be in the Catholic Church. Was it from your study of psychoanalysis or an innate wisdom that led you to conclude at such a young age the necessity to maintain a healthy transparent accountability from all institutions? Now you most certainly were not anti-cleric or anti-religious (admired the work of many). You were quite spiritual in an open tolerant circular way, I would say. However, I do remember how strongly you felt on this. Religious orders will always claim to have their God on side and their obedience, you claimed, was disastrous. This obedience to their superiors whom they saw as God's representive would always take precedence. You were all for religious orders coming and working in our institutions but never controlling them. It's really only in recent years since you left us and the explosion of information on the hidden scandals in the church that I, now in my sixties, am thinking through and genuinely reflecting on such.

"Horses for courses" they'd always say in
the deep and serious tone of the living dead.
Young heart strings were severed prepared
for their fate of a dreamless, lifeless prewritten
state. I told myself this for many a year, believed
those death tones that bellowed in my ears.
Was I not then as pathetic as they though
I'm proud to say while I might not own my
yesterdays I own my today.
I've chanced all courses and lost and won the
important thing is the rules have
been overcome The legacy no longer passed on
from Mother to daughter
or father to son.
Today's horses live with unbolted doors.

by Ailbhe Hannon Dunne

They'll never see the things you
see and
only dream of being the
way you'll be.
What they search for is what
you've got, that's
why they'll claim you've
lost the plot. They have to try,
by quoting books, despotic theories,
academic crooks. You see
answers with your eyes.
Questions you ask they'll
ignorantly despise.
Answers lost in hungry yearning, no
soul thrives through such learning.
A blind less look, A blind
less stare can
easily uncover all that's there.
What you belittle is
what they fear.
They'll cloud your
judgement unless you steer clear.

by Ailbhe Hannon Dunne

I came across an interesting article in the Messenger magazine - you'd remember the little red Catholic booklet Mrs. Brady distributed in school for years and how you would all want to be postmen delivering them to the various houses. Well I took over their distribution after she retired and made a quick copy of the article. I think it was published some months before your death. We had a conversation about this and I remember you saying how you agreed, Indeed, I heard Aidín quote you recently as saying you failed to see what all the disagreements and fussy complicated interpretations of Christianity were about when, "Jesus was most likely just an ordinary kind person." I hope I do the article justice, as I jotted it down quickly and at the best of times my handwriting never merited compliment, I beg forgiveness if I do a disservice to its author. Anyway here goes, From Jesus Family Life James McPolin S.J.

Published in The Sacred Heart Messenger Feb.2002.

Jesus was an ordinary layman with no special credentials or power base. He would have seemed at first negligible to the high priestly families in Jerusalem until he began to appear dangerous. He was a Galilean nobody on a collision course with the Jerusalem Priesthood. He was a charismatic wonder worker in conflict with the priests who were very concerned about preserving the central institutions of their religion. Jesus conducted his ministry as a Jewish layman and died a Jewish layman.

"That Jesus was a layman was not just a neutral datum. It played a role in the drama of his life and death. The image of high priest we owe to a writer of the first century - the author of the epistle to the Hebrews." Has religion hijacked Jesus Ailbhe? You certainly exuded great liberated humane spirituality. Thankfully you never allowed a hierarchical image of God projected by the rigid authoritarian structures of a religion which had kept previous generations in meek submission - reducing Christianity to a particular narrow code of practice to colonise your mind. I remember shopping with you in Cavan on a Christmas Eve - you were in about third year in secondary school. The town was buzzing, queues in every shop we visited. There was at that time a shop opposite the Post Office with the name The Christian Bookshop written over its entrance in big bold lettering. We climbed the stairs and went in. To my surprise, we were its only customers. We were greeted by a very pleasant lady and we admired some of the bric-a-brac. As we left our oasis, facing again into the crowded streets of seasonal shoppers. I voiced my surprise as to why this nice shop was not attracting some of the many shoppers in town and you replied,

"It is a lovely shop inside but if they want to get people in they should change its name. Not many people would go into a shop with the name "The Christian Book Shop."

"Why?" I enquired

"You know what people would think with a name like that," you quickly replied.

"What would they think?" I asked.

"Ah, all priests and religion and holy Joes," you answered.

I remember at the time thinking how awful - what have we done to the message of Jesus. But reflecting on it now, I can see how the Holy Spirit was secretly at work. I would now compliment the courage of many of your generation in challenging and breaking loose from a repression that previous generations had bowed to, while some people today bemoan all this as the secularisation of society and an attack on religion. I welcome it and I would contend that secularisation rather than leading to an end to spirituality is opening up to a new understanding and experience of God working in the world. You Ailbhe simply regarded Jesus as a true friend and was it St. Teresa who said that she, "found God among her pots and pans." You always had such empathy for the marginalised in society Ailbhe. Aidín reminded me of how you would say of people we referred to as autistic, "These people are probably the most real and nicest of people." When you went to hospital aged eleven to have your kidney removed you made friends with a young man with special needs called Gabriel whom you supported, talked with and included him as a friend. It seemed to mean a lot to him and indeed to his very dedicated mother. Shortly after you left hospital you got a letter from Gabriel's mum saying he had died and thanking you for your friendship and support to him.

Strangely when you started in Loreto College, the class you were allotted to for your five years there was Saint Gabriel's. I wonder have you met up again - yourself and Gabriel. On July 8th 2002 as you neared your last breath Aidín was the bus on her way home from work in A.I.B in the I.F.S.C to Castleknock. She said how she felt very down and a terrible weight of sadness fell on her. A little down syndrome boy on the bus started banging on the window and some passengers expressed annoyance at this. She said she could hear your voice in her head repeating, "God you know they are some of nicest people" and how she felt such empathy towards him. When she got to her flat, news had reached her housemates that she was to rush to the hospital. One of her housemates kindly drove her there. The song, "Last Breath" was played on the car radio as they approached the hospital. The day before had been that famous world cup day. The staff in the office where she worked were all interested so they took time out to watch the match on TV while Aidín stayed and manned the phones alone - (Aidín was never a keen follower of football). You rang her from the hospital. You were feeling totally fed up. Aidín had had the test done to see if she would be suitable kidney match and had offered to give you one of her kidneys. You had a long, long chat. Strangely she said not even one call came to interrupt your chat - most unusual - you told her how much you appreciated her offering you one of her kidneys and Aidín assured you that she was delighted to do it.

"If I had a burst tyre and you had a spare wouldn't you give me your spare?" Aidín said.

You both had a great laugh and Ailbhe you sure had a hearty laugh. Aidín said how then there was a silence and you said, "Aidín I love you" and she replied "and I love you" - your last words to each other as she wrote in her poem.

"Ailbhe" written by your sister Aidín.

It was like life was the sight of chocolate cake, when I had no appetite until... "The day you died I was on the bus after work, I didn't yet know...and there was a little Down syndrome boy banging a bottle off the window and singing to himself. Other people were kinda irritated but I liked it cause I remembered you saying to me "they're probably some of the nicest people in the world." I'd gone for a test a few days before to find out would I be a suitable kidney donor, you asked me was I sure I'd do it if I was a match? I said if I had two tyres and you had a puncture of course I'd give you a tyre. You said but what if you got a puncture. I was frivolous cause I knew if you had part me I'd still be okay. We named your dialysis machine Kivin for the laugh, and we did laugh, you died and we never did find out if I were a suitable match. I do think of you when I'm looking through celebrity magazines, at the fashion, best and worst dressed. I nearly turn to you and take off slating all their bland, ridiculously expensive attire as we so often did.

I look at my own face you bequeathed it to me, always with the quibble "not just as pretty." At your anniversary some people looked at me and said "Ah God, she'll never be dead" and now cause of you neither will I. When I see frogs I smile at them, cause you said once you were fond of frogs cause nobody really appreciated them. Assumpta and I would often slag your "frog eyes" that I was secretly jealous of. When I see people at their showcase weddings I plan to have one like yours. You wore a pair of your old brown boots up the aisle with your white dress. When I meet someone and I hear their mobile ring I giggle at our conclusion that peoples mobile tone sound like their theme tunes. Sometimes when I'm listening to my mp3 playing, I realise I've downloaded songs you used to like without even thinking.

I buy clothes now and when I lose an item for a split second I wonder did you nick it cause I know you'd pinch and wear them and I'd be mad but flattered.

When I'm worried about something and obsessing, I remember you saying to me "Oh Aidín you worry about stuff that doesn't even exist." God it is such a relief to say that to myself. When I walk around Crown Alley in Dublin I remember you bringing me and mum there years ago and you bribed mum into buying you an expensive pair of black-laced tank girl boots. You never wore them out and now I do.

When I'm stuck on the 130 bus in city rush hour traffic I say to myself like you used to "Jaysus it's like something out of Hard Times."

The memory of meeting you on Grafton Street, we going to a cafe, I had no appetite but you insisted on buying us both a large slice of chocolate cake. I sat there looking at it and you said to me "Go on you know you want to," so I devoured every crumb like you did life.

Mum told me that after you died she used to go all round the house looking for you. When she retrieved your wedding dress from your flat she smelt it for you, you probably never knew how much she loved you and I didn't until now, how much she loves us all. I read one of your poems about your husband "the strongest of silent men" you called him and since you died he hasn't said much but he can still laugh at a joke.

The last words you said to me "I love you" I said it too, but I was shocked cause we rarely said that in our family back then but since you died we do. I make sure I say it all the time. It is the most important sentence in the English language you must have known that and now cause of you I do.

I found Aidín's reference to your fondness for frogs quite poignant as I too remember when you said how you felt for frogs as they were mostly ignored. The year after your death, on your birthday I was putting together a group of poems for my class on the theme, "Our Favourite Animals through Poetry." I must admit the frog never crossed my mind but to my amazement when I randomly opened a book of poems to prepare my lesson and make my selection, a poem entitled "The Frog" appeared in front of me. I immediately thought of your stance and decided it would be given pride of place in the lesson. I said nothing of course of your regard for the frog. However when I went back to visit the class after my retirement the class teacher told me that the class were anxious to recite a favourite poem for me, guess what they all recited off by heart "The Frog" and they included a copy in the goodbye retirement card they gave me.

The Frog by Hilaire Belloc
Be kind and tender to the frog
And do not call him names,
As 'slimy skin' or 'polly-wog',
Or likewise 'ugly James',
Or 'Billy Bandy-knees',
The frog is justly sensitive
To epithets like these.

No animal will more repay
A treatment kind and fair,
At least so lonely people say
Who keep a frog (and by the way
They are extremely rare)

The frog gets a mention too in the following poem titled 'Ailbhe' Written by Aidín.

Ailbhe

Big eyes, pudgy cool cheeks,
Chewed nails, a smell of lived in skin,
Crisps and frogs and fags,
Sprawling boxes of cheap jewellery,
A pair of jeans, a t-shirt,
With a star on, big bubbly runners,
Sharp, angel clean, Padre Pio,
Lady of Lourdes "Love"
A favourite and final word.

Chapter 2

Caterpillar To Butterfly

Well Alli you seem to have grown up so quickly, off to primary school, nine years there, five years in secondary plus five in university but I'd suspect you would claim that it was the University of Life that gave you your real education, the interacting with peers plus of course your considerable travel experience. Now the child abuse reports woke me up to the realisation of how relatively lucky you and your siblings were in having an affirming early life experience. Then again, I'm wondering if you were here sitting at this table writing about your childhood, what experiences and memories might jump on to the page. I've mentioned wheeling you out, you sitting in your pram under the magnificent beech trees at the front of the house, these trees later home to the family swing, the playroom with all your toys, little tea sets, teddies. Your tiny red bike, riding down to visit your friend Paula and telling me how much you enjoyed the cool breeze on your face as you cycled along. Visits to Derryvella, Tipperary, your neighbours, the Duignan's, McKeowns, Paula and your cousins coming to the birthday parties. Later friends from school and of course your pony club friends, who came on sleepovers bringing the ponies with them and how you would all ride off or do a round or two of the cross-country jumps at the house.

You'd remember your loyal friend Clair, now married with three beautiful children, who talk about you and visit your grave. She named her eldest girl Chloe Ailbhe. It was so strange how Clair rang the hospital the morning of July 8th (your last morning with us), she was very anxious to talk to you. The nurse told you Clair was on the phone and as she and I encouraged you to take the call, I noticed a great sadness come over you and you just could not face it. I've since wondered if perhaps you had a premonition of what was approaching. John O'Donohue, in his book 'Divine Beauty' suggests that for the person dying there may be extreme sadness at leaving the world,

"In our tradition the loneliness of death is usually described with reference to those around the death bed and the heartbreak that death brings. Yet for the one dying how lonely it must be to lose the world." Hope you did not find it too difficult Ailbhe? I desperately hope that the wishes expressed by John ODonohue in his poem "For The Dying" was the reality for you - that death came "gently towards you, leaving you time to make your way through the cold embrace of fear to the "place of inner tranquillity" and that your spirit felt the surge of true delight "when the veil of the visible was raised, and you glimpsed again the living face of departed family and friends."

It is nine years to the day since we sadly and reluctantly took your beautiful young body to Coronea Church for your funeral service and burial in the graveyard there under the majestic ancient Bruce Mountain. I'm reliably informed that Bruce Mountain is 350 million years old. What memories it must hold and what a noble backdrop it provides for the graveyard which had become the resting place of your older brother Aodhghan, who died in infancy and now was to be home to your beautiful young body.

When the day arrived and we had to take you to the church for burial, Kerill was like fiddlers elbows, in and out of the house all agitated and distracted. Then out of the blue I noticed an unexpected calm and control had come over him. He called me privately and said, "Look what I've just found" holding up a tiny battered dirty toy teacup which he said was just peering up at him in a wild unmanicured space at the side of the house. He said he had been pleading to you all morning to send him a sign that you were happy. He could hardly believe his eyes when he saw this little cup peering up at him. He then remembered you telling him how you buried your toy tea set there for the fairies. You also told him that you saw a fairy on two occasions but that he would never see one. That space where Kerill found the toy cup had as I said remained uncultivated and wild. I remember you saying, "Don't tidy that space - leave it natural." I have since learned that there was a Celtic belief that fairies were the guardian angels of nature and that they liked these wild undeveloped spaces. Well for better or worse Ailbhe, we did not follow your instruction. The space is now neat and trim and manicured to perfection. I did apologise to the fairies. One of the poems you liked dad to recite when you were young was "Up the airy mountain, down the rushy glen..." So perhaps Ailbhe you've been dancing with the fairies. You would sure be a beautiful fairy queen. Anyhow we have kept the toy cup and it is indeed very precious.

Remember Trevor your pet cat? When you were doing your Leaving Cert exam he was such a comfort to you, not that you got stressed, too wise, you were able to take it all in your stride. But I do remember you stroking and nursing him as you revised. Do you remember the other cats and when the kittens were born in the loft and you enquired on first seeing them, "Where is the father. Why isn't he here?" Well our cat family has increased and multiplied. Since you left us Aidín has found great comfort in her magnificent tom cat Felix. He was such a comfort to her when she was unwell, a life saver she would claim. And yes, he has even made it into the realm of poetry! We now have charge of Assumpta's twin cats too, Izzie and Phoenix. Town life did not agree with them so they have taken up residence here, plus our outdoor cat Aine, making at the moment a grand total of four. You made sure to get a good home for Trevor when you were leaving for college in Dublin - remember?

I'll bet you'd mention the two faithful dogs you grew up with Bánín and Sioda and how they looked after each other in their old age. Dusty the Alsatian was a bit scary but very protective of family and home. When he died you would remember us getting Jack. We were on our way from one of your checkups in the hospital and we collected him from his owner, a lady in Finglas who tearfully handed him over to us because of her changed circumstances. Jack too became a much loved and loyal family dog. It sure could never have dawned on us that Jack would outlive you Ailbhe. He lived to be a ripe old age. On the night he died, Aonghus and Michelle, heard three dog barks from their apartment in Edinburgh. As this was most unusual they went to investigate but found no evidence of a dog in the vicinity.

Next day they got the news from home that Jack had died the night before at about the time they heard the three barks. We now have our three dogs Tobie, Frankie and Sam, all with their own personal histories and personalities. What memories would you have of the caravan holidays, forest park, the bike rides, Tipperary, Corlough, your first trip aboard when your aunt Mags (who has since joined you R.I.P) took yourself and Aonghus as young teenagers on a tour of Europe? Very brave of her to head off with two teenagers but I suspect it's one thing she never regretted, a rewarding and memorable experience for all three and it certainly whet both your appetites for travel.

Would you recall your delight at being the first in the house to discover our first newborn foal? In fact today being a glorious sunny day I'm writing sitting on the veranda in full view of the paddock where you stood that morning having left your bed at dawn to make the discovery and joyfully proclaim to the sleeping house hold "We have a new foal." You started your riding on our now deceased angelic Daisy as all four of you did; a real treasure was our Daisy. Then you graduated to Comfy, and then Blackie (Aonghus' ring master). You'd be sure to remember Breffni who I'm glad to say is still with us, blind in one eye (you'd remember the accident) but enjoying a well-earned happy retirement while acting as a good role model for our latest arrival, Assumpta's foal, Iona and her horse Woody.

Have I left any out? The sleepovers I've already referred to when Clair and your other pony-club friends would arrive - ponies in toe, stable here for a few nights and off you'd all go on a hack. Then every summer you went to pony camp - made many friends, had a lot of fun, competed well. Those caravan holidays -Tipperary forest park and all the cycling you did - remember the Aran Islands and how proud you were of the long cycle you did to Dun Aonghus?

You started primary school at just gone four years. It all seems just like a flash now. You did a short stint in Bruskey N.S. - yourself and Aonghus - due to an unwritten rule -thanks to a brain wave on the part of the Rev – chairman of the School Board of Management. The numbers in the school where I taught were increasing and the school was due an extra teacher. But his reverence had a problem with money being spent on facilities for school children and did not want to build the classroom required or indeed in any way modernise the school - not entirely unusual for chairs of Boards of Managements of the time. Indeed a good book could be written on same. Anyway his bright idea was that as few children as possible would be allowed start school in Scoil Mhuire that year and no children from outside the parish would be accepted. We lived in the neighbouring parish and as I was far from flavour of the month with the said Reverend, I knew that no exception would be made for me. So having started Aonghus in Bruskey N.S. you then joined him as a temporary measure. It was the most convenient way travel-wise and the teachers there, our friends Owen the principal and Evelyn, his wife and class teacher agreed to collect both of you from me on my way to work and take you back to the crossroads - the agreed collection point in the evening. You found the school day so tiring at the start that Dad and I often felt guilty that we started you off too young, But then you were so keen to start and once there you did seem to enjoy the comraderie of it all. It was difficult for us to then change tack but definitely with the benefit of hindsight I'd advise not starting so young - hope you can forgive us.

After your year in Bruskey, circumstances had changed in Scoil Mhuire Lacken where I taught and yourself and Aonghus moved to Scoil Mhuire to the caring competent care of Mrs Brady -who taught you both in infants and first. You then moved to my class and spent three years with me in second, third and fourth class. I loved having you in class and you did not show any signs of having any difficulty with mum as teacher but then we never got the chance to discuss it Ailbhe. I did discuss it with your other siblings to some extent since and found that they did find it difficult at times having mum teach them even though they have very positive happy memories of Scoil Mhuire. So perhaps you were relieved to move on to the principal Kevin Foley's room and to get away from me.

There is one incident from your primary school years that stood out in my mind. It was coming up to confirmation day for sixth class. As was customary then, the bishop would visit the school if confirmation was in the parish. It was our school parish's turn. You were in high infants, Mrs Brady your teacher happened to be off sick and her class was shared out to the other two rooms. Your class joined mine in the prefab so I had wall-to-wall children in the old prefab as we awaited the visit of the bishop. You requested the "An bhfuil cead agam dul amach?" translated as "Can I go to the toilet?" I responded with the obvious Tá (yes).

At the time the toilet facilities were dry toilets at the top of the school yard (thank goodness for the more proactive Board of Management and Parents Councils of today who keep an eye and an ear to see that school childrens legitimate rights and needs are met. Power to the parents I say in these areas. At that time practically every family in school with us had running water and flush toilets at home, yet many in charge of schools saw these primitive conditions as acceptable standards for schools. Well his lordship, in his flowing floor length robes arrived while you were spending a penny. You arrived back to class to me as he was doing his quick dash around the room shaking hands with each child as he enquired "What is your name"?

You entered the room, stopped, watched his performance for a few seconds, looked at me, and asked "Mammy is that the bishop?

I replied "yes" and you responded "why is he wearing women's clothes"?

Out of the mouth of babies - you made many friends in Lacken School. I'm afraid to start naming, as I'd leave someone out.

You'd remember the birthday parties. I wonder if you'd remember the fascination with shoes that you had from very early on Ailbhe. You'd come home from school when in early primary having swapped shoes with one of your friends. When Aonghus was preparing for his first communion we went to Longford to buy the style. You got your outfit - a nice blue and white dress- I can still see it in my mind's eye the Cavan G.A.A colours but what gave you most joy was the tiny pair of black patent shoes. You just loved them. You would peep into the box at them on the way home making sure they were real. We came home - sorted things out, had something to eat and got into our regular routines. To our alarm sometime later, you were missing - plus the shoes. We called and searched, but there was no response. Then it dawned on me that you might have taken off to the main road as you had mentioned how you liked the sound your shoes made on the floor and that they would be great on tarmacadam. The thought nearly paralysed me with fear as you would have had to walk up our avenue, out the lane and on to the main road where there was a dangerous busy crossroads to negotiate. This was a journey none of you would at that stage have ever taken alone. With my heart in my mouth I rang McKeirnans - neighbours who lived at the cross enquiring if perhaps they had seen you. Ann answered and responded "Yes, Ailbhe is here she came to show us her new shoes. When I collected you, you said how you just wanted to hear the "dick dock" sound your shoes would make on the tarmacadam and as we had no tarmacadam at the house you decided to travel to where there was some. The shoes were christened "the dick dock shoes" and I hope they brought you much pleasure.

Later when you were at university in Dublin myself and Aidín met up with you and you introduced us to Crown Alley - (a place you loved). You charmed me into buying you this pair of lace-up boots. I remember afterwards on my way home thinking - Ailbhe will have to be up out of her bed an hour earlier if she is to get these boots laced up and make college in time. Aidín makes reference to this in one of her poems "Ailbhe" when I walk around Crown Alley in Dublin I remember you bringing me and mum there years ago and you bribed mum into buying you an expensive pair of black-laced tank girl boots, you never wore them so I rooted them out and now I do".

Then Ailbhe, we went on our last shopping outing in Cavan town, the week before you died, when you had a week off work which you spent with us as Kerill had to go down south for a few days on work-related business. With hindsight what a blessing that was for me. Yourself and myself set off shopping in Cavan. Remember you bought a long black cardigan and a black skirt for work. We visited practically all the shops in town, as the ad says shopped until we were about to drop – we had a lovely time. Red-laced flat shoes were very much in vogue and again you were smitten but felt it unwise to indulge due to financial constraints. Despite your weariness, you were so keen to see Paula your friend who worked in town and you insisted on going to where she worked to say "Hello." I can still see the two of you automatically locking in a total embrace as soon as your eyes met. Paula told me afterwards that she just did not want to let you go - a week later she was at your funeral. When you said goodbye to Paula I decided to heck with poverty and we went back to the shoe shop where I did buy you the red shoes and you were delighted. On the way home you told me how one of the doctors you knew in the hospital had been wearing a similar pair of red shoes when you last were in and how you had remarked to him, "Next time you see me I'll be wearing your shoes." Sure enough at the end of the week when I accompanied you to hospital for your check-up, you wore your new red shoes and as we walked up the corridor we happened to bump into the said doctor who remarked, "And you did get the shoes Ailbhe".

Well sadly you never got to wear your new long cardigan and pretty black Celtic skirt. I wore your cardigan at your wake. Aidín took charge of the skirt - still wears it on occasions and has great warmth and regard for it. We put the red shoes on you when you died, along with the long Celtic dress you had for your post-wedding wear. They were your going away outfit Ailbhe.

Recently I met a lady who claimed to have psychic powers. She knew nothing of me or my background. She told me she could see various people dear to me who had passed on. Initially she said the information wasn't very clear, but later she saw a youngish person with a younger child by the hand, both had passed on young – they were extremely happy - something came through about annoyance and questions around the circumstances of the death of this young person but she was to tell me they have no concerns about that now, to tell me that I was a good mother. These were the messages she was to pass on. Then the lady started banging her feet on the floor, "This person," she said "is doing this with her shoes - they are shiny black children's shoes, I don't know what religion you are but they are the type of shoes Catholic girls wear for first communion." This person says, "The shoes - you will understand" and I did.

Through school you remained a pleasant content, lovable, academically middle of the road child. Middle of the road was a term we used to describe children who presented as balanced, sensible students but not necessarily the most competitive. I remember you saying as a child when taking part in a race, "Sure someone has to come last - what difference." I can now happily say, with my hand on my heart, that we never over-pushed or got over-anxious about the academics so long as you stayed on board. Ours was not a home where hours of homework was encouraged for young children. I personally think that so many children have their childhoods blighted by an over-anxiety about school exams and narrow academic achievement. Our aim for all four of you was that you be given the opportunity as far as we could to reach your full potential - be it practical, academic or a mix of both and that you would all be able to enjoy a good, broad, liberal education acknowledging that the university of life is where the real education takes place.

While happy to see you do your bit of homework we were equally anxious that you have plenty of free time and opportunity for playtime and leisure time with your friends, pet animals plus your own "me" time. A philosophy which I think you yourself followed. "In life there is no winning and no losing only the taking part and getting better," expresses it well. I was always aware of the limitations of the poor "educated fool." So fun roundedness and an open questioning mind and healthy competition were encouraged in Farranseer - happily none of our four A's in adulthood would equate with the bleak plight of "the achiever" so poignantly expressed in Pat Ingoldsby's poem

"The Achievers Lament" published in his amusing evocative book of poems entitled "Poems so fresh and so new.....yahoo."

"I can specify quantify classify verify modify but I don't know how to talk to my children - I can motivate dictate update delegate activate but I don't know how to talk to my children. I can rationalise decimalise analyse capitalise marginalise but I don't know how to talk to my children".

A Fly on the Wall

A fly on the wall laughed out loud and said
"You people are all mad in the head,
there in your cages surrounded by pretty
things you waste your lives
thinking your living like
kings-your car
outside and huge big telly ensure you're
trapped just like a fly in jelly.
It may smell sweet as it appeals to
your greed but
it will close around you and disallow
you to breathe
Smart flies like me, we have our fun as we puke on
your folly-living our lives from the inside out.
Now you may think we're worthless but live
no doubt you'll discover what's worthless
and tis you'll get some fright.

People flock as they always will
Individuality makes them awkward and unstill,
Words of sorrow and sympathy floating
In the air like a threatening bee,

Suddenly in the click of a switch I feel
uncomfortable-a relentless itch.
Leave me alone, go way
I'm still the same person I was yesterday.

Love me and care and give me support I'm not
a story for you to report, conversation filler or
a prayer at mass, an unfortunate invalid put out to grass.

In the game of life I play my own hand and remind
you of something you fear in yourself you'd crack
and crumble like delicate delf
I've on the other hand gained
a power that alongside yours is a
strong sweet smelling flower.

Chapter 3

All Is Not Well

When in sixth class with Mr. Foley, you started complaining periodically of severe headaches. We would on occasion have to put you to bed in a darkened room. This bothered your teacher as it did Mrs. Brady, your former teacher. Both spoke to me about their concerns for you. Mr. Foley wondered if it might be something in his class that might be causing your upset. I spoke to you about this and I was able to assure him that you were more than happy in his class and school was a positive experience for you. Mrs. Brady wondered if something outside of school might be bothering you. Various possibilities were suggested; migraine, your age, but no definitive cause could be found. Yet these headaches seemed to strike at the most inopportune times for you. We now regret that we thought you might be faking these headaches at times and there were times you were pushed to go on, especially riding your pony when you were unwell. It must have seemed so awfully cruel to you, please forgive us Ailbhe. When it came close to your confirmation date you asked me to request Mr. Foley not to ask you to do a reading at the service as you felt you might not be able to see the words if you got a headache. An eye test had shown you did not need glasses but I'm now glad to say I did convey your request to your teacher and your wish was adhered to.

Your confirmation day came. Style brought family and extended family on site, but poor you had such a severe headache that after the ceremony you were unable to celebrate. Your brother Aonghus, sisters Aidín and Assumpta, along with your cousins. Granny and Ava (Ava was the name Aonghus invented for granddad) your aunts and uncles and Paula, plus dad and myself, did what we could, to make the day memorable for you. Mary as usual had lovely food prepared and I remember being so sad that the headache should strike at this time. Mags (Margaret) my late sister had just completed a study of reflexology and she sat you down comfortably to do reflexology on you lovely little feet. As she massaged them she inquired, "Ailbhe where exactly have you this pain?"

You replied, "In my head."

True to style, she retorted quite authoritatively, "I think it's in your kidney area, are you sure it's not your kidney that's bothering you?"

Now at that time reflexology was little more than a word to me but how right Mags was. One G.P. later told me that he would just love to have a reflexologist in his medical practice for diagnostic purposes. It would lead he felt to quicker, more exact diagnosis and free up time for him to spend on treatment.

Some week's later, dad and I were attending a school function in Cavan town. I think it was an end of school year celebration. You went to stay with your good friend Paula Sheridan in her home, just across the fields from us. Next morning Maureen, Paula's mother phoned us to say you were unwell and she did sound very worried. She mentioned how your eyes were rolling in your head. This frightened us. We remain very grateful to Maureen for her quick action. I dashed down to Sheridan's, collected you and drove to the G.P's surgery. Dad stayed home minding Aonghus, Aidín and Assumpta. You had a severe headache. The doctor carried out routine medical examinations. Nothing presented. We recalled your medical history. I recounted your falling on ice one day in the school yard and banging your head and the concern about it, but how after a short while all seemed well and you were off playing again. Then doc took your blood pressure (apparently not a very usual procedure for someone your age). Alarm. This was serious and urgent. Your blood pressure was sky high, you had to be taken to hospital at once. If you or I had blood pressure that high we'd be at deaths door I was informed. What hospital would I choose? I hardly knew one from that other. They were all just names to me but luckily, thinking on my feet, I made for the hospital as my sister lived just down the road in Drumcondra and I knew we could depend on great support from her. I rang home, gave dad the news, he would be ready to drive us to a wise choice immediately. Gwen, a neighbour, kindly took charge of your three siblings, collected them on hearing of the urgency, telling us not to be rushing back or to be concerned about them as she would see them.

So before we knew it we were on our way to the hospital, the G.P. having made the necessary arrangements by phone. I still remember the long, long wait. There were cutbacks and the staff were run off their feet, what's new? I kept begging and badgering them to see you and do something as you were in such agony with the headache (sounds familiar). Finally you got some attention; a head scan was suggested, again the fall on the ice at school surfaced as a possible source of your trouble. Dad left for home as it was agreed that I would stay with you in the hospital. Mags arrived to support. You were admitted to the children's ward. They were able to stabilise your blood pressure and you had some relief. You were to stay in the children's ward for the night under observation and further tests were arranged for the next day. Your blood pressure stabilised further and you became relaxed gradually becoming drowsy and sleepy. Mags suggested that I go with her to her house for an hour or so for a break and then return to stay the night with you in the hospital. I agreed to do this. Later, she dropped me back at the entrance to the hospital and I made my way to the children's ward where I had left you. Alarm again.

I was greeted with the message, "We were looking for you (words that were later repeated)

"Ailbhe has become very unwell and we have moved her to intensive care, we were unable to contact you (no mobile phones then). They took me to intensive care. You seemed comfortable and two marvellous nurses were caring for you. You were quite calm and we joked about all the tubes you were connected to, but one of the nurses informed me that your situation was very serious and that a hospital counsellor was available to talk with me if I wished. I remember I just froze with the shock. I was then taken to meet this warm capable empathic lady with a distinct American accent who spent about half an hour with me. Now while I honestly cannot recall one thing she said the encounter enabled me to move from a position of paralysed shock and fear to that place where I could take charge, and see what needed to be done. Would I ring home now and alert dad as to the seriousness of the situation? I considered but decided it would be wiser to wait till the morning to make contact as he had just driven the double journey to and from Dublin and would need his rest and of course there was not a thing he could do. Things were beyond our control. This was my first experience of counselling and up to then I would probably have dismissed it as of little value. It was a new enough concept in Ireland I think at the time, but the experience had been most helpful in enabling me to get some balance, face the reality of the situation, take responsibility and so I think I was better able to support you Ailbhe rather than falling all over the place in shock and fear. Did you remember much of this Ailbhe? I don't think we ever spoke about the experience except just in a factual way. I'm amazed at how vivid all this is in my mind and how easily the memories flow out as I write. "Those hardy weeds in ones memory. How does one kill them off? They have the effrontery to flaunt themselves in dreams like flavoured flower and if one used some poison which would shrivel first them or me." Author unknown.

I spent that night anxiously by your bedside in intensive care. There was some improvement during the night. I rang home, the difficulty of having the right coins for the phone, they kept getting stuck I remember. Thank goodness for mobiles. I contacted Mags and once I connected with her, my troubles with the phones were over. Practically all phone calls and information was channelled through her house phone. It was just sheer inspiration that I suggested a particular hospital to the G.P. as Mags was on call 24-7.

She'd arrive up in the morning to the hospital and question proceedings in her usual way. We decided we would do shifts. I would go and have a few hours sleep in No 3 (her house) while she stayed at your bedside keeping watch. Dad came to visit but we were advised to keep visitors to a minimum and of short duration. I can quite remember an empathetic doctor telling me how relieved he was when he came back on duty the day after your arrival in hospital to see you had pulled through. When you were released from intensive care to a ward, Mags brought board games and cards which we played to pass the time. There was a nice lady in the ward who joined in the card games. I remember your first walk with me downstairs to the entrance hall after your release from intensive care, how appreciative you were to have your freedom. You greatly admired the Remembrance Garden the hospital had erected to the memory of the people lost in the Stardust fire. The sight of this bit of greenery seemed to ignite a new hopefulness and brightness of Spirit in you – 'Oh isn't that beautiful' You'd repeat. This was your first connection with nature since your admission to hospital and I distinctly remember the healing, enliving effect it had on you.

Following considerable investigation, the source of your problem was unearthed. One of your kidneys had ceased to function, had probably never functioned, and had now damaged the other kidney. This had caused your blood pressure problem and hence the headaches. Mags's reflexology determination had been correct. The prognosis was, you were to have your diseased kidney surgically removed. You would have about enough functioning in your other kidney to keep you going for about five years, we were informed. After that we would be looking at a kidney transplant for you. It was such a relief to have a determination. It all seemed perfectly manageable. You were in perfect health bar this, so we were assured that the disruption to your life would be minimal. Your blood pressure would be monitored and medication was prescribed for you. You could lead a perfectly normal life. What a relief. There was great joy at your discharge from hospital. Many friends came to visit. When the time came for you to go back to hospital to have the kidney removed you protested loud and clear. You poor thing, how you cried and screamed. It must have been so hard for you and I only hope we gave you all the support we could.

The surgery went well but you did have severe pain post-operation and although the doctors would say that there was no need for pain, that they had excellent medication to manage it, this was not the reality. You'd often be screaming with pain and I'd practically have to beg for pain relief for you. It seems the pain relief was due at allotted times and there was a reluctance to give any relief outside these times but your pain was not so predictable and I still can't understand why they were not more liberal with your pain relief for the period your discomfort lasted post-surgery. Indeed I wonder if they can do this procedure via keyhole surgery now. It would seem to be a great advancement and relieve a lot of the pain. Anyhow too late for you Ailbhe, but we all survived and you were back home to a hero's welcome.

You said goodbye to Scoil Mhuire, your primary school education complete and started your secondary in Loreto where you had five equally happy years. You made many new friends, stayed on board workwise, never becoming over-concerned about points. In fact the points race was never an issue for you. You worked at your own pace as your letter to granny and Ava (granddad) shows, discoing now and then of course and riding your pony, competing and having fun in pony club and on the social scene.

Beaumont Hosp.
Dublin 9.
Tuesday 17th August.

Dear Gran & AVA,

I hope you're both well. i'm fine. I get out tomorrow so i'll come and visit you once I come home. I might spend a few days with maggs in Dublin. The weather is quite good here and i'm allowed to walk around outside because i'm not sick. i'm only in for a [illegible]p and all my tests have been clear [illegible] everything is fine. I got out on Sunday for the day mam and Dad and Clare came up and we all went to the beach. It was a lovely

2

day and we had a good laugh.

Aonghus is eagery awaiting his exam results. I'll be home for when he gets them so we can celebrate together. I don't get my results until September but I'm not really worried about them they ar'nt important.

I have radio and T.V in my room and I read a lot so I don't get too bored. I go around talking to the other Patients so it Shortens the da[illegible] Considerable amount. Clare bought me a [illegible]ddy toy. Its a big brown Furry bear. Mum bought me slippers with Cats on the Front. my friend Gavin sent up Flowers. I'm spoilt am'nt I?.

There

3

aren't that many young people on my floor but there are a few who are waiting for their results. I'd better go because my Dinner will get cold if I don't eat it.

Love

Ailbhe

Farranseer, Cornafean

Dear Gran and Ava,

I hope you are both keeping well and enjoying this recent yet sudden spell of simply terrific weather.

I am getting ready to go back to school. I dont really mind going back to school but the good weather makes me want a prolonged holiday. Its such a shame to be sitting in a classroom when there is such beautiful outside to be enjoyed. I have got all my school books now most of which Aonghus already had.

Aonghus dose'nt know as of yet what he wants to do. Clare sends her best wishes. Shes a bit sad lately as a boy from Killeshandra got killed in an accident on Sunday.

myself and Clare were out on Friday night as you know and we had a good time. We will both be getting our exam results in a few weeks but we ar'nt under pressure they ar'nt really important. I've almost forgotten about them. I'm only thinking about the school year ahead. luckily I'm not the type of person who worrys about exams or school. I do what I can and do my best to enjoy it. I only have seven subjects this year comparded to nine last year and I like the subjects I am doing this year so that will also help. Anyway see you in the not so distant future.

Lots of Love
Ailbhe

Healthwise, things went relatively smoothly. You kept your medical appointments, monitored your blood pressure and took your medication.

The initial prognosis proved accurate and you now, five years post-surgery were a candidate for a kidney transplant. We weren't greatly alarmed at this, as we had been well-informed along the way as to what to expect. You were prepared for and settled on your portable kidney dialysis machine having opted for home dialysis. This machine was to act as an artificial kidney for you until such time as a suitable transplant could be performed. Your name was placed on a waiting list. We did enquire about the possibility of a family member donating a kidney but the powers that be assured us there was a good steady supply of kidneys coming their way but if you were to remain too long on the waiting list, they would consider going that route. The machine plus all its trappings had to go everywhere you went as you had to perform your dialysis every night. So prior to going to bed you had to set up your machine then hook yourself on to it for the night. Then next morning unhook, and do some sterilisation before breakfast. The machine as wonderful as it was, like all modern technology could have a mind of its own at times and did not always obey orders. There were frustrating times when you must have felt like flinging it out the window.

You decided after Leaving Cert that you would be interested in a psychological-related area of study. You also thought of teaching too, felt drawn in the direction of social-caring work. However when you were better informed as to the actual content of the psychology course and discovered there was a substantial mathematical component in it, you felt it was not for you. So you came across a course in psychoanalysis which attracted you. We checked it out with a neighbour whose daughter had studied the course and it seemed to fit the bill. I went to Dublin with you for the interview. You had the required academic qualifications. The interview went well and you were offered a place.

Mags came to the rescue again. As you were now on dialysis, the machine would have to travel with you and there were strict hygiene requirements to be adhered to in order to avoid infection.

Mags offered to set up a room for you in her house. So come the following October you were living in Dublin, travelling in and out of university daily and studying psychoanalysis while awaiting your transplant. Your student life was in no way constricted by your tie to dialysis. You did your work, socialised and really had a ball, making many new friends, male and female, many of whom were extremely supportive to you. You were always very lucky in the friends that came your way Ailbhe, some wonderful friends. "So of course were they," I hear you say "to have met a gal like me." Indeed, indeed.

You wrote this light hearted poem in July 1997.

If only kidneys could grow on trees
Life could be lived with such ease,
You'd never need to watch your intake,
Or decline the pints for your kidneys sake,
Potassium could go up or down or
Pack its bags and just leave town,
Figures and levels could all be ignored,
Never needing anything heightened or lowered.
If only we had kidney trees
We could take a kidney whenever we please,
Then use it up and spit it out.
Sure isn't that what life is all about,
The easiest way, the shortest route,
Forget the long term only the immediate will suit.
Well kidney trees may sound great
But sometimes too it's worth the wait
Cause what you learn won't be forgotten and
Kidney trees may go rotten.

Well Ailbhe, we discovered that this was one of the many poems you wrote while resident in No 3, Gracepark. As I mentioned earlier I was quite surprised at how much digging you did with your pen. Initially I felt a sense of guilt at reading your personal diaries (don't worry I'll not be exposing any personal details of what you wrote)

– but they did let me get a glimpse at what life was like for you internally as you worked through the various challenges that life brought your way. You wrote practically every day of your leaving cert year and daily during your college life. This consistency plus the depth of thought and reasoning of your diary entries amazed me. While to me your persona was of a happy-go-lucky student devoid of worry and concern, your diaries exposed many feelings of confusion, fear, anxiety, frustration, expectation and hopes that I wasn't aware of. Was writing a way to self-reflect and search? Perhaps it was therapeutic and cathartic? It probably was pivotal in you achieving your strong sense of identity and in enabling you to become the autonomous, creative, complex thinker with a capacity for mature, moral reasoning that was beyond the norm for your years. Your own positive self-concept and independence left you quite comfortable in resisting pressure to conform. You had, I feel, arrived at a place where you were quite comfortable in your own skin. Is this what you would refer to in psychoanalytical terminology as "ego integrity?" I'm grateful to the diaries for the extra insight.

However I feel much more comfortable in reading and quoting the many poems you wrote. Most of your poems were written on ordinary school copies, while the diaries had this personal sacred aura to them and I felt like I was invading your private personal space. Do you remember getting a prize for a poem you wrote while in primary school? I think we spoke about this earlier, you entered the competition for what was I think the first "Window Publication" here in Cavan run by the Arts Society and Cavan County Council. Unfortunately I can't find it and I don't remember what it was about but I do remember both of us attending the prize-giving in Ballyhaise agricultural college and we had a most enjoyable evening surrounded by a variety of friendly people, animals and fowl. But guess what - I did find the invitation and complimentary tickets. I'm glad to say "Windows Publication" have gone from strength to strength.

Aidín wrote a poem in 2002 after your death, which was published in the September edition of that year, the poem she read to family and friends as we encircled the copper beach tree we set on the side of the avenue in your memory (now known as

Allie's tree) a month following your death. Its shiny brown, black leaves remind me so much of your lovely black shiny hair.

Poem Eternal Home
For Ailbhe my sister, by Aidín

Eternal Home
Is this life really sacred or at all profound.
As into clay and earth I know I'm someday bound.
There to rest forever in the deep peace of fresh
Assuring breeze 'neath those tall and stately leafy trees.
Sometimes, I see beyond, glimpses of eternal home,
She lets me see in the candle light.
But I won't live each day as if it's my last nor try
To understand for I only long to become one with nature, grass and weeds.
O let wild winds set me free and I'll only ask to feel her
Heart again so I mightn't be so alone.
Her spirit is free. She is complete. She dwells in the candlelit world
In timeless limitless joy, in DEEP DEEP PEACE OF ETERNAL HOME.

We remain so indebted to your kidney donor Ailbhe. Thanks to her you left college in 1998 with your degree under your belt and a successful kidney transplant behind you. Words could never express our gratitude.

I remember how delighted I was when you rang that morning in 1998 with the good news that you had passed all exams and obtained your B.A hons degree on Psychoanalytic studies. You also at this point had met Kerill and he simultaneously got his hons degree, so both of you graduated together. Dad and I, you'll remember, used our trip to Dublin as an opportunity to meet Kerill's parents and family, as we stayed overnight with them and had a most enjoyable time.

/7

Ailbhe Hannon Dunne 19-06-77 To 08-07- 2002.

Farranseer House, Cornafean, and Clontarf, Dublin.

Ailbhe spent the first two years of her primary education in Bruskey N.S. prior to transferring to the neighbouring Lacken N.S. where her mother taught.

Ailbhe had many happy memories of her time in Bruskey N.S. where she formed many good friendships. She reconnected with many of these friends in Loreto College and again while studying in third level in Dublin. She was always delighted to meet up with past pupils from Bruskey when socialising in Quinn's in Drumcondra.

It was while studying for her Primary Degree that she met Kerill whom she later married while both were studying for their Masters, she in U.C.D. and he in Trinity. On completing her Masters she went teaching in a third level college in Dublin work she really enjoyed.

Sadly while undergoing a routine medical procedure in July 2002 due to a mishap Ailbhe died most unexpectedly. While she is greatly missed by her Husband Dr Kerill Dunne, her family and many friends she has left a generous legacy of fond memories.

After her death Ailbhe's family were surprised to find a small collection of personal poems she had written some pointing to a premonition of an early death such as this poem written by Ailbhe (23-01-97).

"I have to leave you now like you knew I would.
I'm off to dance with the fairies and live in the magical world.
I long for the morning music and the twilight calm.
I long for my fairy friends and love to embalm.
I can hear the seashores beauty I feel it in my blood.
I'm off to dance with the fairies and live in the magical
wood I'll spend my nights on the beach whispering to the sea.
There is nothing more I need now I've got my fairy wings.
Listen to my heart beat and hear how it merrily sings.
Don't be sad at my departure you knew I'd have to go.
Think of me in winter while you are dancing in the snow
Remember me in Autumn when leaves learn to dance
Love me in spring when fresh life gets a chance
Talk with me in summer while I'm floating in the breeze
See me smiling down through the opening in the trees.

Ailbhe Hannon 23/01/97.

32

On reading through your C.V. Ailbhe, I'm amazed at the variety and extent of what you managed to fit into the four years post-degree. Without doubt, the highlight has had to be the day you walked down the aisle and said "I do" to your husband Kerill. What a memorable and totally relaxed occasion that was for family and friends. Talking of "relaxed," did I already mention how one of your wedding shoes went missing (must have been those fairies). You were not in the least perturbed – you just put on your knee-length boots and said the dress would cover them and how comfortable they were to wear. Off you went, happy out. Something old - were you the only bride to wear her everyday boots on her wedding day. It certainly did not dull your enjoyment or anyone else's to my knowledge. You will remind me of when yourself and Kerill told us you intended getting engaged, we were not exactly delighted and excited (claiming you were too young, that's parents for you). But while we initially advised strongly against it, fortunately we went with your decision, encouraging you all the way. Later, as your life was cut so short, we felt it was one of the best decisions you could have made. You did however take my advice re education Ailbhe, "to get a good broad liberal education." Both yourself and Kerill continued in education, culminating in both of you getting your Masters - you in U.C.D and Kerill in Trinity in 2001. Kerrill, much to his credit, has since your death got his doctorate. Do you remember me asking you after you got your masters if you would ever see yourself doing a doctorate and you almost automatically replied, "No, but Kerrill will." Did you sense something the rest of us missed? After you left us Ailbhe, I was surprised to find among the collection of poems you'd written, quite a few on the theme of death. Some such as the following suggest to me that you had some premonition of your own early death.

15

F

Open the window
I need to fly
I'll never return
From my home in the sky.

I belong among the stars
Where I can sing my song
I live among the dreamers
Where ther is neither Right nor wrong

I can't be bound by ties
Or others expectations
I can't be held by kisses
Permanency destroys intimacy

OVER

Wave to me as I'm passing
I'll give you a smile
I'm heading to my home now
I was only meant to stay here a while.

The stars are whispering
Calling out my name
telling me to fly home
in time for fun and games

I continue to live out an experience for
which I have yet to find a name.
My reality has its own
rhythm which I float to wide
eye/and hungry.
Today nothing inhibits me I care
little for others
thoughts of me but I am in love
with their own
secrets. Some live their thoughts
when they speak,
they speak their dreams. My dreams
speak me. I am secondary.
There is such ecstasy
and freedom in
the rhythm of the float. Lips reveal
and deceive me. Symbolism is sickening
Something unvoiced connects us a
reality un changed by time.

She was born in a bubble
filled up with love
and then carried to earth on the
back of a Dove.
Never losing her virtue she
floats through
life's hurdles, always ready
to show you how
to get through your worries.
With arms that bring
comfort, strength and support she'll
find your best
qualities and help bring them forth.
Courage is
something you'll find through
her love and
she'll never forget you when she
returns up above.
She is not a being any different from us.
She's just that much more human and
without all the fuss.
If like me you're lucky enough to have
such a mother you'll know
such happiness could
not be got from any other.

I wish my wings were ready my spirit
is losing patience
its ready for a flight I'm holding on by
the skin of my teeth

Both you and Kerill were keen travellers. Having explored Europe pre-college days you set off further a field, fitting in a three-month working stint in Australia. Then there was a world trip taking in Asia, America, Australia, New Zealand and I can't remember where else. There was no Skype then, so I remember how delighted we always were to get the letter on the mat. You also had a variety of jobs all bringing their own experiences. I never heard you complain much about any of them. I think you enjoyed the various experiences, though I do think you were especially happy in your last position working as a teacher in C.E.S and you made some real good friends there and had a great admiration for how it was run. You always claimed that it was your intention to eventually work in the psychoanalysis field but that you felt you needed more life experience. Well Ailbhe, you certainly cannot be accused of living the unlived life or letting the grass grow under your feet. You totally embraced life and lived every moment of it to the full. Well done!

Tuesday. 27/7/99

TempTeam
Permanent, Temporary & Contract Placement

①

Things To Do

62/7 Elizabeth St
Sydney
NSW 2000
Australia

Dear Mam + Dad,
How are things?, everything here is going well. We have a lovely apartment. We live right in the City Centre, which is brilliant. We can walk down to Darling harbour and the opera house. Its lovely at night time when its all lit up. Thats where the 2000 Celebrations are going to be so we'll have a birds eye view. our apartment costs $300 (£150) per week which we can easily cover between us but we decided to get some others in to stay to help so we could save some money. We have 3 others staying

ADELAIDE	MELBOURNE	PERTH	SYDNEY
Tel: (08) 8410 6800	Tel: (03) 9866 2838	Tel: (08) 9221 1211	Tel: (02) 9231 5415
Fax: (08) 8410 6866	Fax: (03) 9867 7499	Fax: (08) 9221 1220	Fax: (02) 9231 5900

with us at the moment. 2 fellows & a girl, the girl & her brother are from New Zeland and her boyfriend is from England he's been travelling for a year ½. They are all really nice and its good crack because sometimes Kerill doesn't finish work till 8:30 and I finish early so its good to have someone here when you come in. There are a lot of Irish and Scotish in the building, most of whom are students. The couple who own the building are lovely. They are elderly and are really helpful.

(2)

TempTeam

Permanent, Temporary & Contract Placement

~~Things To Do~~

They run a travel agency downstairs and are always about. Which is good because I've already locked myself out twice! We have a spare bed for anyone who wants to stay. And theres plenty of floor space. The apartment is much nicer than the flat in Phibsboro Its like the apartment we had in the Canaries. We nearly moved into an apartment which had a rooftop swimming pool but there was 2 guys living there & they were a bit strange (pity). We are happy where we are for the time being. The plan is to stay here until Jan/Feb and then to go travelling. The lads staying with

ADELAIDE	MELBOURNE	PERTH	SYDNEY
Tel: (08) 8410 6800	Tel: (03) 9866 2838	Tel: (08) 9221 1211	Tel: (02) 9231 5415
Fax: (08) 8410 6866	Fax: (03) 9867 7499	Fax: (08) 9221 1220	Fax: (02) 9231 5900

us have made their way down the coast so they have been filling us in on the best places to go and how to travel. The couple downstairs do cheap packages so they said they'd help us out too - mind you I'll have to sell half of my clothes before that.

Most things are cheaper over here - clothes shoes jewellery and so is food. Theres so much choice of food. Its cheaper to eat out than to cook. They have lovely asian food thats really cheap. Myself and the girl who lives with us (Liz) are going to go on a shopping tour. Its a bus that goes to all the warehouses and discount shops.

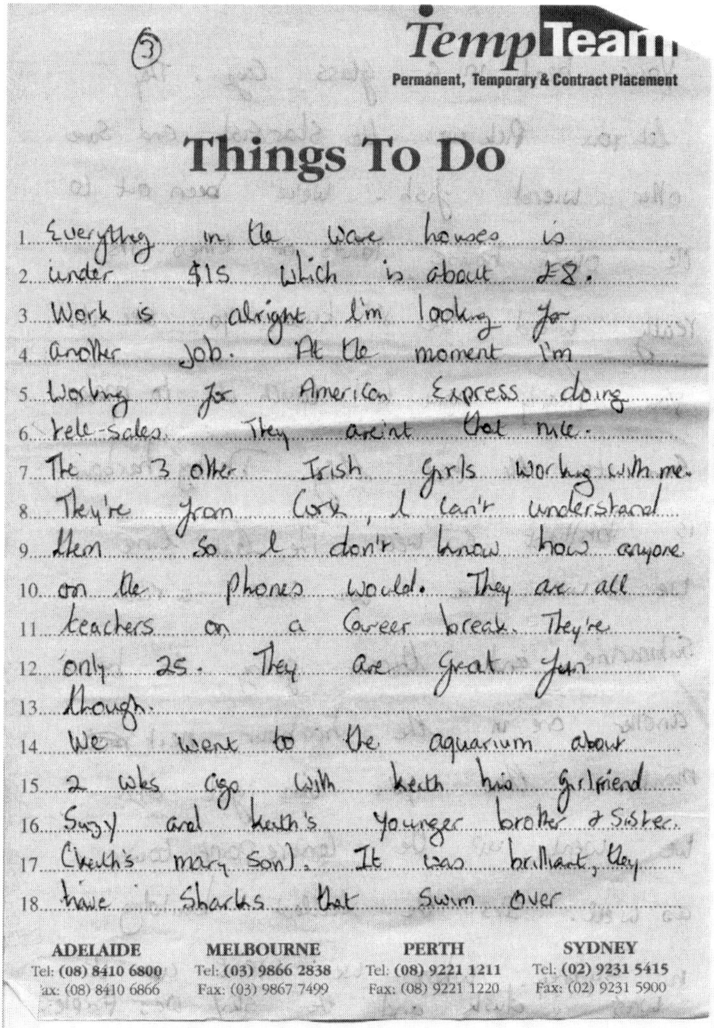

③

TempTeam
Permanent, Temporary & Contract Placement

Things To Do

1. Everything in the ware houses is
2. under $15 which is about £8.
3. Work is alright I'm looking for
4. another job. At the moment I'm
5. working for American Express doing
6. tele-sales. They aren't that nice.
7. The 3 other Irish girls working with me.
8. They're from Cork, I can't understand
9. them so I don't know how anyone
10. on the phones would. They are all
11. teachers on a career break. They're
12. only 25. They are great fun
13. though.
14. We went to the aquarium about
15. 2 wks ago with Keith his girlfriend
16. Suzy and Keith's younger brother & sister.
17. (Keith's mary son). It was brilliant, they
18. have sharks that swim over

ADELAIDE	MELBOURNE	PERTH	SYDNEY
Tel: (08) 8410 6800	Tel: (03) 9866 2838	Tel: (08) 9221 1211	Tel: (02) 9231 5415
Fax: (08) 8410 6866	Fax: (03) 9867 7499	Fax: (08) 9221 1220	Fax: (02) 9231 5900

ur head in a glass cage. They let you pick up the star fish and some other wierd fish. We've been out to the opera house loads of times. Its really wierd the 1st time you see it. You nearly want to touch it to make sure its the real thing. Darling harbour is brilliant as well. The last time we were there we saw a real submarine and there's going to be another one in the harbour next ~~moth~~ month that you can get on. We went up the Centre Point tower as well. Its the tallest building in Sydney. When we went up it was dusk and the sky was purple.

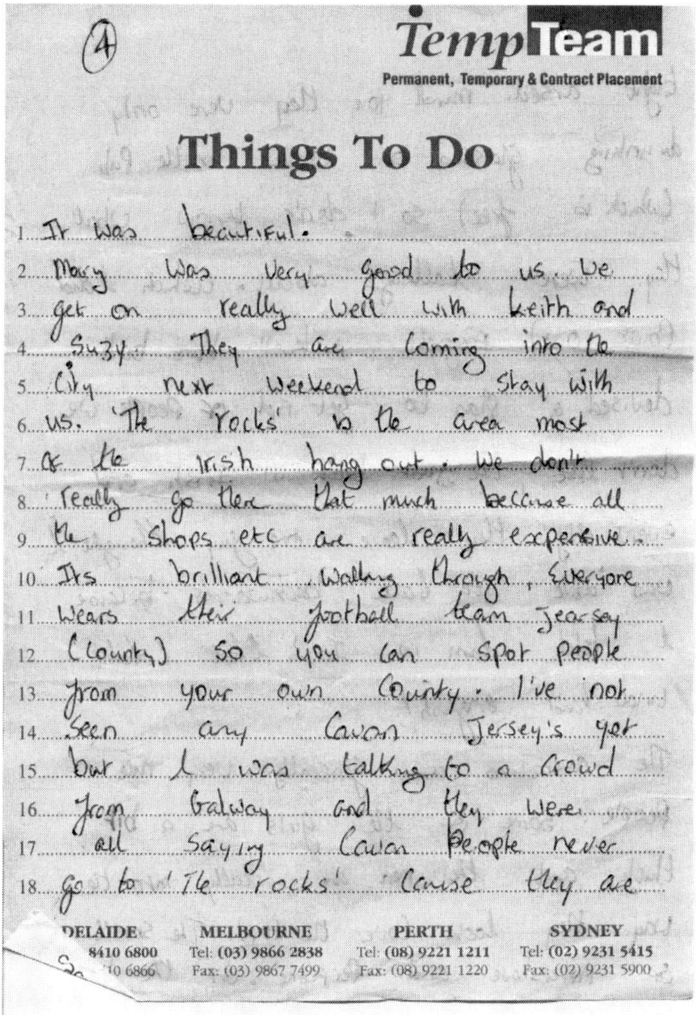
4

TempTeam
Permanent, Temporary & Contract Placement

Things To Do

It was beautiful. Mary was very good to us. We get on really well with Keith and Suzy. They are coming into the city next weekend to stay with us. 'The Rocks' is the area most of the Irish hang out. We don't really go there that much because all the shops etc are really expensive. Its brilliant walking through, Everyone wears their football team jearsey (County) so you can spot people from your own County. I've not seen any Cavan Jersey's yet but I was talking to a crowd from Galway and they were all saying Cavan people never go to 'The rocks' 'cause they are

DELAIDE 8410 6800 10 6866
MELBOURNE Tel: (03) 9866 2838 Fax: (03) 9867 7499
PERTH Tel: (08) 9221 1211 Fax: (08) 9221 1220
SYDNEY Tel: (02) 9231 5415 Fax: (02) 9231 5900

tight arsed. mind you they were only drinking Glasses of water in the Pub (which is free) so I don't know what they were talking about. (which I did Point out) myself + Kerill have both devised a plan to Get rid of People we don't like, we just talk in Irish and eventually they leave. One guy thought I was able to talk backwards because I told him in Irish that I didnt understand english!.

The australians are Generally very nice People. Some of the Girls are a bit thick and the men are really into the way they look (over the top). The smell of Aftershave and Perfume on the buses

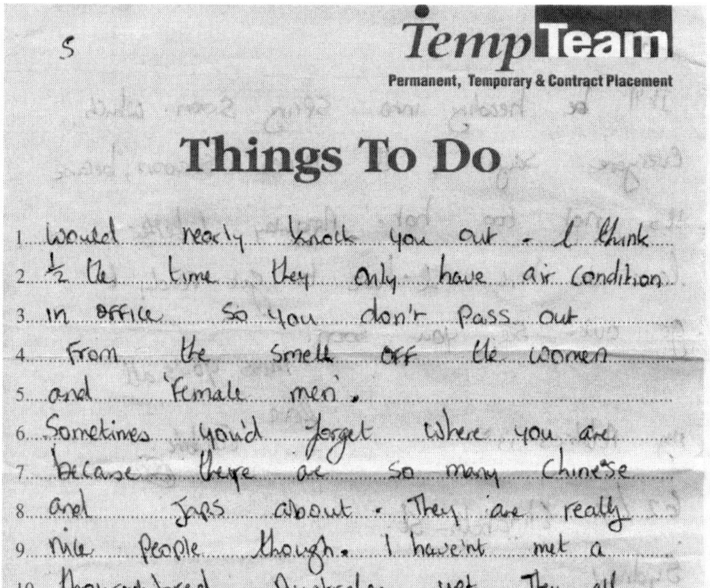

5

TempTeam
Permanent, Temporary & Contract Placement

Things To Do

would nearly knock you out - I think ½ the time they only have air condition in office so you don't pass out from the smell off the women and 'female men'. Sometimes you'd forget where you are because there are so many Chinese and Japs about. They are really nice people though. I haven't met a thorough bred Australian yet. They all have oriental/European parents. Dana Eric's friend is from Yougaslavia, she's the one who dyed my hair and Kerill's hair. It looks good although a lot of the colour is gone. The weather here at the moment is wet although its still warm. It gets really cold at night time.

ADELAIDE	MELBOURNE	PERTH	SYDNEY
Tel: (08) 8410 6800	Tel: (03) 9866 2838	Tel: (08) 9221 1211	Tel: (02) 9231 5415
Fax: (08) 8410 6866	Fax: (03) 9867 7499	Fax: (08) 9221 1220	Fax: (02) 9231 5900

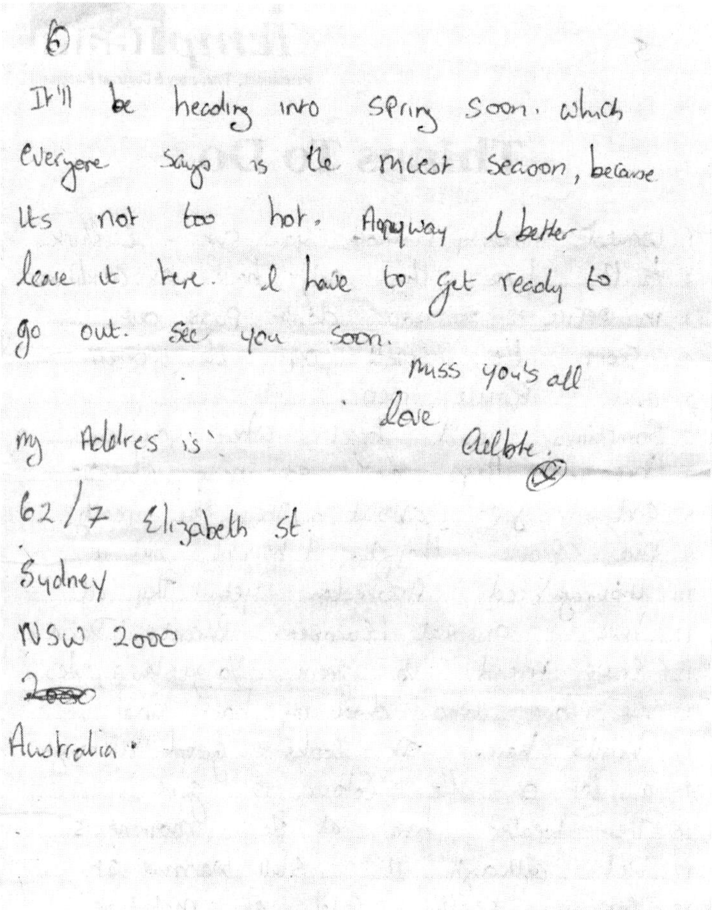

6

It'll be heading into spring soon. which everyone says is the nicest season, because its not too hot. Anyway I better leave it here. I have to get ready to go out. See you soon.

miss you's all

love

Adele.

my Address is:

62/7 Elizabeth St

Sydney

NSW 2000

~~2000~~

Australia.

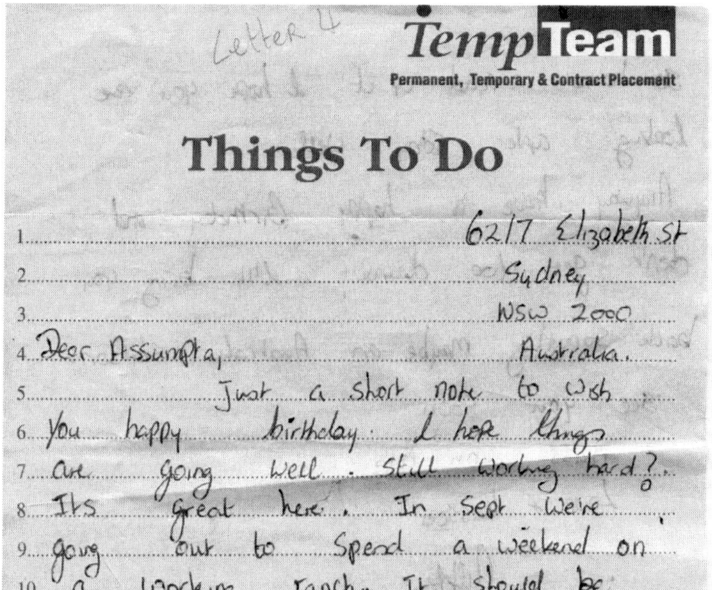

Letter 4

TempTeam
Permanent, Temporary & Contract Placement

Things To Do

6/7 Elizabeth St
Sydney
NSW 2000
Australia.

Dear Assumpta,

Just a short note to wish you happy birthday. I hope things are going well. Still working hard? It's great here. In Sept we're going out to spend a weekend on a working ranch. It should be great fun. The ranches over here are constantly looking for people to work for the holidays. You don't get paid much but you get free food & accomodation. I'll let you know how our short stint goes. I'd say it'll be good crack. All my news is in the other letter

ADELAIDE Tel: (08) 8410 6800 Fax: (08) 8410 6866
MELBOURNE Tel: (03) 9866 2838 Fax: (03) 9867 7499
PERTH Tel: (08) 9221 1211 Fax: (08) 9221 1220
SYDNEY Tel: (02) 9231 5415 Fax: (02) 9231 5900

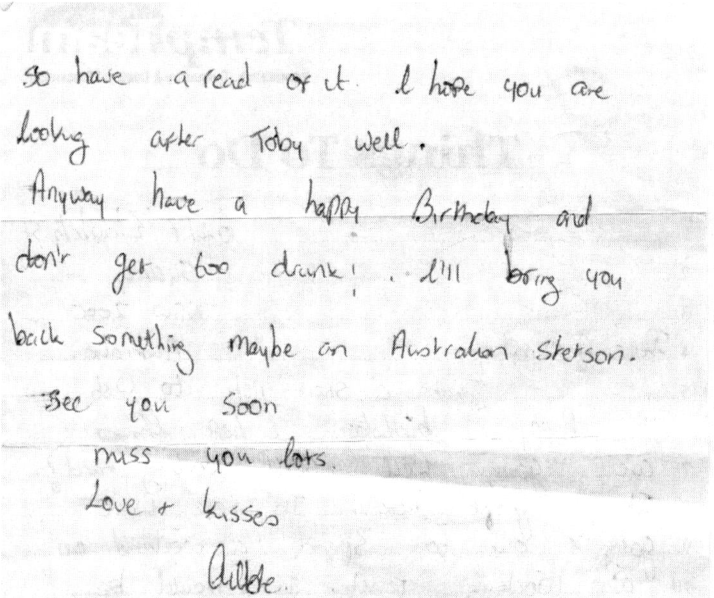
so have a read of it. I hope you are
looking after Toby well.
Anyway have a happy Birthday and
don't get too drunk! .. I'll bring you
back something maybe an Australian Stetson.
See you Soon
miss you lots.
Love + kisses
[illegible]
PS Don't Forget to fill me in on
all the news, send me a letter.

Chapter 4

The New Millennium Last Orders

The much heralded new millennium brought us our first encounter with death in our immediate family Ailbhe. Yes dad's parents had passed away some years earlier but you were all too young then to have any real memory of that loss. They both died in their late eighties following protracted illness. They also lived quite a distance from us and sadly you never got the chance to build a personal intimate relationship with them. You were too young to travel to the funerals and I remember you enquiring as to what a funrail was as you called it and asking if we would soon be going to another one as yourself and Aonghus had such fun with the kind family who looked after you while dad and I were away. They lived at the top of a hill and the older children had some sort of buggie and gave you rides down the hill. So I think you may have confused funeral with funfair Ailbhe. The deaths that came to our door in the year 2000 were different and definitely more apparent for you. My parents both your beloved grandparents also your God parents died within three months of each other in the year 2000 having just welcomed in the new year hosting a family barbeque at their house which we all attended and enjoyed. Granny died suddenly on March 26th 2000, just fell to the floor as she dusted and tended to her plants in the downstairs shower room. You would have to have fond memories of that room Ailbhe. We called it "Lucy's Room" and when you visited as children Granny would have special goodies stored there for all of you. So it became a no go area for all the grandchildren. We convinced you that this rather cross lady named Lucy lived there and that it was best never to disturb her. It worked I think. At least I can't remember anyone breaking ranks and it was marvellous what granny could bring back to all of you, sweets, crisps, presents when she'd suggest that it might be alright for her to quietly visit Lucy's room as she felt Lucy was sleeping. An anticipatory silence would fall on all until Granny returned armed with surprises. Well as granny and granddad (Ava) got older they must have had Lucy evicted as this room was transformed into a spacious purpose built shower room. Granny for some reason loved this room. She kept some of her favourite house plants in it and she told me how she found the room so peaceful and relaxing and how she now and then would go in there sit and relax. I wonder if this had something to do with this room's former function perhaps places do hold memories. It was in this room on that Sunday March 26th 2000 as she tended to her plants that Granny collapsed. The doctor reckoned she was dead before she reached the floor. She was born 13th March 1914 so she had just seen in her 86th year and the new millennium. Her health both mental and physical (bar a minor heart and blood pressure problem which she monitored and had controlled by prescribed medication) was pretty well perfect. So it was quite a shock to all of us. Granddad was in the kitchen-heard the bang and rushed into find Granny on the floor dead. He himself sadly rapidly progressed into acute dementia and died in hospital June 2nd 2000-not quite three months later. A great loss but it was lovely to have the memory of the barbeque new years eve 2000, the chats, laughter song or two good food and a few drinks. I am so grateful that both Grandparents lived long enough to get to know their grandchildren. You brought them such joy Ailbhe -your letters phone calls and visits. Grannies death was so sudden. We were more prepared for Grandad's and really felt I think that the dementia had robbed him of any quality of life. He always said he felt people who died suddenly were lucky. He would say. "They got away handy" and "when your number is up you've got to go". These phrases became almost personal mantras for him when considering death and its inevitability. I've thought it weird Ailbhe that the night before you died (Sunday July 7th 2002) just over two years later as yourself Kerill, Assumpta and myself were enjoying our meal in Clontarf Castle you quite spontaneously started repeating "When your number is up you have got to go, when your number is up you have got to go", and you reminded us that Grandad would say that when referring to death. We were not talking about Grandad and certainly death never entered our minds. You were so bright and breezy full of the joys of life and enjoying the get together and food so what on earth could have put thoughts of death into your head at that time. I remember you choose and enjoyed a fish dish-to bring up your something-in your blood you said. It was and has been as huge comfort to me since your most unexpected death the following evening to get a glimse of Granddads countenance at your death bed opposite me and to sense the message from him. " I got this job" you shortly afterwards raised your hand and gave us a lovely wave and a calm serene peace seemed to imbue your presence as Kerill and myself huddled around your death bed less than twenty four hours later. Now in his book "Divine Beauty" John O'Donoghue, suggests that prior to their death some people begin "to see the eternal tracings of the invisible world". He supposes that there must be excitement for the soul at the edge of such transformation and joy in bringing the bright essence of a life's harvest into eternity". I've learned since your death Ailbhe that many people who tend to the dying speak of how often a dying person will tell them that they have just seen the countenance of some departed relative or friend and how comforting this seems to be for the person dying.

Colm Keane the award winning journalist and author has documented his personal years of research into the personal accounts of peoples experiences at the time of death – in two interesting books "Going home" Irish stories from the edge of Death and "We'll Meet Again" – Irish Deathbed visions who you meet when you die. Case histories of people dying and those left behind are recounted, many of whom report having been greeted and helped by dead relatives leading to the conclusion that we do not die alone.

I hope you too felt Granddad's comforting presence and that he came to shelter and guide you through the travail of departure. I know just how enormously reassuring and comforting it would be for you to see or feel his presence at that time. It would certainly make your leaving less painful and frightening. Certainly for me been there with you as you died Ailbhe was a privilege for which I will be eternally grateful. Sometimes I worry at my stage of life with the advances in modern science-(great though they are)-might some of us be kept alive too long when there is no life to live. Is some of what happens now more about delaying death than sustaining life? Big questions Ailbhe now I'm not in any hurry away at the moment and I don't think any of those near me are in any way wishing on my exit but when I think of poor Granddad getting the dementia and how in his periods of lucidity he wished for a quick death. Is there not alot to be said for the quick exit? This lovely poem entitled a blessing for death by John O Donoghue expresses beautifully the sentiments we would wish for our friends and ourselves and indeed all human kind

Entering Death by John O Donoghue

I pray that you will have the blessing of being
consoled and sure about your death.
May you know in your soul
There is no need to be afraid.
When your time comes, may you
Have every blessing and strength you need.
May there be a beautiful welcome for you in the home
You are going to.
You are not going somewhere strange, merely back
To the home you have never left.
May you live with compassion
And transfigure everything negative within and about you.
When you come to die, may it be after long life.
May you be tranquil among those who care for you.
May your going be sheltered
And your welcome assured.
May your soul smile
In the embrace of your
Anam Cara"

That meal we had together in Clontarf Castle that night before you died Ailbhe was, to use bible speak our last supper. The restaurant was quite busy with lots of people coming and going, eating, socializing like ourselves. Now I've thought to myself afterwards if anyone present had been asked to look around the clients and surmise who present would be dead in twenty four hours you'd most probably be bottom of the list. Yourself Kerill and Assumpta were among the youngest and liveliest there. I remember well yourself and Assumpta going off on a tour of the castle and on route you came on a manager or some authority figure training a group of hotel staff. He called the staff by numbers not names. Now I'm sure this manager was following what was normal acceptable practice but when you came back to kerill and myself you voiced your annoyance at this and told us how you had called out to him from the top of the stairs "These people have names". Now while you were not one to go breaking your shin on a stool that was not in your way Ailbhe you would not be slow in speaking up for someone you felt was being wronged, especially if they were being robbed of their dignity. You certainly picked up on this. Your sentiment would concur with those of James Connolly way back when he wrote in 1916 "Workers are regarded by their masters not as people but as numbers on a sheet". Perhaps the more things change the more they stay the same.

All too soon our last supper came to an end. The hands on the clock indicated we had considerably over stayed our time. Reluctantly the four of us left Clontarf castle and headed for the hospital where you were due for an overnight stay to have an unpleasant yet necessary routine enough medical procedure performed next morning. Do you remember the lashing rain that night Ailbhe? Perhaps Mother Nature had an awareness of what lay ahead and was crying its eyes out at the immediacy of your departure. You had already gone through the admissions process at the hospital and as it was now quite late, well past the agreed time for your arrival so we rather gingerly accompanied you to the twin bedded room that had been allotted to you for the night. Your bed was ready. We saw you tucked into bed, chatted for a while. As we said our "good nights" "see you in the morning" you said "I wish I was going with you". The wish was reciprocal Ailbhe. It must have been hard for you.

Yourself and Kerill were both working at this stage and living happily and comfortably in Clontarf, able to look out on to the sea. Your transplanted kidney had started giving your trouble and a second transplant seemed a likely necessity but we were assured by the experts that there was no alarm or rush, that a transplant kidney at this stage of you development would see you through many years probably life. Anyway no definitive decision had as yet been made. Aidín and Assumpta had offered you one of their kidneys should the need arise. They had the required test done to see if they were a match or rather if their kidney would be a match. You had been having terrible discomfort with your legs, this tingling uneasiness through them, kind of pins and needles feeling I think but again there seemed no great worry medically. From talking to others in your situation it seemed to go with the territory. You had been to hospital a few weeks prior to this for observation, you will remember being in on your birthday June 19th your last, and the nice Chinese nurse who spotted from your chart that it was your birthday (most observant of her I thought) I was downstairs with you waiting for some test that was to be carried out and the nurse went off came back with a slice of cake, a lit candle on top and wishing you happy birthday. It certainly brightened up things for us and took some of the dullness out of our wait. Yes kindness is a blessed gift in a broken world. Reflecting on how circumstances evolved the period before your death I now wonder if an unseen hand had been guiding us Ailbhe. The weekend before your birthday, Saturday June 15th I as was quite customary went into Cavan town to shop. I parked the car in Dunne's car park and headed down town but this terrible bleak feeling overwhelmed me as I walked down Main Street, a feeling I'd never experienced since or before. I tried to logic it away. I became anxious for you. Felt all is not well. I made my way back towards the car feeling disorientated. A neighbour spoke to me and I told her how anxious and unwell I felt. She supported me and took me in for a cup of coffee. I was afraid to drive home, this awful dark feeling got into me that all was not going to be well with you. Now there was absolutely no medical evidence to suggest this. Bridget got me settled, walked me to the car and I drove home minus the shopping. Bridget later called to the house and left a bottle of "Rescue Remedy" (you might remember Rescue remedy from your pony club days) for me, again so kind. Later I wondered what all that had been about and felt quite foolish. I chatted as usual with you on the phone over the weekend and all seemed under control. However when driving to work the following Monday June 17th, two days before your birthday, the same desolate dark feeling hit me out of the blue. My car suddenly stalled. A lady came and helped me push the car to a safe space on the roadside and dropped me off to work. Try as I did I just could not settle. Again I tried to logic it out but I just felt this over powering urge to get to you. I rang dad to come and collect me, made work arrangements and prepared for home with this irresistible compulsion to get to Dublin to you despite the illogicality of it. After all you were just having routine tests. We were all quite accustomed to that.

Dad had been in bed with a severe enough flu but he came immediately and I insisted that he take me to the bus stop which he did and I headed for the hospital. You were delighted to see me as Kerill was working and you were feeling very disappointed at having to take the time off work. You felt you were letting the principal and college down. The consultant had felt it now necessary for you to take the next three weeks off to get things fully sorted. When I saw your concern I offered to ring the college, speak with the principal and explain your situation. You agreed and I can see to this day the relief that came over your face when the principal responded with such understanding. She told me to assure you that there would always be work there for you, not to rush back, that your dedication and skill were appreciated and that you were a much valued members of staff. Three weeks later members of staff came to support us at your funeral and we were comforted by an empathetic letter the principal sent us.

Letter from Princip

[redacted]

[redacted]

Dear Maura,

I can't tell you how shocked and saddened I was to hear of Aibhe's death, as were the teachers who worked with her.

Although she only worked with us for a relatively short time, she was so popular with everybody at CES ... teachers, admin staff and most importantly, the students. She was a lovely lovely girl, who was always smiling and positive and was an absolute joy to work with.

Many of the teachers yesterdays, both male and female, were visibly shocked and moved to tears at the news and I think thats a testament to the respect and love in which she was held here at the school.

I can't even begin to understand or imagine what all her family and husband are going

[redacted]

through right now but I hope some of words written in this card will bring some comfort to you in the months ahead.

On a personal note, I am saddened that I will not be working with Ailbhe again. She was so good at her job and was able to jump into any class at a moments notice. Qualities such as the ones she possessed are rare these days and I, personally will miss her.

Everybody here is thinking of all you at the moment as you go through this terribly sad time in your lives.

Wherever Ailbhe is now, I really hope she is happy and at peace and watching over all of us, smiling.

With fondest love to all of you
and my deepest deepest sympathy

[redacted]

Indeed you had mentioned to me on a few occasions how you admired the principal's efficient holistic attitude in managing the college. Our words can have consequences well beyond the obvious. 'The Lines Winning Words' by Kathleen Gillum and published in a friendship book, a thought for each day gives us wise advice,

"Say to someone something kind,
Speak praise sincerely meant,
Express appreciation and give encouragement.
For we inspire and influence,
Just through the words we say,
Within us lies the power to bless
And change somebody's day"

Well the reassurance you got about your work lifted your mood and you returned to your bright cheery self. I certainly never regretted my impetuous trip to Dublin. I was able to be with you on your last birthday, share the many cards, sort flowers and presents with you. Auntie Teresa says she remembers thinking as she posted your birthday card going through her mind was the idea of this been your last birthday. When I returned home dad told me how he had got a local mechanic to come to my stalled car along the roadside where I had had to abandon it on route to work. It mysteriously started first try. The mechanic could find no problem and it continued to work perfectly. Dad himself tells how around that time he had a disturbing dream. He could quite vividly see a coffin as the words "A coffin for Ailbhe, A coffin for Ailbhe" reverberated through his head.

While you were interested and knowledgeable about religion Ailbhe you were not what might be termed churchy, spiritual yes but for some reason you had taken a shine to Padre Pio, he was not at that point Canonized but much revered. You had his picture in your place in Dublin and also in your bedroom at home here. You mentioned to me on your birthday that you had been given the phone number of a lady who was willing to have the Padre Pio glove taken to anyone in hospital should they wish to access it. You seemed interested in taking up this offer. We rang on several occasions but with no luck. There was no reply. However when I came home to my surprise I discovered on reading a local paper that the glove was to be made available in a neighbouring church the following weekend. You were down with us for the week and we were able to go and attend the ceremony. As we walked to the car to come home the kind parish priest whom you'd not previously met bumped into us and handed you a sizeable statue of Padre Pio which he had just purchased at the stall that had been specially erected for their special ceremony. The experience was a positive for you. An extra sense of peace and contentment seemed to come over you. I got holidays Friday June 21st. The hospital at this stage had discharged you with a view to calling you back within the week to have a permcath inserted to initiate possible haemodialysis with a view to undergo a transplant nephrectomy later. As Kerrill was to be working out of Dublin for the next two weeks you decided to spend the next week with us. That too with hind sight was a great blessing as it gave us a chance to have a relaxed time together. We went shopping remember? You got your red swede shoes, black cardigan and black skirt and met your old friend Paula. You surprised me at how much you seemed to have come into rhythm with yourself. I remember my taking your advice and going for a rest for an hour or so. You were hoovering the hallway downstairs when I got up and I got a great whiff of the lavender shake and vac you were using. You were very partial to lavender Ailbhe. As I looked down at you hovering away in the downstairs hallway from the top of the stairs I saw a luminous circle surrounding the top of your head. It lasted a few seconds and there was this almost tangible aura of serenity and wholeness emanating from you. I experienced a somewhat similar transient radiated glow as I greeted you on my arrival to your pad in Clontarf on that for me very memorable Sunday evening July 7th 2002, the evening of our last supper' in Clontarf Castle, your last evening alive.

Now I expect many reasonable people would write off these phenomena as wishful thinking on my part or at best a figment of my imagination. Perhaps a consoling figment. I have no difficulty in empathising with their scepticism. Prior to my own experiences I'd probably be foremost among the sceptics so I quite understand. But I cannot deny my own experience however unbelievable it may seem from a rational view point. I was so perplexed by the whole unusual coincidences that I felt an urgency to write them down in detail at the time of your death. They were so real to me that I wanted to have them documented immediately lest with the passage of time my memory might become blurred and I might begin to doubt the accuracy of my recall so I'm so glad that the day after your funeral I found a quiet space and detailed the events and my experiences leading up to your death Ailbhe. I titled the script,

"Details leading up to Ailbhe Hannon's Death as observed by me her mother Maura Hannon" written by Maura Hannon.

I tucked the script away in a safe place secure in the knowing that knowledge of the details and experiences would not be dependent on word of mouth or remain the prisoner of my memory. Almost a decade later I now congratulate myself on my foresight at what was a most poignant time. Your unexpected or indeed what now seems quite surreal questioning me about death, that week you spent at home with us, just two weeks prior to your death, surprised me at the time but later became a source of disquiet to me. Remember how I would sit on the side of your bed where you lay unable to sleep because of the discomfort in your legs, chatting away and drinking cups of tea into the early hours of the morning. Quite out of context came the very deliberate question "Mam, what happens when you die"? I sort of shrugged off the question with something about differing traditional beliefs and changed the subject as your question was totally disconnected from the this and that we had been chatting about. Certainly there had been no conversation around anything to do with death. It undoubtedly was the farthest thing from my mind. But you pursued your enquiry asking "Who dresses you when you die?" and you stated categorically that you would want your family to do this and not strangers. Then you queried where the idea of taking the dead person to the church the night before the funeral and leaving them there over night came from. I explained how it was a tradition in the Catholic Church and that others had different customs. You quickly replied "why can't they leave the house with their family and friends the day of the funeral?" I suggested it was choice and you stated emphatically that you would want to leave with your family and friends and you said "how lonely" it would be if one were left on their own through the night in an empty church. I mentioned how this conversation became for me a source of concern Ailbhe. Not you're questions but my own reaction and response. I realise now too late how inadequate my response was. I see it as a lost opportunity to have engaged with you in an in-depth exchange. It might have given you an opportunity to unburden some concerns, fears, thoughts or premonitions you might have had around death. I felt I failed you here. John O Donohue refers to how "we prefer to avoid talk of death..... Aside from minimal and superficial reference the theme of death is absent from most of our conversations. Our culture avoids it too. Where time is money no one wants to focus on that edge where time runs out on you. Our education system never really considers it. We have no pedagogy of death consequently; death is something we are left to deal with in the isolation of our own life and family".

It seems so strange too that how the evening before your death as we had that last meal you repeatedly quoted Granddad's philosophy about death. Well we just do not get back yesterday Ailbhe and I can only hope that any fear or isolation you felt became sheltered by some loving secure reassurance. We did carry out your two stated preferences. You were dressed by family, not strangers and beautifully turned out in your long Celtic dress plus the new red Swede shoes I had bought you on that last shopping venture. You left the house with family, friends and neighbours as we did not have a removal, which I notice is now quite common practice but in 2002 it was quite rare in our area. Now the disappointment I've felt around what

I deduced as a missed opportunity to enable you to open up and speak about your thoughts on death keep being mitigated by what I can only describe as a sort of telepathic response from you telling me not to be hard on myself that I was there for you and that I did the best I could with the understanding I had at that time and you are reminding me of one of my own mantras that I frequently used when teaching "A mistake is not a mistake if a lesson from its learned." The last week of June and first days of July you spent with us was such a blessing Ailbhe. You returned to Dublin July 3rd for observation and tests and it was then that the hospital arranged to go ahead with insertion of permcath the following Monday July 8th so that you could avail of dialysis pending a future kidney transplant. We were all relieved that a definite determination had been made as that tingling in your legs had become very annoying for you. There was of course no serious worry as medical evidence indicated your general health was normal and dialysis followed hopefully by a successful kidney transplant should at this stage of your life see you into a long healthy life spell. The specialist consultant indicated that should a suitable match not arise by Christmas that he would consider your sisters' offer, but there seemed no great urgency at that point in time. Wasn't it a great stroke of luck that I decided to get that 4pm bus from Cavan to Dublin Sunday July 7th- the day before your death and I do remember as I taxied out to Clontarf having an overwhelming feeling of urgency and excitement. I just could not wait to get to you. Intuitively I felt the need to be with you and now with hind sight it gave us, myself, yourself and Kerill and Assumpta that last opportunity to share a last meal. I remember as we left you in the hospital that might how adamant you were that I was to stay at your place with Kerill in Clontarf for the night and you insisted I was to take the main bedroom. We obeyed your instructions and I remember yourself and Kerill joking that for once I'd find it difficult to get any tidying to do. The place was so tidy, sparkling; everything in place, not your usual casual style Ailbhe-and you had the bed made up so comfortably for me. When I awoke the next morning I went out walking along the sea front opposite your place thinking of you all the time and wishing you well. You rang to confirm that they were going to do the procedure. Kerill arranged the day off work to stay with you. Again I remember been very anxious to get to the hospital as Kerill drove through the heavy traffic, this strong urge to be with you again surfaced. When we got to your room you were in bed. You said something about them having wanted you to go down earlier for the procedure and how you refused to go until we arrived. You seemed reluctant and anxious about the procedure. I sensed negative karma around. When your good friend Clair rang very eager to talk to you it was as though a deep sadness welled up in you and you just seemed unable to face talking to her despite the encouragement and gentle pressure discretely applied by the nurse and myself. We thought it would lift your spirits as I knew how much you enjoyed talking to Clair, be it day or night and I could feel the disappointment in Clair's voice but I had to accept that for whatever reason you were at that point unable to go there emotionally. I've wondered Ailbhe had we given credence to the vibes and postponed the procedure what might have been the outcome. The consequences could hardly have been worse. Well go ahead we did. A porter duely arrived into the room and wheeled you off to the particular area in the hospital where you were to have a haemodialysis catheter inserted. Kerill joined you on the journey walking along side you. As it was the hospital policy that patients could not be accompanied while the procedure was taking place Kerill had to part company with you at the door of the room even though he had specifically taken a days holiday to be with you to support you and he knew you would like him to be present. Unfortunately Ailbhe rules took precedence. This too was later a source of annoyance for us-that Kerill or myself were not allowed be with you to support you. I later learned from the report prepared for us at our own request and substantial cost by an independent interventional radiologist that the procedure you were undergoing- (cv's) the placement of central venous catheters (cv's) takes place in a variety of hospital settings and how (outpatients of cv's is becoming increasing frequent particularly in haemodialysis and oncology centres". I've also been told that in America it can be usual practice for nurses to do the procedure at the patients beside. I would so wish that we had been with you when things went so wrong to be your support and advocate and to know at first hand what actually happened rather than be left to depend on the word of professional strangers who's responses have often been found to be motivated by the protection of their own vested interests. Kerill returned to your room where he and I obediently waited for your return. Assumpta went down to Mags to collect some clothes that aunty Mags (fairy godmother) had washed and ironed for you. Shortly after this a nursing sister with a porter pushing a bed entered the room where Kerill and I were awaiting your return. I exclaimed in impulsive delight "Great Ailbhe you are back to us. The sister quickly retorted. This is not Ailbhe. Ailbhe is going up to the ward. I automatically interjected no Ailbhe does not like the ward she must have a room. Then came the dejecting news, Ailbhe she said is on the corridor she is been taken to the ward to be near the nurses' station for observation. Where were you she was calling you, there were complications. This message stuck in my psyche Ailbhe. The words she was calling you have semi haunted me. Ailbhe I was and remain so annoyed that Kerill had not been allowed stay with you and that no one bothered to get us to comfort you. Who writes these rules and to what purpose. Were I now to have someone I cared about going for a similar procedure I believe I'd break down the door to be with them. I can only hope Ailbhe that it was not too awful for you and that those present acted in a kind way. Now I don't blame the sister of course she did not write the rules. She did seem to be stressed, under pressure. I responded with a loud angry expletive and pointed out that we had been in the room available all the time. Seeing my alarm she then assured us that things had been righted and not to worry that we could accompany you up to the ward where they would be better able to monitor your position. Do you remember when we joined you on the corridor just outside the door of your former room? You were waiting for the bed at the nurses' station to be readied.

Well you seemed to be hooked up to all kinds of everything-tubes all over the place. When you saw us you immediately pulled yourself up in the bed and very angrily exclaimed "and they fucked this up on me too". We assured you that the sister had told us all had now been righted, the worst was over and that we would stay with you. We followed you up to the ward where you were positioned right beside the nurses' station. Three or four doctors and a nurse were seated at a desk. On and off they checked the monitor over your bed while communicating very little with us, were quite aloof but anytime we requested information the feedback was positive. I sat to one side of your bed towards the bottom. I kept rubbing your little soft hand as you lay seemingly quite relaxed and in no discomfort. At one stage I told you how I had got holidays and would stay with you all night would not leave your beside, you leaned forward and said "Do you mind Mammy" I replied not at all I'll be delighted to. I'll be here for as long as it takes" You seemed pleased and relieved and an added air of calm came over you. Assumpta joined us around your bed. You slept snored woke up talked a little certainly seemed relaxed. I so hope my deduction was accurate and that this was as peaceful a time for you and that we did and said the right things. A decision was taken to do an x-ray on the ward. The consultant spoke assuring us that it was quite routine and would only take a few minutes. Assumpta took off to meet Mags who had phoned to say she was parked at the front door and had some clean glad rags for you. The doctor (x-ray complete) spoke briefly telling us how all was going well-that the former mishap had been sorted and while it could slow developments by a few days even this might not now even be necessary. As he left a cousin who worked in the hospital came to say hello. Her mother was a first cousin of Granddads and like her mother was a nurse. I'd never met her but knew who she was when she introduced herself- I remembered the confidence Granddad had in her mother's opinion and although he did not visit her that frequently should any family member be hospitalized he was sure to pay her a visit and get her opinion. So I introduced her briefly to you as Granddad's cousin and she kindly placed a magazine on your bed, looked at the monitor and expressed her optimism with what she saw. I thanked her and she left. This visit turned out to be quite poignant as she was the last visitor you had. I remained sitting-to the foot of your bed rubbing your hand-Kerill to the side stroking your forehead. I told you the doctor had told us everything was under control. From the earlier time that you had been taken to this ward and we had settled down with you at your bedside I sensed this all-encompassing tranquillity and serenity but despite the medics reassurances the intuitive message being relayed to the deepest space in me was that all was over and this was waste of medical time. The definitive message emanating from you Ailbhe was "I'm going to fox them". "I'm going to get away". I was in no doubt internally but that you were telling me you were dying. It amazed me afterwards that I remained calm and just seemed to go with the flow and facilitate your dying Ailbhe. It was as though I was giving you permission to die. Then that gentle wave you gave us as if to say a last good bye-you seemed relaxed and peaceful also that transient vision I experienced of Granddad to the side of your bed wordlessly announcing the news -"I got this job". I immediately took this to mean that he had come to take you through to the un-seen. While this was all of course mind talk this experience has been a great source of consolation to me Ailbhe. Of course I can't be sure as to what it was like for you but I did feel great empathy and connectedness with you at that time. John O Donohue puts words on the experience but only to some extent as of course the personal experience can never be fully articulated. We can but aim at an articulation. As I think I said before Ailbhe I did not come across John O Donoghue's work until post your death so I don't know what resonance it would have had were I to have read it minus the experience of being with you as you died but his depiction of a death bed in his book Divine Beauty fits perfectly with my experience.

"A death bed is more like an altar than a bed. It is an altar where the flesh and blood of a life is transformed into external spirit. Rather than being unsure, anxious and bungling, we should endeavour to be present there with the most contemplative priestly grace-regardless of the shock and pain of our grief; our whole attention should be dedicated to the one who is setting off on their solitary journey. We will have plenty of time later to engage our own grief. Now we need to provide the best shelter, the sweetest love, the most sensitive listening and the most wholesome words for the one who is dying. This is the most significant time, the last moments of time on earth. Therefore it is vital to attend and listen".

Well I hope Ailbhe that the period of your death and dying was as devoid of fear and struggle for you as it was for me. The vibes I got were in no way to the contrary and while obviously we were restricted to the perimeters of the event as death is not an experience any of us can have. We can but see it from one side. For me looking back it was as if my normal thinking and functioning had been transcended and that I was spiritually at one with you enabling you to make your exit in a calm comfortable way. While John O Donoghue acknowledges that "Death is the great shadow that darkens every life it is a huge mystery". When the individual life flows towards death, he says, it also flows through death. It travels like the music of the river sustained by its passion and belonging and within the sureness of its flowing the river is alive. It has a future and urgency for new possibility. It has no fear of death and yet at the end of its flow, a river always seems to be dying into the huge embrace of the ocean. Yet there is no break between the end of the river and its flowing life. The song of its end continues to sing back to the river towards the first moments of its visible infant flow"- "At death the music of the heart becomes one with the unheard eternal melody". For me it was the greatest privilege to have been present with you as you died Ailbhe and I hope the shelter Kerill and I provided was what you needed. I hope Grandads presence was as real and as comforting for you as it was for me.

The assuring doctor gone. Assumpta gone to collect your clean glad rags from fairy godmother Mags. Your last visitor gone. A kind looking young nurse stood silently resting both her hands on the bottom of your bed and looking straight up at the monitor over your head. Kerill stood at the top of your bed to the right. I sat at the other side towards the bottom of your bed gently stroking your hands. Three doctors took up position to my left at the top end of your bed. They were from what I could see huddled around a wall connection to which your tubes were connected. They were bent forward looking downwards. One doctor seemed to be down on his knees doing something with connections and sounding cranky and censorious, raised his voice complaining about connection while the others watched him silently and submissively. I had this urge to shout at them and ask if they knew what they were doing and to remind them that the connection they were manipulating were connected to my daughter and suggest-they get help. I had the feeling rightly or wrongly that they were unsure about what they were doing or supposed to be doing. Regrettably this gut feeling never got beyond the intuitive. I'm sorry to say Ailbhe I lost courage-hesitated-telling myself it would be an arrogance on my part to interfere,- these were the professionals after all. So I quelled the notion (quite dissimilar Ailbhe to the courage you showed the previous night in challenging that manager for what you considered a demeaning of the staffs dignity by his addressing them numerically rather than using their individual names). While I still feel I should have expressed my alarm earlier the episode was over in minutes. I noticed that you were trying to push yourself forward in the bed. I got the feeling you were uncomfortable. Your breathing had changed so I did say "Ailbhe wants to sit up". I remember the words so clearly nurse standing at the bottom of the bed took her eyes off the monitors took her hands off the bed and quickly walked forward and put your pillows to your back to support you sitting up. You sat up-head bent down as nurse repeated breathe slowly Ailbhe look at your mother and breathe. I kept rubbing your hand; Kerill rubbed your back assuring you that you were just having a panic attack. The doctors had stood up and were staring at your monitors with a look of total paralysis. I screamed "THIS IS SERIOUS". You fell backwards and Ailbhe I just can't forget the size of your eyes as you stared directly into my eyes. They were wide open and huge, huge, huge. The eyes we are told are the window to the soul. Alarm bells, crisis declared, summon to arms, medical personnel seemed to automatically appear from all corners as the emergency team swung into immediate action with admirable precision. Kerill and I were dispatched to the day room, told to remain there and we would be kept informed as to developments. I knew in my heart that it was all over Ailbhe, that they were wasting their time. As we walked to the day room we met some more medical people on route. We met Assumpta coming skipping up the corridor full of joys of the carefree student embarking on her long summer holiday, a bag swinging from her shoulder, containing your clean clothes that Mags had washed ironed and packed. I remember how I hated to rain on her parade but I had no choice. I told her further complications had arisen for you Ailbhe and that we had to leave you to the care of the medical staff and wait in the day room. She looked at us in utter disbelief as she turned and walked to the day room with us.

I've just listened to Pat Kenny on the radio interview (I forget the interviewees name) but he worked as a geriatrician I think I heard him say. Anyhow the interview was to do with a recent seminar on "End of life care ethic and legal challenges". I found what he had to say very interesting. He posed the question "What is a good death? What is a good life? Who decides?" He went on to explore how many of us in this part of the world were brought up influenced by Religions that inculcated the notion of the merits of suffering and the value of a painful death. While we have moved on from this belief we rarely enough feel comfortable developing a policy for our own death. He spoke of how his personal experience of being with his wife as she died from cancer in her fifties had left him questioning how he had handled the situation. He felt on reflection it would have been better for both of them to have talked through the reality of their situation. Both knew her death was imminent. She did not believe in God and religious rite would not have been appropriate for her. Her physical pain was successfully managed by use of drugs. He felt it was his own inability to face the prospect of losing her that thwarted any talk about the reality of her death. He like myself felt it was a missed opportunity. I was glad to hear about the "advance directive" becoming available. Debate and reflection about death can only help us to think ahead and create a better awareness of what is unavoidable for all of us, a most seriously significant occasion. John O Donoghue writes of the possibility of death resembling birth, and how if a baby in the safety of the womb were to be told that it was about to be catapulted out onto this vast earth how frightened it might be. Indeed when I was growing up birth like death was veiled in a similar kind of secrecy. It was not spoken about as openly as today, more in whispers. Now of course that has all changed. Many parents now speak openly and some talk to the baby in the womb pre birth. I've digressed Ailbhe.

Kerril immediately rang his parents and they were on their way to the hospital immediately. Assumpta felt optimistic. A nurse came in, said no news yet, trying to get a heartbeat, she would be back to keep us informed. Kerril's parents arrived. All present seemed optimistic that you would be fine Ailbhe. I said little but could not share their optimism. I knew inside me that you were truly gone and there would be no coming back. I felt sorry for the nurse as she came in and out informing us. My whole being knew it was work in vain. Then nurse returned flanked by the doctors. Poor things their faces told it all. Is Ailbhe gone I asked, is she dead? Yes came the tearful reply. We never did get the heartbeat and they stood in silence with us. A kind nurse came with a tray of tea and biscuits. To our astonishment the biscuits Ailbhe were your very own favourite biscuits "Traditional Scottish all butter shortbread", each biscuit enclosed in the traditional Scottish wrapper. We could hardly believe our eyes.

I remember feeling so awful at the thought of having to convey this news to dad, Aonghus and Aidín but felt I should do so myself. The nurses were so helpful. Rightly or wrongly it was my conviction that each family member be given the straight bitter truth. There was no way to sugar this pill. I've always found for myself that I manage best when presented with the truth, worst case scenario, I can then work backwards. I hate been fed false expectations but then I suppose there is no right or wrong way to deliver such news. I remember been worried at the prospect of dad setting out from Cavan to drive under such distress. Scotland, where Aonghus was now, seemed so far away. I can still hear that wail of grief that came back down the phone to me as he digested the news Ailbhe, your big beautiful brother was heartbroken at loosing you. I did have the presence of mind to ask in advance if he was alone and was relieved with his response that Michelle was on her way and would be there with him in a matter of minutes. I said I'd hang up, give him a few minutes and ring back. When I rang back I found he was over the initial shock. Michelle had arrived and they were able to start the necessary arrangements to get home the next morning. Assumpta was on the phone letting all who needed to, know the sad news. Aidín was in Dublin living just out the road in Castleknock so we were able to contact her as she arrived home from work before you were pronounced dead Ailbhe and she arrived into the hospital a short time after you left us having got a lift from one of her kind housemates. I think I already mentioned how as her friend drove her to the hospital minutes before you died the song "Last breath" was played on the car radio. She had never heard the song previously, but found it in keeping with the sadness she felt and the feeling that all was far from well with you.

One Last Breath (Ringtone)
"One last breath please come now, I think I'm falling.
I'm holding on to all I think is safe, it seems I found the road to nowhere
And I'm trying to escape. I yelled back when I heard the thunder but I'm down to one last breath and with it let me say one last breath.
Please come now I think I'm falling. I'm holding on to all I think is safe. It seems I found the road to nowhere and I'm trying to escape.
Hold me now I'm six feet from the edge
and I'm thinking that maybe six feet aint so far down.
I'm looking down now that it's over reflecting on all of my mistakes.

I thought I found the road to somewhere, somewhere in his
grace.
I cried out Heaven save me but I'm down to one last breath.
And with it let me say hold me now I'm six feet from the edge
and I'm thinking six feet aint so far down. Sad eyes follow me
but I still believe there is something left for you and me for you
and me. Hold me now
I'm six feet from the edge and I'm thinking that six feet aint so
far down".

Aidín tells then of how she arrived in the hospital looked at our faces and decided she would not listen to what she knew we had to tell her.

Kerrils family contacted all the relevant people on their side of the family. Mags started into arranging beds and food, always so practical. We were surrounded by kindness. Dad arrived safely and said how he just talked away to you on the journey. We were told that our time back with you would unfortunately have to be restricted, due to post-mortem regulations. Your lovely young body would have to be taken away within a legally specified time because of the suddenness of you death. We were allowed gather around your bed in the ward. A Chaplin came and said some prayers. I vividly remember a big cold looking steel casket arriving at your bedside. A very polite empathetic porter informing us that he now had to take your body away for post-mortem. I wanted to object, putting your lovely body into that cold looking contraption seemed such a cruel violation.

Reluctantly we said our goodbyes and obediently stepped outside as he lowered your body into the casket. We walked along the corridors staying with you for as long as was allowed touching the cold casket as we dreaded the imminent parting. Wishing this journey might never end as we approached the door with the big sign STRICTLY NO ENTERY my mind flashed back to that day about fourteen years previous when you were having your kidney removed. I walked what looked like the same corridors with you as the porter wheeled you for the required surgery to the operating theatre. I remember how when we came to what looked like the same door with big writing and I think "No Entry Staff Only" glaring down at us the nurse telling me I could go off for a few hours and meet you after surgery as I was not allowed into theatre. That parting I'd found difficult and I walked up and down the hospital drive way wishing the hands on my watch would move faster. But this parting was much more brutal. I was perfectly aware of the harsh reality. Our meetings and chats were over, confined to the realm of memory.

Kerills parents kindly suggested dad and I spend the night with them in their home. We did so and a great idea it was. The girls, your sisters in law in the midst of their grief had food ready, beds made and we all gathered together, stayed up remembering you and feeling you very close to us as we sheltered each other in our great loss.

The hospital told us your body would be released sometime the next day. Aonghus arrived next morning and dad, kerill and myself met him at the hospital. Your consultant plus another doctor met with us briefly, seemed sad and a little tearful but the consultant could not account for what happened said that the personnel involved in your care the day before had had a long meeting earlier that the doctor who was in charge of inserting your permcath, an Australian, had gone home for a rest and was unable to meet us. I remember thinking briefly I hope it's not home to his native country he has gone as that might make it difficult for us to meet him and be told what exactly had happened. Anyhow as none of the team who were pertinent to your care at the critical time the day before were present at the meeting I assumed a meeting with them would take place at a later date, following post-mortem and at a time when we would be in a more balanced frame of mind. Well I was wrong. I'll talk more about that to you later.

Kerill agreed that we take you back home to Farranseer, to have your funeral service in Coronea Church and to have you buried there in the cemetery in the shadow of the ancient Bruce Mountain, the cemetery where your brother Aoghdhán had been buried thirty years earlier. As the hospital were not now able to release your body until the following day we decided it was best for Aonghus, Aidín, Assumpta, Dad and myself to return home and set about the practical arrangements. So we left Kerill in Dublin to be close by you and to be available for the heart wrenching task of formally identifying your body.

Dad, Aonghus and Kerill sorted the grave, undertaker and coffin. I set about having the house especially the sitting room ready for your arrival. I just felt you would like to spend your last days there, where you so often stretched out on the floor in front of the open fire relaxed in the bosom of the family. I made sure to give the carpet a generous sprinkling of the lavender shake and vac to have the fragrance to your liking Ailbhe. The girl's helped. Neighbours too came as did extended family all offering help and condolences.

While as the old Irish adage on death contends "Death is a very direct individual who sends no story before him", "*Is fear díreach é an bás ní chuireann sé scéal ar bith roimhe.*" Yet now looking back I'm amazed Ailbhe at how despite the unexpectedness of it all we kept equilibrium and managed to stay in charge despite for my own part anyway been fully aware of the devastating finality of the unexpected traumatic event that was been visited upon us. Everything seemed to, fall perfectly into place. Wednesday July 10th-our wedding anniversary-(thirty one year's previously Dad and I had got married)-now all five of us set off for Dublin to bring you home to Farranseer. We went to Mags house en route and true to form she had an open house for us all-plenty of food. Mary came with her delicious cakes tarts buns-generous as ever. Thanks Mary. Many friends came to offer their support-but of course no Ailbhe-how I thought you would love to be in the midst of the gathering, all the happy mischievous escapades you had got up to while staying there when you were in college. Some people suggest that places hold the energy of what happened, hold memories and that some people of particular psyche can get that energy. Just four years later, this house was host to a similar get together when Mags herself died very suddenly having only reached her mid fifties. She left us on that unique date 6-6-06-

her death too very much sans warning sans anticipation. While I would have regarded Mags as quite pivotal to you becoming the great Ailbhe that you were. I know how you did not always see eye to eye but well I knew how much you appreciated her wonderful support so I was a bit taken a back at first when her first reaction on hearing of your death was to exclaim "I only wish I had been better to her". We can be hard on ourselves. We then set off for the hospital mortuary where poor Kerill had to identify your body-so brave, "the strongest of silent men". I think you defined him in one of your poems. A porter wheeled you into us and I remember feeling a surge of delight at seeing you and having you back. Kerills sisters had decked you out beautifully. Your lovely long black hair and quoting Aidíns poem "Ailbhe" your "pudgy cool cheeks, a smell of lived in skin, sharp, angel, clean" and you were clad in your lovely long Celtic gown and the recently purchased red shoes. A priest came to us offering his sympathy. He wisely and humbly said he had neither answers nor explanations for our tragedy. I was so relieved that he didn't go off on a "God's will speil". People gathered around your open coffin. Many of the nurses who had so kindly and expertly looked after you came to say a final farewell. For me as we surrounded your coffin and I introduced the various people I knew to you, the overall atmosphere was of a shocked sadness - a sense of disbelief. However I was well aware of the stark reality-that never again would we hear your voice, your hearty laugh see your unique smile, the glint in those big beautiful eyes-"frog eyes" as Aidín was later to describe them. The thought of burying your young beautiful body seemed an outrage but this desolation was somehow tinged with a calm warm assuring comfort of manageability and the overriding conviction that everything was going to be alright. All the time I had an innate perception of your inherent presence in our midst. Kerill travelled in the hearse from Dublin to Farranseer with his lovely young wife. We followed behind you and I was very impressed by the respect shown to the hearse. As it was the busy time of evening we came on heavy traffic-people going home from work but so many were so patient allowing the hearse and funeral cars out and so many making the sign of the cross or gesturing in a reverent way as the hearse passed. As we approached Cavan town, coming along the main Dublin road the hearse indicated turning left into Mac Donald's restaurant. We thought initially-a mechanical fault. Then Kerill got out quickly and went into the restaurant so we assumed to answer the call of nature. He promptly returned to the hearse package in hand. He placed it along side your coffin. It was a Mc Donald's Happy Meal. A meal that both of you had been fond of and so often enjoyed. When we reached home family friends and neighbours were out on the front street to meet us providing a supportive shelter for your final return Ailbhe. There was not a sound. I can still hear that silence. It was as if W.H Auden's instructions in his poem Funeral Blues were been strictly adhered to –"stop all the clocks, cut off the telephone, prevent the dog from barking with a juicy bone. Silence the pianos and with muffled drum bring out the coffin, let the mourners come". Visually we could see that a sizable group of people had assembled but I think was I to have lacked the faculty of eye sight I would have deducted that we were completely alone with you Ailbhe-such was the atmosphere as I experienced it-this reverent surreal silence. We took you into the sitting room-that room -that down through the years had been a sanctuary of refuge, relaxation and jollity to all four of you. The following lines penned by our own poet your sister Aidín again captures the mood-in her poem Absence "The house shocked, The Chair listening out, The T.V. listening out and I listening out-But nothing bar a chronic echoless void in reply". Silence broken-tea and sandwiches arrived, more tea more sandwiches. People were so kind just carried us. Neighbours and family had just taken over and everything just got done. People came and went. We talked endlessly about you, explained your sudden departure as best we could. We were in no doubt but that bringing you home was right for us. I introduced you to people as they came Ailbhe. It all felt quite cosy but now and then I'd feel the dread of the brute reality of the situation. I remember looking at you and thinking how unfair it all was how you loved life, had so much to live for, you looked so young and the words of the song-"If those lips could only speak, if those eyes could only see, if those beautiful golden tresses were still a reality" and the lines from Tennyson's poem "But o for the touch of a vanished hand, and the sound of a voice that is still..................But the tender grace of a day that is dead "will never come back to me". Kept coming into my head. I mentioned to a neighbour how I just could not contemplate taking you out of the house to the church to bury you. She advised just let it all go over your head. I reflected on this well intentioned advice. It seemed tempting-should I get medication to see me through-I wondered but the voice inside me said no engage with every bit of it. So this is what I tried to do and in hindsight I'm glad I was able to do so-not suggesting that this would be the best option for everyone in similar circumstances. One size never fits all. We went through old photographs that had not been looked at for ages and these photographs have become very precious Ailbhe. Time kept ticking away. Father Sean McGoldrick who had officiated at your wedding just a mere twenty months previously was waiting here to receive you when we arrived from Dublin and was most helpful and arranged to take your funeral mass on Friday July 12th. He himself of course has since joined you Ailbhe, an untimely death and a great loss too. We sat in the kitchen-Dad, myself, Kerill, Aonghus, Aidín and Assumpta tossing out different ideas and options as to what we felt would be an appropriate funeral service. When it was suggested that some of the notions under consideration might not meet church protocol there was a chorus from all four to the effect. This is our funeral arrangements for Ailbhe if the church has a problem with what we decide on "we will go ahead ourselves". That last sentence stuck in my memory. I felt it was just the attitude you yourself would take Ailbhe. Now Father Sean and the clergy involved could not have been more accommodating and kind. But I felt it was so healthy to see your siblings claiming their own power and taking personal responsibility. We followed your wishes, so we decided to keep you with us as long as possible, skip the removal as you had told me of your dislike of the practice so we agreed we would all leave the house together. I mentioned how Kerill was so distraught and how finding your old play tea set cup brought such comfort to him. Now I don't think you had to my knowledge, ever spoken of any preference you had regarding the actual funeral service. We never did discuss your experience of funerals. Perhaps if I had been more tuned in and comfortable and encouraged the conversation you opened the week before-asking me "what happens when you die"? I might have got an insight but no point in sending myself on a guilt trip at this stage. My own earliest memory of attending funerals services in church is of this black austere clerically dominated scary event. In our diocese during my childhood we had a tradition of offerings at funerals. A most despicable practise I think you will agree Ailbhe when I explain. I think now a day's funeral services are one of the areas where the Catholic Church excels-can be so compassionate, inclusive and personal. But back to the past during the funeral service of my youth a table would be placed inside the altar. The grieving male members of the immediate family of the deceased person "sons-brothers) would take up position at this table. (Never women if my memory is correct and not because women could not count then but at that time women were not normally allowed inside the altar rails. That seemed to be a male only arena except of course to clean and arrange flowers). The priest would stand or sit to the side while the congregation would walk up the church to the altar and place their offering (money) on this table. We had our own money at that time as we had not joined the euro so the usual offerings would be (a pound)-(ten shillings) or (half a crown=two shillings and sixpence). The social status of the deceased would determine the amount of offerings and status seemed to be determined by the social standing in the community-based on property owned size of farm business or professional ranking and family connections, of a deceased-"very Christian" I hear you say. Now if an adult could not attend the funeral personally but wished to be associated they would put their monetary offering in an envelope, write their name and address plus the amount of money enclosed and send same with a neighbour or friend. As children we were often dispatched to do this errand –a task I often did. Well when all present in the church had filed through, placed their offerings on the table and settled back in their seats the family members at the table would proceed to open each envelope taking the money out and placing the empty envelopes in a neat pile. They would then count this money. Job completed- A whisper would pass between the counters and the priest as they returned to their seats by the coffin of their loved one. The priest would then read out the information on each envelope-name, address, amount paid eg. "Thomas McGovern Derryvella two and six, "John Duffy Derryna ten shillings, "Pat McGovern Coronea, one pound and on and on and I'd often think will this ever end-and where I lived so many McGovern's the name was ringing in my ears. Finally he would run out of envelopes. His reverence would then step back to the centre of the altar and announce-"The offerings amounted to five pounds"-"Thank you for your very generous offerings of twenty pounds" or some such speak. One can easily imagine-human nature being as it is, what comparisons, gloating's and humiliations must have followed. It was awful and I can well remember as a child getting a vile sensation from the experience. It was like an auction. For a long time I thought this money was to help out the grieving family at this difficult time but imagine my consternation Ailbhe when I discovered that not at all not a penny went to the family. It all went to the priest. How such a barbaric practise went un challenged for so long is beyond me. I'm surprised some of our reflective writers have not penned a chapter or two on this particular phenomenon now perhaps they have and I've just missed it. Most families in the area would not have had money like that to give and often had to borrow it to avoid shame and humiliation. Well back to more civilized times. The automatic reaction of your siblings to the mildest of a suggestion that they might have to defer to a prescribed format when preparing for your funeral service Ailbhe exposed the gap of epic proportions that have arisen in one generation. Our neighbour Gerry (a whiz kid on the computer) worked tirelessly with my sister Margaret your brother sisters and extended family on getting your funeral booklet sorted. I think you would approve of the finished product. A last minute urgent request was conveyed to Mary Spooner to iron Kerills white shirt for the funeral-which she tearfully did reminding us that the last white shirt she had ironed was Kerills wedding shirt twenty months earlier-you'll remember Ailbhe how Kerill and the best men had stayed in Marys house the night before your wedding. For me to have had those last days with you at home in that sitting room that you had found so relaxing and in the environment you knew and so loved is such a consoling memory. John O Donoghue's depiction of a home in his book Divine Beauty is what I would wish Farranseer was to you. "A home is not simple a building it is the shelter around the intimacy of a life. Coming in from the outside world and its rasp of force and usage, you relax and allow yourself to be who you are. The inner walls of a home are threaded with the textures of one's soul, a subtle weave of presences". While I can't know if you had any awareness of where you were Ailbhe but if you did have I suspect the thought of having to leave the warm shelter of Farranseer never again to return would be for you tinged with immense sadness. Certainly for me the realization that such was inevitable and now imminent was excruciatingly painful. Aidín's poem written the October following your death perhaps gives a pertinent insight. She titled the poem "Farranseer" but for rhythmic reasons interposed Manderly for "Farranseer"

Manderly

"O what of these worldly woes when resting in beauty such as here
I fear naught for friends or foe
Now that my Manderly is near,
TEAR ME AWAY OH NO
OH NO NEVER TEAR ME AWAY,
The autumn leaves are swirling in
A fresh sweet lullaby breeze
My heart is comforted, my soul is

Sooted in-gentle whisperings of
The trees. Oh the breathtaking beauty of
This green land. Where I was born and raised.
Quiet now, welcome-autumn, winter, spring summer,
Each with such miracles to be praised"

Well time running out, the undertaker arrived-put well again by John O Donoghue in his poem "Coffin"-" The undertaker has a low, slow voice without echo and immune to sorrow, that fits itself to the silence of death will not alert the mourners, lets them feel secure in the script of the funeral". Friends extended family members and neighbours vacated the sitting room leaving you all to ourselves Ailbhe. Yes our time with you was running out. Time to take you to church for your funeral service and burial. What a brutal desolate reality but there was no alternative, no escape. Radical acceptance our only sane option. So Dad, Aonghus, Aidín, Assumpta and myself and of course Kerill circuled you in your coffin in the sitting room for our last look at our beautiful Ailbhe. We touched you, rubbed you, kissed you whispered personal messages to you, put personal little memorabilia that had sentimental connections between us into your coffin. I felt your shiny thick black beautiful hair. These were and still remain the most poignant and sacred of moments. Too soon however we were respectfully interrupted by the re-entry of the undertaker as he wordlessly conveyed the inevitable brutal sentence -Time up Ailbhe- your coffin had to be closed. Surely this has to be the most heart wrenching of moments experienced by humans. Now perhaps if a loved one dies following a painful terminal illness or where life had lost all quality and become a burden there might be an understandable sense of relief that their pain had ended and this realization might ease the sting of their loss. But this was very different Ailbhe, you had been so full of the joys and adventures of life, you had so much to live for and so much to offer life and so abruptly this great life with all of its potential had been cruelly snatched from you and here were we now left helplessly facing this harsh grotesques naked reality of that loss.

Again John O Donoghue gives verbalization to the stark reality of these final moments in the poem Coffin- "Weeping heads dip deep into her cold form. Hands enshrine her face; lips tip the forehead as they enter whispers in her thick sleep. A son sows a locket under her neck. The lid is brought down, the light sealed out, the screws with crucifix heads would down tight. A twitch arches her corpse against the dark" Reflecting back Ailbhe with a cold factual look at our situation it is easy to empathize with the utter despair and loneliness expressed by the poet W.H Auden in Funeral Blues or indeed the Irish poem " An Bhean Caointe" written by Padraig Mac Piarais-poems I expect you came across in school- but paradoxically while I was aware of the awful finality of our situation and certainly all artificiality and pretentions were well and truly excoriated thankfully I never did experience the depth of despair expressed in these poems. There was for me this overriding atmosphere of peace. It was as if a transcendent ether was carrying me through with a silent internal assurance that all would be well. Call it grace or blessing, or survival instinct or the inestimable power of intention. Perhaps the sustenance came not only from the kindness and compassion of the many people who thought of us, wished us on and sheltered and supported us but also from our ancestors among the dead who too helped carry us through. Thankfully we were able to remain in charge and I am now comforted at having been able to enter fully into what was unfolding. As we wheeled you in your coffin out the sitting room door into the front hall and through the porch-(that porch that down through the years had been the place of so many arrivals and departures Fáiltes and Sláns for all of us down through the years) thinking how it had been through this same threshold you had made your first entrance to our home here some twenty six years previously as Dad and I carried you in your new little carrycot to be greeted by your little brother and ecstatic Granny. I knew there would be no returning for you this time Ailbhe but all I could hope was that wherever you were now you were surrounded with as much love and support and joy as had greeted you on your first arrival home here twenty six years ago. A crowd of supportive family friends and neighbours had assembled in the front street and stood in reverent silence as we wheeled you over the street to the awaiting hearse to take you on your final journey for your funeral service and burial. I remember how you had as a child played here, rode your bike-learned to ride, through the trees, rode your pony played on the swing and –now silence. I still remembered that absolute silence-so appropriate as this was well beyond words, no dog barked, no bird sang it was as if the wind too had taken a temporary vow of silence. It was so comforting for me to discover from the poem you yourself wrote entitled Silence and indeed you're other poems Ailbhe after your death that you had reached such a personal depth and wisdom in your short life.

Silence

Written by Ailbhe Hannon Dunne

It is only in silence you will hear what you so attentively listen for.
It is only in silence you will find the peace you seek so desperately.
It is only in silence you will see the things your eyes have been straining for.
It is only in silence you will reach the place you longingly seek.
It is only in silence your soul can hear, see, find and know.
It is only in silence you can rest.
There is a voice you ignore or maybe it's just you can't hear,
You are listening with your ears and forgetting about what your ears can't hear.
You are searching with your eyes and forgetting what your eyes can't see.
You look so useless so near yet so far. If only you'd listen with your soul you'd get to the whole.

Otto Frank, on reading the famous diaries of his daughter Anne remarked how he did not know his daughter until he read her diaries.

Kerrill travelled in the hearse with you to the church as we followed behind. A Garda directed traffic at the cross roads. We were astounded at the number of people. So many made such a personal effort to come and support us and bid you that final farewell. Now as your funeral was at three pm on a Friday many must have had to make special work arrangements and many travelled distances to be with us. What did you make of it all Ailbhe? As we approached the church Sean Kelly a local piper kindly played his pipes as we took you from the hearse. He piped you right up the church. This brought back memories of that day twenty months previously, your wedding day, when this same piper piped you up this same church where the same priest Father Sean had celebrated your marriage ceremony and now we were back to say our final goodbyes. My mind went back to that happy day and I remembered how beautiful you were so calm and real not in the least into vanity or image just happy to be yourself. I remembered the problem with the shoes Ailbhe.

The weather on your funeral day seemed more obliging, brilliant sunshine not a whisper of rain. Remember how we often joked about the rattling sounds of wind and rain through the church on your wedding day, nature having its input providing unique background music giving the ceremony a haunting ghost like quality. Now for your funeral all was so still and quiet. My much quoted guru John O Donoghue in his book 'Divine Beauty' writes "There is a deep silence in death". He says "Death is the master of stillness. In silence it takes you into silence from which no echo returns". Kerril gave a fabulous eulogy. You must have been so proud of him. When he told us of his intention to write and deliver his personal eulogy we tried to persuade him that it might over stress and upset him but he stood his ground and insisted. We were proven wrong again Ailbhe and your "strongest of silent men" won the day. So many people spoke to us afterwards as to how deeply moving they found his sentiments and indeed many spoke of the privilege it had been for them to be present that day at your funeral. I found the service sad but empowering. There was this feeling of "peace that surpasses human understanding". Prior to your funeral Ailbhe I would have believed the custom of the people present in church coming forward , shaking hands with the bereaved and verbally expressing their condolences an unhelpful intrusion on the bereaved family even if well intentioned, a custom that we should drop. You probably heard me say this after funerals that I'd attend, how I'd felt it unfair of us all keeping the poor bereaved exhausted relatives waiting for all present to file past shaking hands. Well my own experience surprised me. I found the hand shake very comforting and reassuring. I could remember each one and how unique each hand shake was. So experience can be the best teacher. We had the song "Time to Say Goodbye" By Andrew Boucelli played at the end of the service in the church before we took you to your grave – we had earlier played this song in the house before we took you from Farranseer. Then of course the piper piped you down the graveyard to your grave. I hate the word grave, what about place of rest, I don't know. Grave to me sounds too static and still for you Ailbhe and I never think of you just resting, more like blowing in the wind, shopping in Dublin, partying or chatting. As the final prayers were been said at the grave side the heavens opened. The rain without the slightest warning lashed down on us. The day had been so good that very few if any had brollies. The undertaker later told us how it was his practice to bring umbrellas for the mourners but that day the weather was so settled it seemed totally unnecessary so he broke with custom and came minus his umbrellas. So we all had to scatter abruptly and make for the shelter of our cars. I remember thinking this is typical of you Ailbhe you don't want us hanging around." You've all done you bit now and get on with it" was the message I felt coming from you and the words of one of your favourite songs started going round in my head to my slight amusement despite the sadness of the situation "Raindrops keep falling on my head... but I'm never going to stop the rain by complaining because I'm free nothing is worrying me" and I hoped and still hope you are free with nothing worrying you. Indeed since your death we have found that when we visit your grave and if we are lingering around this quite un announced shower comes as if again you are saying " Get on with it!". Poor Kerill found it difficult to visit your grave after your funeral. He made a few attempts but had to turn back until one day he begged you to send him a sign that you were happy. He set off from the house here having asked me to follow in about half an hour. I did so and when I got to your grave I found him there very peaceful and relieved. He said how as he arrived at the grave this robin flew around your grave singing; then flew down onto your grave for a few moments, then took a drink of water circled your grave singing and then flew off. This had given him the assurance he sought at that point. It was pretty similar to your little tea set cup making its appearance out of the blue the morning of your funeral that I already mentioned.

Family and friends came back to the house for food and although we did not have you physically present with us Ailbhe I felt your spirit very much in our midst and the get together despite our sadness was tempered with humour and fun. Strange to say despite the heavy rain and so many people getting a soaking no one suffered any ill effects. Aonghus' friends, Aidín's, Assumpta's and of course your own and Kerill's friends were so supportive and generous. I'd have only the height of praise for your vintage, the way they looked out for each other. Now there is the little added extra here, you casually mentioned to me some weeks prior to your death that Aonghus had a girl friend in Scotland. You were texting him so you said how Aonghus played his cards close to his chest and how he had not told you her name but you had deduced that she was a nurse so you were including in your text to him "next time you're coming back bring Florence" Well wasn't it strange that Florence who turned out to be the beautiful Michelle now Mrs Aonghus Hannon paid her first visit to us to attend your funeral. I do so regret you never got to meet Michelle but as Aonghus said in his wedding speech I know you'd both get on well.

You will remember Peter, Assumpta's boyfriend, you did meet him in Dublin but the romance ended shortly afterwards. Well on hearing of your death he rang Assumpta, came to the house and as the old saying goes the half quenched coal was easily lighted. So Peter is now your brother in law and a very welcome addition to our family. So in a strange way beginnings and endings converged.

I think you will agree Ailbhe that we have all done very well with getting on with our lives since your death and as you had no time for moaning Minnies I know you'd approve. All went back to work and muddled through with getting on with getting on. Kerill of course while he returned to work for a period of time decided to try for a post grad, got accepted and to his credit completed his course and is now Dr. Kerill Dunne. This you predicted, remember?

Getting on with life without you was not easy Ailbhe. I can and will only speak for myself and my own personal experience. There were times very bleak times after the rituals and drama of your funeral when a desolate sense of loss would overwhelm me. It might strike out of the blue. I could be getting on fine to be just suddenly ambushed. I remember blissfully walking through Dunne's Store one day, an outfit caught my eye, "that would be something Ailbhe would wear" I thought and then this awful sense of loss hit me and I had to head for the car and get back to the shelter of the house. To this day I can be going along the street in town see someone who reminds me of you, would be about your age, usually dressed in a Celtic style and I'd be off wondering had you lived would this be how you would now look? I remember a day in Dublin having such an experience. This lady seemed to cross my path a few times, at Bus Áras, again in Penny's and yet again crossing the street at the spire. Each time she looked more like you and just dressed as I'd imagined you'd be, with that pleasant "happy in my own skin" air. I wanted to go and speak with her and hear her voice and look into her eyes but of course I did desist. As I walked along with my thoughts of loss this poor unfortunate girl stepped out begging for money obviously heavy on drugs, again looking about you age and build and I could hear you on my shoulder saying "This too could have been my lot". So my grief abated and the lines of Anne Bronte's poem A Reminiscence rang in my ears,

Yet thought I cannot see thee more,
Tis still a comfort to have seen,
And though thy transient life is o'er,
Tis sweet to think that thou hast been.
To think a soul so near divine,
Within a form so angel fair,
United to a heart like thine,
Has gladdened once our humble sphere.

The poet Moya Cannan calls poetry "A conversation between souls". After you funeral dad and myself took to reading all the poems on the theme of death we could find and I compiled a personal collection of poems that best spoke my feelings. Some lines in James Russell Lowell's poem "After the Burial" would express the sad empty despair that at times engulfed me.

To the spirit its splendid conjectures,
To the flesh its sweet despair,
Immortal? I feel it and know it,
Who doubts it of such as she?
But that's the pangs' very secret-
Immortal away from me!"

Console if you will, I can bear it,
Tis a well-meant alms of breath,
But not all preaching since Adam
Has made death other than death.
It is pagan; but wait till you feel it,
That jar of our earth, that dull shock,
When the ploughshare of deeper passion
Tears down to our primitive rock.

I already spoke about your love affair with shoes Ailbhe. Well I kept some of your clothes. I take them out now and then to look at them, feel them and smell them. You will remember the dark green laced runner you had. They were kind of old faithful's. You had them for quite a while, were very fond of them, spoke how comfy they were. When I take them out and put my hand inside them where your dainty little feet would so often have entered I think of all the places you went to wearing them. I can picture you legging it up Grafton Street or heading for the craic in Quinn's in Drumcondra, the memories they hold, and in what are my thankfully rare moments of paralysing grief the final lines in "After the Burial" speak for me,

"Communion in spirit? Forgive me,
But I, who am eartly and weak,
Would give all my incomes from dreamland
For her rose-leaf palm on my cheek.

That little shoe in the corner,
So worn and wrinkled and brown-
Its emptiness confutes you,
And argues your wisdom down".

Then the time after your death I went back to the place in Clontarf where you were so happily living at the time of your death and as I walked the strand and remembered how much you loved this walk and view Tennyson's poem "Break, Break, Break" said it all.

Break, Break, break,
On thy cold grey stones, O sea
And I would that my tongue could utter the thoughts that arise in me
And the stately ships go on to the haven under the hill
But o for the touch of a vanish hand,
And the sound of a voice that is still.
Break, Break, Break,
At the foot of thy crags, o seal.
But the tender grace of a day that is dead will never come back to me.

Those last lines expressing the harsh unambiguous reality of the loss-

A former friend with whom you had lost contact with for the year or two prior to your death on hearing the news of your death kindly paid us a visit to express his sympathy a few weeks post your death. In the course of our chatting he mentioned how your paths had not crossed in a while but how some weeks earlier he was driving through a part of Phibsborough where you had lived when you were friends and how he saw this female walking along on the footpath. He was convinced it was you so he pulled his car over and let down the window to enquire how life was with you Ailbhe-were you married? Had you children? But to his amazement you had vanished, there was nobody there so he drove on about his business somewhat taken aback. On checking date and time we discovered it happened at the exact day and time of your funeral. Yes Ailbhe the unanswerable question would continue to surface. Where exactly had you gone to? Where were you?-the age old philosophical question where does the flame go when the candle is quenched? Some of the questions are so well articulated in the poem November Questions written by John O Donohue in memory of his uncle the late Pete O Donohue-for example

"Where did you go when your eyes closed and you were cloaked in the ancient cold? How did we seem, huddled around the hospital bed?

Did we loom as figures do in dream?
Did your new feet take you beyond to fields of Elysia
Did you have to go to a place unknown?
Were there friendly faces to welcome you, help you settle in?
Have you someone there that you can talk to, someone who
Is drawn to the life you carry?
With your new eyes can you see from within? Is it we
Who seem outside?"

Life without you Ailbhe often felt strange and empty but slowly the raw wound of loss began to heal and I appreciated more and more the great years we had with you. I realized no one, nothing not even death could rob us of our precious memories. The ancient third century poem by Callimachus - showing how grief is tempered by the qualities of memories expresses this reality - I substituted your name Ailbhe in place of Heraclitus to give the poem a more personal resonance.

They told me, Heraclitus,(Ailbhe)
They told me you were dead.
They brought me bitter news to hear
And bitter tears to shed.
I wept as I remembered,
How often you and I
Had tired the sun with talking
And sent him down the sky.
An now that you are lying
My dear old Carian guest,
A hand full of grey ashes
Long long ago at rest.
Still are thy pleasant voices
thy nightingales awake.
For death he taketh all away,
but them he cannot take.
Callimachus
540-480 B.C
T

That verse reminds me of the late night chats and discussions we had in the kitchen at weekends, me with my hot toddy and yourself with a glass of wine or two. Remember Ailbhe how we would comfortably hibernate in the kitchen, enjoying food, drinks, crisps, chat, discussions debates open agenda, no no go areas. Well Aidín wrote a poem aptly titled "The Big Friendly Kitchen" and had it framed as a present for me for my 60th birthday. It now hangs on the kitchen wall.

The Big Friendly Kitchen
The big tom cat curled up in a yellow weaved basket,
The red and blue tartan covered chairs,
Briquettes burning in the brown warmlser cooker,
Mam perched on the wooden box leaning on the singing kettle
The table that dada so often sat at on Christmas morning
Tapping his nails, cosy in his scarf and sheepskin coat.
Ailbhe sat on these big chairs eating crisps and smoking
And talking about psychoanalysis,
Grannies and granddads, cousins and neighbours and friends
Communions, birthdays, weddings and funerals.
Discussions on philosophy, politics, life, death and love.
Tea, hot whiskeys, chips in the deep fat fryer,
Kittens and puppies and babies and
EVERYTHING
By Aidín Hannon

We were surprised to learn from historical research done by a member of a neighbouring family that our house here in Farranseer very likely dates back to the 16th century so just imagine the memories it holds.

Speaking of memories, some time back Aidín mentioned how when she was about fifteen or sixteen years old, she watched a film or drama on T.V. in the sitting room, now the name and details of the film or drama escapes her but it had to do with a young girl left alone in life following the deaths of all her immediate family. What stuck in her memory was the palpable grief of this girl standing alone in a church like building singing a song with the repetitive line "They have only gone out walking and now they will be coming back home". She said how the plaintiveness of the denial and sentiments expressed would unexpectedly resurface much later in her life when she personally was faced with the deaths of loved ones engulfing her in a sense of her own loss and grief. Well recently she decided to go to Google in search and was delighted to get the background to the song (modern technology can be wonderful). According to her research the song dates back to 1833-34. An Austrian father named Friedrich Ruckert distraught with grief following the death of his two daughters to scarlet fever took refuge in writing poetry to cope with his loss. He is said to have written 428 poems in a year, in his "attempt at poetic resuscitation of his children punctuated by anguished outbursts" but above all his poems show a final quiet acquience to fate and to a peaceful world of solace. While the poems were not originally intended for publication later in about 1901-1904 a composer named "Maher" selected five of these poems and set them to music which he personally composed. The music reflected the mixture of feelings-Anguish-Fantasy-Recutitation-the final song ending in a major key and mood of transcendence. Sadly for Maher he lost his own daughter Maria to scarlet fever four years later. Interestingly he later wrote to his friend telling him that when writing this song "I placed myself in the situation that a child of mine had died but when I really lost my daughter I could not have written these songs anymore". Aidín downloaded the song "Now the sun wants to rise as brightly as if nothing terrible had happened during the night. This misfortune had happened only to me but the sun shines equally on everyone. You must not enfold the night in you. You must sink it in eternal light. A little star went out in my tent. Greetings to the joyful light of the world. Now I see well why with such dark flames in many glances you flash upon me. Oh yes as if one look to draw all your strength together. I didn't realise because a mist surrounded me woven of tangled destinies that your beam was already returning home wards to the place from which all rays eminate, you would tell me with your brightness, we would gladly stay with you, now that it is denied to us by fate. Look at us soon, we will not be far away. What are only eyes to you in these days in the coming night shall be your stars. When your mother steps in through the door and I turn my head to see at her, falling on her face my gaze does not first fall but at the place nearer the doorstep there where your dear little face would be. When you with bright joy step inside as you use to my little daughter. When your mother steps in through the door with the glowing candle, it seems to me always you came in too, hurrying behind her as you use to come into the room. Oh you of a fathers cell, a too soon extinguished light. I often think they have only just gone out and now they will be coming back home. The day is fine, don't be dismayed they have just gone for a long walk yes indeed they have just gone out and now they are making their way home. Don't be dismayed the day is fine they have simply made a journey to yonder heights. They have just gone out ahead of us and will not be thinking of coming home. We go to meet them on yonder heights in the sunlight; the day is fine on yonder heights. In this weather in this windy storm I would never have sent the children out. They have been carried off. I wasn't able to warn them. In this weather in this gale I would never have let the children out. I feared they have sickened, those thoughts are now in vain. In this weather, in this storm I would never have let the children out. I was anxious they might die next day. Now anxiety is pointless. In this weather in this windy storm I would never have sent the children out. They have been carried off. I wasn't able to warn them. In this weather in this gale in this windy storm they rest as if in their mother's house frightened by no storm sheltered by the hand of God". Such poetry reminds we humans how death has always been a lonely visitor, producing a dark forlornness, inducing feelings of denial, anger resentment, guilt and questioning. I certainly experienced all of the above Ailbhe. Where had you gone? Were you really gone? Life was strange and empty without your voice, your face your physical presence. The thorn of your absence could emerge through the best of days or happiest of memories re igniting the depth of our loss. The brazen unfairness of it all. Had I done enough to protect you? What if we had delayed that fatal procedure that morning-you were very negative about it when Kerill and I arrived into you. Should we have taken more seriously your mood. Were your instincts telling you something? The regret that we did not insist on been allowed stay with you while the procedure was been carried out as had been our intention-the words of the nurse "Ailbhe was calling for you" as she told us that there had been a complication haunted me-anger that they did not come and get us as we submissively waited in your room. We could so easily have been with you to comfort you. Guilt that I did not go with my gut and shout at the doctors as they agitatedly manipulated these drains that were connected to you as my perception at the time was that they were confused unsure and out of their depth and I had that urge to shout "Are you sure of what you are doing those drains are connected to my daughter should you get help". Regrettably I quelled the urge. We don't get back yesterday. Despite all thankfully we kept balance and played as best we could the hand life dealt us. The poem by John O Donohue- For a parent on the death of a child expressed how grief is a journey that knows its way and I like to now think of you Ailbhe as that "unseen angel" he refers to.

For a parent on the death of a child written by John O Donohue

Verse 2.
Now you sit bereft
Inside a nightmare,
Your eyes numbed
By the sight of a grave
No parent should ever see.

Verse 3.
You will wear this absence
Like a secret locket,
Always wondering why
Such a new soul
Was taken home so soon.

Verse 4.
Let the silent tears flow
And when your eyes clear
Perhaps you will glimpse
How your external child
Has become the unseen angel
Who parents your heart
And persuades the moon
To send new gifts

There were the poignent practicalities to be dealt with after your funeral. We set to work on designing a suitable memorial card for you. Indeed the various print companies kept our postman busy delivering their various samples. Apparently they check the papers for info on deaths. We were glad of their suggestions but decided we would formulate our own and selected a print company to produce it. They requested a photograph of you and said they would send us a large sample memorial card, photo intact, free and we could then negotiate our personal design and they would produce the number we required. A large sample card arrived with your enlarged photo on the outside I was quite thrown when I read the particular sample verse they used.

Now it's a common enough verse for memorial cards but I remember when you were about nine or ten years old you taped on to the wall of your bedroom just alongside your bed this very verse written in your own hand writing. I often read it but never really discussed it with you. It remained on that wall for years I'd imagine. It has been comforting for me to know that you obviously had empathised with these positive sentiments and I so dearly hope they express what will be the reality of death for us all Ailbhe. The verse I refer to is titled Togetherness and goes.

Death is nothing at all
I have only slipped away into the next room.
Whatever we were to each other,
That we are still. Call me by my
Old familiar name, speak to me in
The easy way you always used
Laugh as we always laughed at
The little jokes we enjoyed together. Play, smile
Think of me, pray for me.
Let my name be the household word
That it always was. Let it be spoken without effort.
Life means all that it ever meant. It is the same
As it ever was. There is absolutely unbroken continuity.
Why should I be out of your mind because I am out of your sight.
I am but waiting for you, for an interval, somewhere very near just
Around the corner. All is well. Nothing is past, nothing is lost.
One brief moment and all will be as it was before-only better,
Infinitely happier and forever-we will all be one together with
Christ.

Then there was the closing over of your grave very difficult quite like the closing of your coffin. For your headstone we decided on a natural Celtic style stone - felt it was in keeping with your psychic. I can imagine you'd be especially pleased with the poem Kerill composed himself and had written onto the stone.

Grave
Poem, on Ailbhes tombstone
Written by Kerill,

Love and Love alone transcends
all earthly creatures and heavenly
bodies.
Bequeath with beauty, your childlike smile
Sweeps down through the empty valleys,
glances across tragedy,
Your strength keeps us from harm,
nestled in the sound of soft whispers
Death between us and our Love
without question logic or demand.
I adore you, until we embrace
Love
Youl soulmate (anam chara) and
husband.
Kerill.

Chapter 5

What On Earth Happened

To mark your months mind we had a great get together in the house and as many of your friends as could make it were here. We had a mass in the back hallway followed by food and drink and the setting of your own memorial tree on the side of the avenue, a lovely copper beech. As we all gathered around the tree Aidín read the poem she had recently written and had published,"Eternal Home for Ailbhe.".

However, the question of what precisely caused your sudden death Ailbhe, did inevitably trouble me. The consultant who met with us briefly the day after your death (Dr G team A I'll refer to him as) appeared personally upset as he offered his sympathy. He said how the teams involved in your care the previous day had met that morning, that (Dr A team B) was upset and had gone home for a rest. He stated that at that point he could not give any definitive answer as to what had caused your sudden death Ailbhe and that a post-mortem result was pending. This seemed like just a courtesy meeting on the part of Dr G. The critical procedures the previous day were carried out by two other teams. So we assumed we would be facilitated with a meeting later when all the evidence would be available, where the medics involved in your care immediately prior to your death would explain what had happened and put our minds more at ease.

So in the immediate aftermath I consciously quelled the urge to investigate the matter and immersed myself in the more immediate tasks. There would be plenty of time and I felt it best to take our fences one at a time. Time passed and occasionally I would take out the diary I'd kept of my experience of being with you in the hospital the day you died. I also studied my medical reference books, familiarising myself with various sudden death causations, such as stroke, aneurysm, heart attack and clot. Try as I did I could not genuinely convince myself that your death was unavoidable much as I wished it to be.

Well, no further meeting or information was offered by the hospital. A difficulty arose in getting a death certificate. Through our own enquiries we discovered that the coroner had difficulty in determining the cause of your death Ailbhe. He had been furnished with the post-mortem report but was not satisfied and looked for clarification. Seemingly he found inconsistencies in the information supplied. Eventually the coroner called for an inquest. We got the date and venue and we were free to attend. I finally felt that we would get full details of what exactly happened. We would, I expected, meet the professionals pertinent to your care on the day of your death and would have an opportunity to ask the questions that had been troubling us. Then with clarity and truth hopefully we could reach a radical acceptance of the situation and I could liberate myself from any niggling guilt as to whether enough had been done.

So, on February 6th 2003, seven months after your death, Kerill, myself and some members of Kerill's family took our seats in the coroner's court and waited for the people who were looking after you on that fateful day on Monday 8th July 2002 to arrive. We were in for a shock Ailbhe. One consultant from the hospital did arrive. We knew him pretty well having built up a relationship with him down through your years of treatment and indeed had been grateful to him for his expertise and the personal interest he had taken in you. He was the consultant who had met with us briefly the day after your death.

When the coroner commenced we were astounded to discover that none of the people who were actively involved in your care on the day of your death were present. The coroner made a strong unequivocal statement that there were people he wished to have present to question who had not presented themselves and how present law precluded him from legally forcing them to present themselves. He referred to this deficiency again during the course of the inquest suggesting to us that we write to our political representatives urging a change in the law. He also stated how he had on numerous occasions made the powers that be, aware of his concerns and his reasoned desire for an urgent change in the law to allow him compel people to present themselves for questioning but nothing had changed.

He conducted the proceedings in what I felt was a very dignified, sensitive and honest manner, but I could scarcely believe what I was seeing and hearing. Written statements were read out, but when the coroner voiced questions regarding certain procedural terminology, the relevant expertise was not present so questions were left unanswered. What an insult to us. It was as if your sudden death and our concerns were trivialised, meriting minimal expiation and no personal accountability. What really gutted me then Ailbhe, was when the pathologist (whom I understand has to be independent) was asked by the coroner whether she would conclude from her investigations that you had quite a normal healthy body for a twenty-five-year old, bar your kidney problem which could be managed with dialysis and transplant. She responded that she found nothing to suggest to the contrary. My worst intuition. I saw red. The coroner again referred to how his hands were tied, outlined his optional verdicts and announced his determination, cause of death "Medical Misadventure." Despite my utter dismay, I got on my feet as he concluded proceedings demanding that I be allowed speak and proceeded to calmly but assertively express my anger at the utter contempt we felt these professionals into whose care you had been entrusted, had shown us, the alarming legal protection afforded them and this apparent culture of a lack of acceptance of any personal accountability on their part. I know you'd approve Ailbhe. Perhaps you gave me a bualadh bos.

We went for tea and supported each other. Then, we parted, deciding we all needed time out. With a heavy heart I travelled home having spoken with Dad and Aidín who were to collect me at the bus station. Aonghus and Assumpta were out of the country. I suggested we defer speaking about the inquest until we got back to the house. I needed time to myself to digest the reality of what I'd experienced. I wanted to be back in the security of the big friendly kitchen before I could contemplate verbalising a coherent account. I was almost speechless, so I was glad of the journey and the space.

I was now confronted with the absolute conviction that you, our beautiful precious Ailbhe Hannon Dunne should not have died but should be alive and well. What had happened? Things rested so but not for long. We considered our options. Our experience of the inquest had been devastatingly dispiriting, having heard the coroner express his concern at how his hands were legally tied, preventing him from compelling people that he deemed pertinent to his investigation to attend. Following his finding "Death by Medical Misadventure," we were shocked and felt totally abandoned. It was as if everything had been grossly trivialised, the enormity of what had happened to you, your great life snatched from you along with our incalculable loss. So, we were all of one mind that doing nothing was not an option for us. Quite apart from any legal requirement on their part, I just could not and to this day cannot comprehend how these people who knew what happened could on a human level think it acceptable not to meet us to explain and sympathise. We all wrote off to our various public representatives including the then Minister for Justice to present our experience and the coroner's concern. Only some replied, including the office of the Minister for Justice. It was just a few lines on expensive notepaper, non-committal, I think it was "under consideration" or some such banal phraseology. Anyway that duty was done Ailbhe. It's kind of strange that we are having this conversation with you now, on Wednesday January 25th 2012 as news has just come through on the radio here about something that sounded similar to our experience , that of the parents of a little boy who died on October 14th 2004. The mother was interviewed, following an apology from the hospital to the family for failures in the care of their son. She stated how for seven years she and her husband had just one question for medics involved and trusted with the care of their son,"How did this happen?" She spoke of the "wall of silence and a culture of denial from the hospital." It took she said seven years, a High Court action "and yes, the Coroners Act to be amended" to finally get the answer.

You died in 2002, apparently it has taken ten years to have the law changed. I must find out Ailbhe what exactly was changed.

Was it the change the coroner referred to at your inquest on Feb 6th 2002? If so how many ministers for justice sat on it for all these years? I have such admiration for those parents, their resilience, stamina and courage. The little boy's artery had been punctured during a procedure to have a device fitted into the chest, it all sounds more than a little familiar Ailbhe. It was ultimately planted in his left jugular vein. His condition deteriorated that evening and clotting factors and blood were administered before he went into cardiac arrest and the poor little darling died later. The parents "claimed the failure to properly insert the device without puncturing an artery led to the child suffering loss of life." "Seven years" later "a high court action and the Coroners Act to be amended to finally get the answer an admission of liability and an apology." (Article written Irish Independent Thursday Jan 26th 2012 by Louise Hogan and Tim Healy).

Rightly or wrongly we decided against litigation. We had no interest in monetary compensation or tarnishing any professional's reputation unnecessarily, indeed we had much to be grateful to them in the past for their care and dedicated expertise. But for our own peace of mind and out of a sense of duty to future patients we felt under an obligation to get a clear honest explanation as to what exactly happened to cause your unexpected death. There might have been deficiencies that required remedying in the interest of future patient safety. After all, you had been out socialising with us just the night before (our last supper) and you were working full time. Yes, we know all was not well kidney-wise, you needed to go back on dialysis and hopefully have a successful transplant. Both your sisters had undergone the test and were more than willing to donate a kidney. You had been through all this before Ailbhe and all had been well. So while this bleep was an unwelcome intrusion into your full young life, we knew all other organs and all other areas of your health were normal, so we were not seriously concerned.

So why did you die Ailbhe? "Medical Misadventure," I'd never come across that as a cause of death. We felt quite entitled to a frank, clear and honest explanation as to what precisely happened. A face to face meeting with the people who were personally engaged in your care was the only way our questions could be addressed. Surely we had an absolute entitlement to such. You had entrusted yourself to their care, you could no longer speak for yourself so we felt duty bound to seek answers and a clear explanation from those in whose care you were when you died, and not some second or third party speaking on their behalf. So we were determined to pursue such. I admit that at the back of my mind I still hoped, now that the inquest was over, these people would as a compassionate duty contact us. It didn't happen Ailbhe.

We decided to try and work with the hospital. We were not out to antagonise anyone. We decided as a first step to get your medical notes which luckily we were legally entitled to under the Freedom of Information (F.O.I). Friends and those in the know advised us that we do all our gathering of information independently, take our time, inform ourselves and get independent expertise. We followed the advice and I'm glad we did Ailbhe even though it cost us substantially, from an emotional, financial and time-wise point of view. You'd do quite a lot of shopping on what we spent. It would probably keep you in shoes for life. With hindsight I don't regret any of it as if we had depended on the hospital and the professionals involved we would judging from our experience have been just jollied along, going nowhere slowly. We managed to get a comprehensive explanation of what exactly happened, the names of the people involved in your care and their particular responsibilities. Knowledge is power and what price can you put on peace of mind? If we had done nothing I would have felt that we let you down and I'd also feel guilt towards future patients in similar situations. I suppose Ailbhe, the old "sin of omission." I don't know that you would be familiar with that terminology but I'm sure you get the message. Much wisdom in the old catechism. Anyway it all seemed to take forever. But we stuck with it and Kerrill invested whole-heartedly although he was busy, out of the country and of course grieving.

I think Ailbhe, I'll do the muinteoir (teacher) on our efforts to get answers and you can mark us out of ten. Remember the timelines in school? Well I'll do a timeline on how long it took from your death, on the 8th July 2002 to 13th February 2008 to finally say enough is enough, six years and seven months. The case I referred to in yesterday's paper that I felt had similarities apparently went on for seven years. Now the parents in that case went to court. With hindsight and knowing what I know now of how these hospitals and professionals work, I'd favour the legal route much and all as I detest litigation. But I think, as things stand, when up against such institutional and professional arrogance and ego it's the only way to have the facts exposed. Of course we would have been denied the advantage of the change in the law, as in the amendment to the Coroners Act, but I still feel from my experience win lose or draw it's unfortunately the only way to get a proper hearing. If we'd got compensation I would have donated it to your favourite charities after taking the legal expenses. Then I often think too Ailbhe at the place we were in life at that time it might have broken us physically, emotionally and indeed financially. There is no going back and we did what we considered appropriate at the time, but personally I do admire people who in these situations have the courage and stamina to take the legal route.

Now back to our timeline.

1. Sunday July 7th, Kerril, Assumpta and myself drove you back to the hospital (late following our last supper in Clontarf Castle) you were booked in for what we understood was to be a routine procedure, premcath insertion so that (a) haemodialysis could be initiated to see you through to a future kidney transplant and (b) to hopefully alleviate the restless leg syndrome which was becoming a bit of a nuisance. Remember how you'd say "these legs are jigging about on me."

2. Monday July 8th, Kerril, Assumpta and myself went into the hospital. Kerril took a day's holiday as he knew you

disliked being alone at times like this. We found you anxious and sad, unable to take Claire's call, most unusual. A feeling of foreboding seemed to have engulfed you. The nurses were very supportive but you were uncharacteristically gloomy. The porter came to take you for the procedure. Kerril went with you as Assumpta and myself settled down in two chairs in your twin-bedded ward to await your return. Kerril came back a bit annoyed that he had not been allowed into the room where the procedure was being carried out. The purpose of him taking a day's holiday had been to be with you to support you. It is 2002 we thought, husbands are no longer excluded from maternity delivery wards, a bit O.T.T. So what was the problem? Anyway we settled down to await your return. I think you'd have left us around midday and it was mentioned that the procedure would not take very long. We could expect you back in about an hour or so. I remember dying for a coffee but decided to wait it out and have you join us in the restaurant with the procedure behind you.

3. It took longer than the hour or so, but I was delighted when a nurse and porter arrived into the room wheeling a patient in a trolley towards your bed. It was about 2.30 p.m.. I said, "Great Ailbhe you are back," but to my disappointment it was not you on the trolley. It was another patient. Then the nurse said, "Where were you? Ailbhe was calling for you, there has been complications and she is going to the main ward." Well I let out a scream of unparliamentary language and protested that we'd been in your room all the time. Why hadn't they got us I asked and stated that you hated those big wards. You had V.H.I. and had been assigned a bed in this room. The nurse assured me that they had righted what went wrong, that all was under control, that they would keep you by the nurse's station where you could be better monitored and that we could stay with you. We went out onto the corridor and found you on a trolley on your way to the ward with all kinds of tubes connected. I was flabbergasted. You were so angry Ailbhe, you pushed yourself forward and announced loud

and clear "and they fucked this up on me." I assured you we would now remain with you and that the nurse had assured us they had now righted things. Myself and Kerill stayed with you. We have talked about that precious time and I am so glad we were there. Assumpta popped in too for a while. So you were surrounded by love I hope you felt it.

4. Very little happened. We became quite comfortable and were left to ourselves. There were doctors coming and going at the nurse's station beside us and the other patients in the ward were just getting on with their own business until our comfort zone was intruded on by a male doctor and a portable machine. The doctor introduced himself and told us he would take an x-ray. We stood outside and curtains were closed around your bed while the doctor (or consultant) had the x-ray taken. He then spoke with us, assuring us everything was going perfectly and that there was no need for concern, that the particular mishap, while disagreeable, would only delay progress by a day or so and maybe not even that. A cousin of Granddad's, a nurse popped in to say hello. I introduced her to you as "Ava's cousin." She looked at the monitor over your head. She too had encouraging words from what she saw. She gave you some magazines, we thanked her and she left. So Kerill and I returned to take up our former positions at your bedside, I sat on a chair at the bottom rubbing your hand and relaying to you the optimistic doctor's report while Kerill went to the top righthand side of your bed. Not long after, we got that good news and settled back with you, a group of young doctors took up position at the top left hand side of your bed. They did not engage with us at all but proceeded to crouch down towards the lower wall and handle connections and tubes. I felt an air of insecurity develop as one doctor who handled the connections spoke in what came across as a loud censorious, anxious tone of voice while the others remained crouched down looking at connections apprehensively. What I picked up were the words that there should be another of these. I felt there was an atmosphere of contention and anxiety

among them as they handled the connections. Now the feeling I got was either these people are out of their depth or they have found something seriously wrong with the connections or the tubes and believing the tubes to be connected to you Ailbhe, I became seriously worried. As I have already told you Ailbhe to this day I regret not following my gut instinct to shout at them to get help that those tubes were connected to my daughter. A nurse remained standing at the bottom of your bed silently watching the monitor over your head. The whole atmosphere changed. We of course had no clue as to what they were about. I noticed you trying to pull yourself up in the bed, you appeared to be distressed. I said to the nurse "Ailbhe wants to sit up" and I screamed "this is serious." The nurse rushed forward placing pillows to your back as support and repeating, "Look at your mother Ailbhe and breathe." The doctors stood up looking at the monitor over your bed in stunned silence. You stared straight into my eyes Ailbhe and your eyes seemed so enormous as I continued rubbing your hand and Kerill rubbed your back supporting you with assuring words as you fell back into his arms. Dead.

5. Kerill and I were ushered to the day room as resuscitation commenced. I knew you had gone Ailbhe and would not be coming back. You were declared dead at 8.40 p.m. on Monday July 8th 2002. What a day that was. Wherever you are Ailbhe, be happy.

6. Fast forward to February 6th 2003, the inquest into the cause of death of Ailbhe Hannon Dunne. Finding: Cause of death Medical Misadventure. On the 12th of February, we sought your medical records under the Freedom of Information Act (FOI) and studied notes. We decided to employ independent relevant experts to clarify medical terminology and procedures. The notes arrived on the 19th February 2003. We were disappointed at how little information had been made available at the time immediately leading up to your death. But we sent all information to the independent relevant experts to

decipher your medical notes and on the 9th of March 2005 we received the reports and analysis. We set about studying them. A clear picture emerged. The people we employed to decipher the notes were able to explain in layman's language step by step the various procedures, who did what and so on. We now had the names of the various professionals actively involved in your care and clear explanations of what their various roles were.

What actually happened? Who did what? It transpired Ailbhe that there were three teams involved in your care. I'll refer to them as teams A, B and C. You went to radiology under the care of the team there (team B) two professionals directly involved in the insertion of a permcath under fluoroscopy and ultrasound for reasons we've mentioned already at approximately 12.40 p.m. on Monday July 8th 2002. Unfortunately their attempts left you with a linear laceration of your brachio-cephalic vein or what medics referred to as an inadvertent arterial puncture and that's all some mouthful Ailbhe. Our independent medical experts on studying the medical notes and reports pointed out in their analysis "that with ultrasound guidance inadvertent arterial puncture" like you suffered "is rare" and while being unaware of any definitive study on the frequency of similar complications associated with central venous catheter placement, from his knowledge was largely due to one or all of the following factors.

(1)"Differences among selected venous insertion sites (2) the degree of prior operator experience (3) the presence of previously described risk factors "while the exact figure for the frequency of venous laceration is not accurately available as many cases are either unreported or undetected because they have no clinical sequelae."

We later discovered that this hospital had carried out 3,000 similar cases over the previous ten years and complications similar to yours occurred on just three occasions. The infrequency of this complication and its tragic outcome I feel, compounds the cruel callousness of those involved in not feeling personally obliged to meet with us and explain what happened. Yes institutions will protect institutions at the expense of the very individuals they are mandated to serve as you always asserted Ailbhe. Well our experts outlined two usual management strategies that could be followed should this complication occur.

(1)The procedure seemingly followed in your case "replace blood loss with replacement fluids, insertion of two chest drains whilst observing ongoing and or continued blood loss" until the condition stabilised or early repair or stent insertion. While claiming not to be personally qualified to comment on stent insertion as it falls within the realm of an interventional radiologist they stated "stent insertion is not universally available and in the absence of the availability of such the only alternative would be to consider open surgical repair. Surgical repair would be reserved for those patients showing substantial on-going bleeding unresponsive to chest drainage and volume replacement." Our experts indicated how "close monitoring would ordinarily be carried out, with intervention in the event of haemodynamic compromise" in circumstances such as yours Ailbhe and made reference to the fact that there is a debate about other interventions in such circumstances as yours such as stent insertion.

At 2.30 p.m. you were returned to the ward, attention was drawn to and I quote "the paucity of nursing and observation records for the period between the time of your return following permcath insertion and "your "arrest." In particular they pointed out that there didn't appear "to be any record of observations having been made for the interval between 14.00 and 17.25 hours on the day of her death" apart from some references in the nursing notes, a critical period. According to the notes at approximately 7 p.m. (team C) suggested that permcath would no longer be used, "they would change the chest tube drain to one with suction." "At seven twenty during manipulation of the chest tube Ailbhe became apnoeic (breathless) and brady? Cardic (slow heart beat)" "An arrest was placed." "At eight forty pm with the consensus of all staff present the resuscitation attempts were stopped." These notes stated "that between five thirty and seven pm the patient appeared in no great distress and her vital signs were stable. She was talking freely with her family and nursing staff."

The clarification we got in March 2005 lifted a lot of the fog and fleshed out in understandable language the chronology of events, identifying the various personnel and their individual responsibilities. We now felt we had a much more rounded understanding of events but needless to say Ailbhe it took time, patience and dedicated effort to comprehend and accept what we were presented with, the notion I had that perhaps you had some internal weakness, the signs of which we had not recognised and that this had caused your unexpected death was totally dispelled when I studied the findings. I told you how disturbed I was at the inquest when the coroner meticulously questioned the pathologist as to your general state of health. He went from organ to organ and when nothing seemed amiss, bar of course the kidney problem, he posed the final question as to whether she could say that you had a perfectly healthy body for a lady of your age allowing for a kidney problem which could be righted by dialysis and kidney transplant, The pathologist replied that she found nothing to suggest to the contrary. Well the detailed written autopsy report confirmed this. Each investigation resulted in the response, "normal" "unremarkable" and finally under the heading "significant negative findings" came the categorical, "no underlying pathology."

Gone too was that slim hope I had been privately harbouring that common humanity would eventually prevail and that one day those relevant to your care on the day of your death would contact us. It was now March 2005 and you had left us July 2002 so I knew it was unrealistic to expect any such gesture. So what now, we wondered, as we reflected on the information and pondered our options. We had, I think you'd agree Ailbhe enjoyed relatively good relations with the hospital and staff. There was no appetite on our part for litigation or interest in financial gain, nor was there any vindictiveness on our part towards any of the professionals. We had however made our concerns public at the inquest. We could not deny our own experience of events but there seemed to be no willingness or interest on the part of hospital staff to engage with us. We had concerns we felt could only be answered by the individuals directly involved in your care at those critical junctures on July 8th. So we needed to meet with them. We also became worried about the consequences of non action on our part for future patients and their families. What if there had been shortcomings, lessons that could be learned that might prevent similar tragedies. So to do nothing and just let things rest, while tempting became disquieting. On reflection we now felt morally obliged to seek honest individual accountability. We came up with the option of contacting the ombudsman. This we figured would be a neutral non adversarial route through which we could have our concerns considered and get the individual accountability we were entitled to. I was the one designated with making contact. The ease with which I got personal access with the ombudsman was a pleasant surprise. She gave her time and actively listened to my story. I felt that I was heard, but then came the sting. She explained to me that because of some restraints regarding the public/voluntary nature of governance of the hospital this was outside her brief. She expressed her personal annoyance at this constraint and spoke of how anxious she was to have the law changed to make it part of her remit and indeed her frustration was palpable but all I could do was express my gratitude for her interest and courtesy.

We felt that all doors had been closed to us until shortly afterwards on the Late Late Show we were introduced to these brave women who had taken a gynaecologist to task and exposed how he had mistreated them (putting it mildly) while they were in his professional care, how the powers that be thwarted their efforts to establish the truth of what happened, discrediting their experiences and trying to legally gag them. To their credit they stuck by their case and against all the odds had now finally come out totally vindicated. A phone number was given out at the end of the programme (remember how they occasionally give out these numbers as points of contact for people who feel disturbed by the contents of the programme Ailbhe). Well I rang and got through to an empathic listener.

I outlined our experience and our desire to have a face to face meeting with the particular professionals and our frustration at how this was not happening. She pointed out the advantage the Drogheda women had. They had been part of a group and were able to support each other, while ours was an individual case and could prove more difficult. She mentioned that all hospitals had an advocacy service for patients and suggested we ring the hospital, get the contact number of their patients advocate, make contact, state our case and request that they facilitate a meeting with the relevant professionals. It was news to us that such a service existed. We'd never heard of it previously.

We followed her advice and spoke with the advocate on the phone who suggested we write up the background to and details of our concerns and post them to her. We prepared a detailed, comprehensive written presentation and posted it off as requested. I think we did get a short written acknowledgement of its safe arrival. After some time I rang to check in and I spoke with the same lady who was now well-informed and up to speed on your case history and our concerns. She sounded most sympathetic and said how we should have been brought in for a meeting when we'd got through the trauma of the funeral to have things explained and afforded an opportunity to have our questions aired. She assured us this would now happen, there would be no question of a cover up, all would be made clear. This was I believe sometime in early September 2005 (mustn't forget our timeline Ailbhe). We were delighted and fully confident that at last we would get our meeting. We were quite specific and clear as to what we wanted in our communications both verbal and written with the advocate. We wanted a face to face meeting with the professionals directly involved in your care on the day of your death. We had of course meticulously familiarised ourselves with the relevant teams and the individual names. I'll use pseudo names but you'll know exactly who they are Ailbhe.

On team B, we wanted to meet with Dr A and Dr B (but most especially and we pointed this out to the advocate), on Team C we desperately wanted to speak with Dr C, Dr D, and Dr E. We felt that it was unnecessary at that point for anyone from Team A to be present as we did not feel they were that relevant to your actual care on the fatal day as they had not been directly involved at the critical times. Initially as I said all was rosy in the garden. The advocate was verbally most positive about our right to our requested meeting and that this would be forthcoming, that a frank, honest and open exchange would be facilitated. She did mention that as some of the people we wished to meet might no longer be employed by the hospital it might take a little time. Well, as it was already over three years since your death we had become accustomed to waiting Ailbhe and we were quite happy to sit it out. Then a letter arrived dated 23rd Sept 2005.

23 September, 2005

Our Ref: PRO/7358-00

Dear Mrs Hannon,

I refer to previous correspondence regarding your late daughters care while attending [redacted] Hospital.

I am sorry it is taking so long to respond to you but I have not as yet received a report from the staff members whom I have contacted in regard to your case. I am today sending a further reminder and hope to be able to respond to you at an early date. If in the meantime I can be of any assistance please do not hesitate to contact me immediately.

Kindest regards.

Yours sincerely,

[redacted]

No panic on our part, the wheels were now in motion. Time passed and as there seemed to be no developments, I rang the advocacy number but the lady who dealt with us was not available so the "message would be passed on," and "they would get back." They rarely did Ailbhe so I kept ringing again periodically, I never seemed to be able to speak with the lady who initially dealt with the case. Often I'd get the answering machine. All written correspondence from the advocate seemed to contain this apology for the delay, for not getting back to us sooner. It seemed to be going on and on. Then the whole tone changed. We were offered a meeting. Don't get over excited, the meeting or their proposed meeting was with Dr G on Team A (who as far as we were concerned was not pivotal to your care on the day nor was his team) plus a Dr H who would speak on behalf of Team B (Dr H's name had not surfaced until now) plus I think a nurse, but strangely no one from Team C would be present, the very team personnel that we had emphasised as being crucial to our concerns. Can we be blamed for being perturbed and more than a little suspicious as to what was at play here Ailbhe?

Well we got more assertive in our communications with the advocate. It now seemed to us as though the advocacy was representing the interests and wishes of the medical professionals rather than as we had been given to understand the patient's interests. They were being allowed call the shots. What had happened to the assurances of support we had been offered at the start? I remember Dad taking the phone and demanding a direct conversation with the advocate with whom we had initially dealt with and reminding her of the sureties given to us. I wrote back expressing our disappointment and bewilderment at how we were being treated and emphatically rejecting the format of the meeting on offer stating our reasons. The response that came offered nothing substantially different. No one from Team C would meet with us, the very team that we had been so eager to speak with. She said how some of the doctors we wished to meet no longer worked in the hospital and could not be located, that they were probably out of the country. This did not seem to me to tally with the letter she had sent on the 23rd of September 2005 stating, "I am sorry it is taking so long to respond to you but I have not as yet received a report from the staff members whom I have contacted in regard to your case. I am today sending a further reminder and hope to be able to respond to you at an early date...." Now months later she claims inability to contact them. Following my questions on the phone she disclosed that Dr C who had been on Team C at the time of your death (in fact the consultant in charge of Team C from our reading of the notes) was still working at the hospital. So I enquired then as to what his difficulty was in meeting us. She replied Dr C will not be at the meeting. I emphasised how important it was to us to meet with him and I remember her voice going into definitive tone as she three times repeated, "Dr C will not meet with you, Dr C will not meet with you, Dr C will not meet with you." I then concluded the conversation by replying in my own definitive tone, "Of course he will meet with us".

I was flabbergasted. Here was this man entrusted to care for people medically, handsomely paid by taxpayers like ourselves, into whose care you had been entrusted, our beautiful twenty-five-year old daughter, Kerill's young wife, sister to Aonghus, Aidín and Assumpta and you had died (partially at least) under his watch. An inquest determined the cause of your death was "Medical misadventure" and although he is still working in the same hospital, he has the gall and the audacity to think it's acceptable to refuse to even meet us. What an arrogant assumption and now it appeared the patients advocate concurred with the assumption that Dr C should have it solely in his gift as to whether he would meet with us or not. What had all the correspondence and apologies for the delay for the last few months been about? Was it a case of just jollying us along, send the fool further? Well the jollying along was well and truly over. We had now completely lost confidence in the patients' advocacy. We found when push came to shove they were on the side of the medics in the guise of representing our interests. I've discovered that they are paid by the hospital so I suppose Ailbhe the old saying, "He who pays the piper calls the tune.

We were now more determined than ever to meet with these people. I was adamant that giving up was not on the cards.

We grew more and more adamant that we would not give up until we met on equal terms with the particular medics to query them and make them listen to us. You our fine relatively healthy much-loved Ailbhe had died we believed unnecessarily. How did this happen from a routine enough procedure? Surely the medical care of people is a solemn duty. We had questions that only those involved in your care could answer. We were determined to pursue all avenues to achieve that little justice even at this late stage.

In response to our request for a written statement as to why Dr. C on team C was refusing to meet with us seeing as he was still employed by and working in the hospital and as to why no member on team C was available to us despite our repeated requests the following letter, dated 27th March 2006.

27 March, 2006

Our Ref: PRO/7358-00

Dear Mrs Hannon,

Further to our telephone conversation I wish to acknowledge your request for a written report from the hospital. I have enclosed a copy of statements, which were received by the medical staff who were caring for Ailbhe on the day of her procedure. However, I do not have any report available from the surgical team who attended Ailbhe on the 8th July 2002 and I regret that [redacted] Hospital no longer employs the doctor in question. [redacted] DR. C *[redacted] as clarified that although Dr.* F *[redacted] who was involved in Ailbhe's care was assigned to his team for the six months of his stay in [redacted] on that particular evening he was not the Consultant on duty and indeed he was out of the country. Therefore* ~~*although in the notes he is described as registrar to*~~ *[redacted] on that evening in question he was the registrar on call in the house and therefore answerable to both the senior registrar of the time and also the consultant on duty for surgery for that particular date. I have not been able to identify which senior registrar was on duty and the Consultant on call could offer no assistance. While I understand how anxious you are to receive such a report however, it is not possible for another member of the medical profession to issue a report based on his / her speculative interpretations of a colleague.*

Both DR. G *[redacted] who was Ailbhe's Consultant and* DR H *[redacted] who is a Consultant Radiologist with considerable experience in the field of insertion of permcath under fluoroscopy, are more than happy to meet with you to help clarify any factual issues within the reports and medical chart and perhaps to discuss areas of speculation. . The*

Divisional Nurse Manager will also be able to attend and she will assist in answering some of the nursing issues. Ms. [redacted] *was the senior sister in charge of the ward on the* 8th *July.*

If you agree to meet I would be very happy to arrange this for you and perhaps you could contact me directly with some dates and times that are suitable to you. Please ring me directly if I can be of any further assistance.

Kindest regards.

Yours sincerely,

[redacted]

We got the copies of the statements she refers to from the inquest and subsequent F.O.I. years earlier. We had made her aware of us having these statements when we first made contact and many of our concerns stemmed from these very statements and our own experience of being present in the hospital with you as some of these procedures were taking place. People we had been requesting to meet for the last year and a half we were now being told were not in the hospital on that particular evening at all, "he was out of the country" even though his name was on the hospital care notes for that evening. She had not been able to identify "which senior registrar was on duty and the consultant on call could offer no assistance." Why not find out who the hospital paid as the senior registrar on duty July 8th 2002 at the critical times in our daughter's care? I wouldn't have thought it a difficult task. Just check back on hospital records. This now nuanced reference to "the doctor in question" did he have a name? How did his name appear on your hospital notes if he was out of the country? To quote, "Although in the notes he is described as registrar to Dr. C on that evening in question he was the registrar on call in the house and therefore answerable to both the senior registrar of the time and also the consultant on duty for surgery for that particular date." Instead of being long-winded and oblique could she not have just stated July 8th 2002 in place of "that particular date."

Now it seemed to us Dr. C was writing himself out of the picture completely. She stated "indeed he was out of the country." Ha ha, not so Ailbhe, hold on, I hope you are still with me. When we got this letter we were livid. We felt this letter was designed to confuse us and we were having none of it. Strange that this same lady acting in her role earlier as our advocate stated on the phone to us that the advocacy had contacted all the professionals we had mentioned as vital to any meeting from our point of view. Indeed her letter dated 23rd of September 2005; had stated and confirmed that "she was sending a further reminder," and hoped to be able to respond at an early date. We had been most explicit as to the staff members we wished her to contact.

Then Ailbhe the statement "It is not possible for another member of the medical profession to issue a report based on his/her speculative interpretations of a colleague"?! We totally agree. That is why we wanted to meet the people directly involved, not some second or third party speaking on their behalf. We wanted first hand information. We found this business of not been able to identify people, "no report available from Team C who attended you on July 8th 2002," to be grossly insulting. To find that they consider this an adequate response to the tragedy that you Ailbhe and all of us had suffered was to put it mildly mind boggling

We researched patient's advocacy to check out their brief lest our understanding of its purpose and function might have been incorrect and I quote, "A patient's advocate is someone who will act on the patient's or the patient's family's behalf when dealing with the hospital or health care service. A patient's advocate will represent the view of those seeking information or making complaints. The advocacy will assist you in dealing with hospitals and other health care service providers, advise you on how to obtain records, write and structure your complaints and arrange meetings with health care service managers and attend as your adviser at the patient's complaint meeting. Sometimes you just need structured answers to your concerns and often meeting with staff will give you these answers."

So our expectation of the service was in no way unrealistic. In fact the last sentence in the above-mentioned quote pretty much stated what we had sought from the start Ailbhe. Well, this letter now claims Dr. C whom we have been so keen to meet "was not the consultant on duty and indeed was out of the country." The advocate had confirmed earlier that Dr C was still employed in the hospital. So why was our request that he'd meet with us and personally clarify his position such a no no? His name had appeared on your chart and at most critical times in your care on July 8th, from 5 p.m.-7.05 p.m. in connection with Dr. D, team C.

She could not now "identify which senior registrar was on duty and the consultant on call could offer no assistance." The Dr. Michael Neary saga comes to mind, almost 200 women damaged by one doctor. This sheer lack of clarity and personal accountability and its acceptance on the part of the advocate knowing the catastrophic outcome we'd been left to face, I feel, exposed a total lack of empathy for us as human beings. Relevant personal identities were cloaked in abstract professional roles such as, "senior registrar of the time" "consultant on duty for surgery," "for that particular date," "consultant on call." Again I ask, don't these people have names like the rest of us? She mentions that Dr. G team A was your consultant. But it was not his department who were involved in your care at the critical times. You were not under his team's specific expertise and we had no questions for him or his team. We certainly did not want an abstract explanation or lecture on how these procedures were carried out. We wanted to interface with the people who were personally involved with carrying out the critical procedures. We had made the position crystal clear in every communication we'd had with her. She herself had stated in her letter dated the 27th March 2006 and I quote again "It is not possible for another member of the medical profession to issue a report based on his/her speculative interpretation of a colleague."

Only today I heard on the national news that another hospital has been found out in court, "the level of care fell short of what was to be expected." Compensation was paid and of course an apology was issued, like the Catholic Church and the child abuse, sorry when they are caught or might it be sorry that they got caught? This last case took a few years and again the poor family was dragged through the courts. What about telling the truth? "Institutions" again I hear you remind me Ailbhe. Yes, I remember those conversations and how I marvelled at your precocious discernment in such matters. That one doctor in Drogheda and the almost 200 women often disturbed me. What if there had been poor inadequate professional performance or operation deficiencies in your case, were these professionals in whose care you were entrusted on July 8th (a) properly qualified (b) properly briefed (c) properly resourced? Well these are questions that surface every time I hear court findings such as, "The level of care fell short of what was to be expected" and again I wonder whether perhaps we were remiss in not pursuing these questions through the legal route lest it happen again and again. Were we too naive Ailbhe, too trusting, in expecting the big powerful ("caring") institution to show sensitivity and accommodation to our request for a meeting to explore our concerns? Well, we certainly believe that the lack of urgency, humanity and seriousness our efforts met with, fell far short of what we justifiably expected and deserved.

An interesting controversy arose last Christmas Ailbhe with regards to an advocacy worker in a psychiatric hospital in Dublin. I happened to hear its initial airing on the radio, on the Joe Duffy show on R.T.E. Louis worked as an advocate in the hospital. She spoke publicly about her concerns relating to the proposed movement of some patients in the hospital from their normal ward to a locked ward over the Christmas break due to staff holidays and staff shortage, that was the gist of it. Considerable public concern was expressed through the media. Politicians became involved and pressure mounted to rethink any such decision. Louis quickly learned that her contract was terminated with immediate effect by the (IAN) Irish Advocacy Network. However, following a huge out pouring of public anger inside a week the IAN admitted that terminating Louis' contact together with that of a colleague was an error and took full responsibility for the mistake.

The chief executive of the IAN told the Irish Independent that Louis, who was an inexperienced staff member, broke the network's code of practice. Louis said she had no regrets about raising the issues as otherwise she would not have been able to sleep at night.

Meanwhile the public expenditure minister Brendan Howlin has announced plans to publish a draft bill that will protect whistle blowers. A proposal is to be submitted in a few weeks. Well bring it on Brendan, I've heard this promise heralded by politicians years back, so hopefully this time round the government will walk the talk. From our personal experience of engaging with patients advocacy, I'd be equally pleased to see the said quango abolished and any public money saved given to some useful health project.

Well Ailbhe, we would need to be profound slow learners not to have concluded at this stage that our chances of getting the meeting we requested via the patients advocacy was negligible. However we decided to take her up on the particular meeting offered even though not one of the medics we had requested to meet would be present.

Now Ailbhe, as you will understand Kerill and myself were both busy people. I was teaching full time plus doing mammy and all that it entailed at home. Kerill of course was in university in London up to his eyes studying for his doctorate. So we came up with suitable dates, the week of the 4th to the 7th of April, any day or time, Kerill had a week off lectures. I made contact suggesting our proposed dates and reasons for our choice. Again a written reply, with the usual apology and surprise surprise our dates were not acceptable, but the letter offered no alternative dates. Instead she had now written to Dr. G and Dr. H and a nurse, asking them to come up with dates. These three people were working in the hospital so why the delay and all this writing just to get a meeting. Surely she could have waited until she'd got an offer of alternative dates before contacting us. Talk about kicking the can down the road Ailbhe.

Letter (3) from Patients

31 March 2006

Dear Mrs Hannon,

Many thanks for your telephone call to-day and I am sorry that I was unavailable to speak to you. I also understand to you rang during the week stating that you would be available to meet from the 4th to the 7th April. Unfortunately staff are not available on those dates to meet and I had intended to contact you in relation to this. I have now written to [redacted] and Ms. [redacted] requesting some dates and times at the end of May and beginning of June that they will be available to meet with you. As soon as I receive confirmation of dates that all three are available I will contact you immediately.

Kindest regards.

Yours sincerely,

[redacted]

[redacted]

April 2006 came and went and there was no further contact regarding the promised meeting.

We had at this stage fully accepted that the patient's advocacy was not going to be of support to us. So we set about enlightening ourselves as to the function of the Medical Council to consider whether this might be an avenue we could pursue. Basically the Medical Council regulates the medical profession in Ireland. Under Part V of the Medical Practitioner's Act 1978, the Fitness to Practice Committee considers complaints about doctors of alleged professional misconduct or unfitness to engage in the practice of medicine by reason of physical or mental disability.

Now I think if I remember correctly at that time it was entirely medics who sat on this council and who carried out the enquiries. Doctors enquiring into doctors, for us not particularly reassuring. Their brief too did seem quite restrictive from our perspective. Anyhow we put pen to paper once again and followed their directions, stating the history and substance of our grievance. "You deserve an honorary doctorate for your efforts," I hear you whisper Ailbhe.

Back to our timeline. We will recap a little first. On March 31st 2006 Patients Advocate responded by letter rejecting the dates we had suggested for the meeting. We waited for them to get back, as promised in the March letter, with suggested dates and in the meantime we informed ourselves as best we could on the Medical Council and made informal contact initially. It was now into April,almost seven months since we first contacted the Patients Advocacy and still waiting. On April 24th 2006, we sent a written formal presentation of our grievance to the Medical Council by registered letter. On the 5th of May 2006, surprise surprise we got a letter from the Patients Advocacy offering dates of Tuesday May 23rd or Tuesday May 30th at 11.15 a.m. with the now usual apology regarding the delay in getting back to us.

[redacted] Letter 4

05 May 2006

Our Ref. PRO/7358-00

[redacted]

Dear Mrs Hannon,

I am writing in relation to dates for the meeting with the consultants as we previously discussed. There is a choice of two dates: Tuesday 23rd May 2006 or Tuesday 30th May 2006 at 11.15 AM. I hope one of these dates will be convenient and I look forward to hearing from you at your earliest convenience. I am sorry for the delay in responding to your request and I look forward to hearing from you.

Kind regards.

Yours sincerely,

[redacted]

Now Tuesday midweek did not suit either Kerill or myself. I had pointed this out earlier to the advocate explaining how Kerill would have to fly in so a weekend would suit better, if possible a Saturday or Sunday or at least a Friday or Monday so he could fit in a visit home rather than having the expense of flying over in the morning and back in the evening. We decided to think it over for a day or two. We had no belief in the particular meeting as we were not meeting any of the medics we had requested. So we really felt this would be a waste of time money and energy on our part. On May 8th we received a letter from the Medical Council informing us that they had contacted the hospital, "seeking the names and registration number of all those doctors involved in your treatment. I will write further in due course on receipt of a response from the "hospital."Would you consider it bad-minded of me Ailbhe to suspect that the offer of the meeting three days earlier by the patients advocacy might have been spurred on by the Medical Council contacting the hospital in relation to the identification of medics we had requested to meet. Perhaps not, but we had been left without any contact since March. Now the inconvenience of the mid-week dates and the early 11.15 time bothered us. I would have to arrange for time off work and make my way from the sticks and be at the hospital by 11.15 a.m. and Kerill would have to fly in the night before and fly back after the meeting the next day and all to attend this nebulous meeting with none of the medics we requested to meet present. As I said earlier Ailbhe we had made our circumstances and time preferences well known to the advocacy. Our first reaction was to call it off but then our wise minds told us it might be in our own best interest to turn up despite the hardship and expense as failing to accept this offer might mitigate against us in our dealings with the Medical Council. We decided to attend. I rang and spoke with our advocate. I confirmed the time, date and venue and our commitment to attend, 11.15 a.m. on Tuesday 30th May 2006 in the hospital building. I think she gave me a general outline of what to do when we got to the hospital, where exactly to go, that she would be there to meet and support us.

The conversation then took what I felt was a peculiar shift. She queried if we had been back in the hospital since your death Ailbhe. When I replied no, she sympathetically suggested that we would most likely find this meeting in the hospital building quite emotionally upsetting. Well I felt her concern came a bit belated. It was she who had arranged the venue. She then again reminded me of the professionals who would be present at the meeting, Dr G, Dr H and nurse Y. I again asked about the particular medics we had requested to meet Dr C, Dr E, Dr F of team C and Dr A and Dr B of team B. She said how Dr E and F were no longer employed by the hospital. She could not contact them and they were probably out of the country. I enquired again as to the possibility of Dr C of team C attending seeing as she had told us earlier that he still worked in the hospital. She again quite definitively replied Dr C will not be attending the meeting. I said that was disappointing but we'd go ahead anyway. She said how she was looking forward to meeting with us. I thanked her and we concluded the conversation.

On Monday May 29th 2006 (the day before our arranged meeting) I was just back in class settling back to work with my little darlings after lunchbreak when I was called to the office to take a phone call. When I took up the phone I was most surprised to find that it was our advocate, as she had never previously rang me at work. On introducing herself she asked if all was in order with us for the meeting the following day. I assured her that all was well and that we'd be at the hospital (Kerill and myself) at 11.15 a.m. as arranged. At that point I assumed the call was just to confirm our intention to attend, but as I was about to say slán she quite casually interjected with the adjunct that Dr F (who had worked on team C) would be attending the meeting as they had discovered he was working in a local hospital. I was pleasantly surprised as we knew from the hospital records that he worked on team C and was at your bedside at the critical times on July 8th and was one of the medics we'd been asking to meet. She then said Dr C would not be attending. I said this was most disappointing. I thanked her and returned to my precious charges.

Well Ailbhe I was hardly five minutes back in role in class when I was called to the office again, I was wanted on the phone. This would have been quite unusual and I do remember feeling a bit guilty at having to abandon my post so quickly again but as you well know, luckily I had an understanding principal. I took the call and was quite surprised to hear our advocate's voice again. This time a short message, Dr. C will attend the meeting tomorrow. Now this was the doctor (still working in the hospital) whom she had categorically ruled out as meeting with us. Remember the letter of the 27th of March 2006, "On that particular evening he was not the consultant on duty and indeed he was out of the country." I thought to myself as I held the phone, the less said here the better and I sharply replied, "Meet you tomorrow, in the hospital as arranged at 11.15 a.m.," put down the phone and returned to my duties somewhat perplexed. The whole scenario was beginning to seem quite surreal Ailbhe.

After work I contacted Kerill and brought him up to speed on the day's surprising development. We went over our concerns. We wanted to strongly get across our annoyance at not having been met by those trusted with and directly involved in your care Ailbhe. We wanted to explore the coroner's findings "Death by medical misadventure." Also, we wanted to find out the precise qualifications and relevant experiences of the individuals performing the various procedures on July 8th 2002, to clarify who was in charge, who did what and who was responsible for making decisions regarding the various procedures, and seeing that instructions were carried out. There were so many questions. Why did Dr A team B and Dr D team C still consider it acceptable not to communicate with us and address our concerns? Both were pivotal at the most crucial times on July 8th 2002. We would of course stress our concerns regarding the contention we witnessed around your bed as doctors on team C manipulated the drains. What was worrying or annoying the doctor so much? It was at this point Ailbhe that you died during this process. Prior to this you had seemed calm and in no distress so Kerill and myself have always had the belief that this was what actually caused your death, some mishap with the change over or delay and we desperately wanted to explore this. What alternative procedures could have been considered? Had any lessons been learned? Had any procedural or other changes resulted? And fundamentally Ailbhe, why and how did you die?

Reflecting on how the process had evolved to date neither Kerill or myself could find much grounds for optimism that this meeting was motivated by any credible desire to mitigate our concerns on the part of the hospital, medics or the patients advocate. We had, as I already mentioned Ailbhe been in contact with the Medical Council a month earlier and had a letter from them dated May 8th 2006, "I have written to x hospital on today's date seeking the names and registration number of those doctors involved in Ailbhe Hannon Dunne's treatment." So on May 29th 2006 they agreed to meet us the next day, a meeting we had been requesting eight months prior to this and indeed since the inquest on February 6th 2003, over three years previously, when I'd spoken publicly in the presence of Dr G. He was left in no doubt as to how disappointed we were that none of the medics actively involved in your care at the critical times on July 8th 2002 turned up to clarify what had happened and of course it was not just we your family who expressed disappointment at this. He equally heard the coroner lament that certain people were not present whom he wished to have present and how the law prohibited him from compelling them to attend. Presumably Dr G reported back to the hospital where he was still employed. Both of us could not help feeling in our bones that these medics had decided to meet with us now as an exercise in appeasing the Medical Council, to cover their own backs. Equally rightly or wrongly we suspected complicity on the part of the patient's advocacy. However we made a decision that we would bury our apprehension for the time being, get into positive mode and go into the meeting with an open mind giving all present the benefit of the doubt.

On May 30th 2006, Kerill and myself arrived at the hospital at approximately 11 a.m. for the 11.15 a.m. scheduled meeting. We followed the instructions we'd been given by the patient's advocacy and you'll understand Ailbhe how well I knew the geography of the place so we had no difficulty finding the meeting room. The room was organised in a formal meeting room arrangement; the usual paraphernalia, water, paper, a long table with nine to ten chairs and in bold writing Ailbhe Hannon Dunne R.I.P., tea and coffee making facilities at the side. You must have carried us Ailbhe, as the memories the place held for us and seeing your name with R.I.P. after it did not phase us in the least. We were met by the advocate given a friendly welcome. She offered us a tea or coffee, outlined the general procedure and then we made small talk. She popped in and out to a room or space behind us. A few minutes after our arrival she told us that Dr. F (team C) had made contact to say he was on his way but had got slightly delayed in traffic. We could sympathise with him having ourselves just worked our way through the traffic. Dr. G (team A) came into the room and sat down at the table. We exchanged basic formal greetings. He left after a few minutes and the advocate came and informed us that Dr. F had arrived and now all involved in the meeting were anseo (present). This would have been 11.25/11.35 ish. We could clearly hear the voices to our back chatting so we continued our small talk.

Gradually our patience began to run out as we became annoyed yet again been left waiting by these medics whom we'd been trying to get to meet us for almost four years. Who did these people think they were? How dare they treat us like this. We had made great efforts to make it on time yet there was a brazen disregard on their part, these were my thoughts. Then we heard this "ha ha ha" a burst of laughter from them right at our backs. Well we'd had enough. I immediately said to the advocate "So here we are yet again left waiting, how dare those people. Document how we have been left waiting and our disgust at how we've been treated." Kerill said, "Get those people in here we have questions to put to them." She left the room and went to where the medics were assembled. There was a bit of a flurry and in a few minutes she returned followed by these four gentlemen who filed into the room in silence and stood behind their respective chairs. Kerill and I were seated. Now they remained standing for a few moments. Why? Don't ask me, protocol perhaps or were they expecting Kerill and I to stand? Gone was any vestige of optimism we'd had of there been any sensitivity or interest on their part in meeting our needs and there certainly was going to be no deference on our part. We were determined to take charge of the meeting. At last we could look them straight in the eye and insist that they hear our concerns. Kerill said, "Let's get on with this. We have questions for all of you." The advocate interjected saying she would introduce everyone. She started on the by now very usual tiresome apology and excuses for delays, but Kerill then cut in saying we wished to start with our questions and took the lead. We had felt that if these medics got the floor we'd probably have been consigned to a medical lecture and we were determined not to let this happen. When asked why we had such difficulty in securing a meeting, responses ranged from Dr A (team B) was in Australia, Dr E (team C) was now gone back to his native America (so we were not deluded Ailbhe, remember how we had maintained one of the doctors involved in the contention around your bed immediately prior to your death had an American accent), Dr H acknowledged on questioning from Kerill that Dr A should have met with the family but he could not give the reason as to why this did not take place as "he could not answer on his behalf." When I asked him if he would have met with the family in a similar situation, he stated that he would have. Dr F stated that he spoke with Dr I (team A) and had offered to meet with the family immediately following your death. What a pity this was not acted on. Such a meeting could have saved us such a lot of stressful hassle. Who or what prevented a follow through? We were very easily contactable. Now interestingly Dr C (team C) and the same team as Dr F took a very different line to Drs A and F. He responded that as you were not his patient "and as he was not the primary consultant it would not be normal practice in these circumstances to meet with relatives, however if the patient were directly under his care he most certainly would have met with the relatives, as is his practice." Well neither were Dr A or Dr F your primary consultant. 'I felt Doctor C took great exception to my questioning him. He seemed to treat Kerill's input with more respect.

After the meeting Kerill concurred with this and told me how on a few occasions he felt like interjecting and asking him to lay off the arrogance and treat me with respect but that I was doing such a good job in holding my ground in a firm, dignified way he felt it best to let the meeting run. You were definitely on my shoulder Ailbhe. "Give me explicit examples," I hear you say.

Well when I asked Dr C as to why it had taken so long to get him to agree to meet us he haughtily replied that it had taken me a long time to raise these issues. I reminded him of how we had expected the inquest in February 2003 to clarify matters and of my publicly expressed disappointment at that time when this did not happen – of the Coroners publicly stated disquiet at how present legislation curtailed his ability to compel people he needed to question to attend and personally answer. So I'd been looking for a meeting with him since February 2003 – it was now the 30th of May 2006. I then asked him to state precisely when he had been personally informed as to our request to meet him. He responded last August (August 2005) it was now the 30th of May 2006 so why this delay I asked. He curtly replied that you were not his patient so such a meeting would not have been appropriate. I then asked him to explain his last minute change in stance. This meeting had been scheduled for some time. According to the patients advocate he had consistently refused to attend despite our repeated requests. Then midday yesterday I got a phone call informing me that he would be in attendance so what constituted this change I asked. He dismissively responded that he normally takes his holidays around the time of your death Ailbhe and anyway ***how could he be expected to remember an incident like that.*** I saw red and told him how grossly insensitive and insulting I found his attitude – reminding him how a 25 year old relatively healthy (according to the pathologist) had died while in his care. Dr G had stated that while the hospital had carried out 3000 similar procedures over the last ten years this type of complication had occurred on only three occasions, none bar yours having a fatal outcome as Dr G also stated that in his 29 years of practice yours was the first case he'd come across with a fatal outcome and he sees fit to refer to this tragedy as an incident like this. He curtly reiterated that you were not his patient. I got the distinct impression Ailbhe that here was a man so resenting having to sit in front of us and doing all in his power to intimidate and break me emotionally. Yes Ailbhe you were definitely on both my shoulders. I left Dr C in no doubt as to how grossely abhorrent I found his attitude and response to the enormous tragedy we your family and friends were left with. I surprised myself.While the others present were less defensive and engaged with us in a more professional, detached manner our concerns were largely met with obfuscatory responses. They tended to take off on tangents going into details of the mechanics of the various medical procedures. They were not short Ailbhe on talking each other up, and assuring us of their absolute confidence in the two absent doctors, Dr E and Dr A. We were left wondering if you were in such wonderful hands Ailbhe why had the outcome been so tragic and why it had taken until now to even get this meeting. As for the patients advocate, there was no clarification as to why the nine months prevarication. Apparently Dr F had no difficulty meeting with us, or so he had said but was only notified the day before. Dr B was in the hospital. We wondered in whose interest had the advocacy been operating. Again I'm amazed Ailbhe at, how clearly I can recall the entire episode. Yes I did keep the various letters and written responses in a special file and it's thanks to that file that I can be accurate on dates. Most of the history I did when I was in school seemed to be based around battles and their dates. I just did not have the memory and did poorly in test in recalling dates accurately. However, the precise detail, emotion and atmosphere of our engagement with the medics and advocacy I can remember clearly as if it were just yesterday.

"How did you feel when the meeting ended"? I hear you ask. Well Ailbhe positive on the whole, delighted that at last we got two of the five medics we'd been trying to meet to the table where they had to engage with us and hear our concerns. We now had a clearer picture of who did what and so on. We no longer had to be content with the vague responses from the patient's advocacy such as "I have not been able to identify which senior registrar was on duty" or "the consultant on call could offer no assistance." We now had names, we felt vindicated in our belief that we as a family had been denied what should have been a minimal justifiable right by those involved in your care. We felt we were totally let down by the patients advocacy. Based on our own personal experience the title patient's advocacy or patient's representative as they also title themselves is now something of an oxymoron. We felt you would have approved of our efforts to get personal accountability. We gave ourselves an A+ for how we held the bone, and did not break down emotionally as this was something that worried me a little in advance of the meeting. So all in all Ailbhe we left with a spring in our step, a sense of achievement, a sense of having done the right thing. We tucked into a well-deserved meal in a comfortable hotel mulling over events and exchanged news. We also wondered how future contact with the Medical Council would pan out, but we held no great expectations. We so wished you could be with us, said our goodbyes and went our separate ways.

Back to our timeline Ailbhe and don't lose interest. I think you'll find some revelations in this final episode of the saga intriguingly significant, perhaps infuriating too but back to our timeline.

24th April 2006 - We sent our concerns to the Medical Council.

8th of May 2006- We received a reply acknowledging receipt of same and outlining the process we were obliged to follow, basically the council had written to the hospital "seeking the names and registration numbers of all those doctors involved on Ms Ailbhe Hannon Dunne's treatment." The letter stated that when they received a response they would write to us to confirm.

/

Comhairle na nDochtúirí Leighis
Medical Council

Your ref: Our ref: C35/06/JS

PRIVATE AND CONFIDENTIAL
STRICTLY ADDRESSEE ONLY

Letters

Letters

Ms. Maura Hannon,
Farranseer House,
Cornafean,
Co. Cavan.

Letters from Medical Council /

8th May, 2006

Dear Ms. Hannon,

Thank you for your letter of 24th April, 2006.

Consideration of a complaint against a doctor is provided for in the Medical Practitioner's Act, 1978, under which the Medical Council was established. Under the Act, the Fitness to Practise Committee, considers complaints against registered medical practitioners on the grounds of:-

(a) alleged professional misconduct; or
(b) fitness to engage in the practice of medicine by reason of physical or mental disability.

Prior to a complaint being considered by the Fitness to Practise Committee it would be necessary that the identity of the registered medical practitioner concerned is established. In this regard, I have written to [redacted] Hospital on today's date seeking the name and registration number of all those doctors involved in Ms. Ailbhe Hannon Dunne's treatment.

I will write further in due course on receipt of a response from [redacted] Hospital. Please find enclosed leaflet detailing the complaints procedure for your in[redacted]on, should you have any queries please do not hesitate to contact me.

Yours sincerely,

[redacted]

Enc/

June 7th 2006- Letter received from the Medical Council informing us that the doctors involved in your treatment had now been identified and that our written presentation had been sent to them with a request that they provide their observations and comments. They would send us a copy for our observation and we were free to respond should we wish, then it went on

"Once the committee is satisfied that all relevant material is before it, it will make a decision as to whether or not your complaint gives grounds for the holding of an inquiry which is similar to a hearing before a court or tribunal....if the committee does decide to hold an inquiry, you may be required to attend before the committee and give sworn evidence in support of your complaint. I will however write to you in more detail in the event that an inquiry is to be held."

.30 Ch-5

Comhairle na nDochtúirí Leighis
Medical Council

Your ref: Our ref: C35/06/JS 6.

PRIVATE AND CONFIDENTIAL
STRICTLY ADDRESSEE ONLY

Ms. Maura Hannon,
Farranseer House,
Cornafean,
Co. Cavan.

Letter 6 From Medical Council

7th June, 2006

Dear Ms. Hannon,

I refer to my letter of 8th May, 2006.

I wish to advise that the doctors involved in Ms. Ailbhe Hannon Dunne's treatment have now been identified and your letter of complaint has been sent to the doctors with a request that they provide their observations and comments concerning your complaint. On receipt of these observations and comments, a copy may be sent to you for your response, if any. Once the Committee is satisfied that all relevant material is before it, it will make a decision as to whether or not your complaint gives grounds for the holding of an inquiry which is similar to a hearing before a Court or Tribunal.

If the Committee does decide to hold an inquiry, you may be required to attend before the Committee and give sworn evidence in support of your complaint. I will, however, write to you in more detail in the event that an inquiry is to be held.

You will appreciate, therefore, that it may take some time before a decision can be made in relation to your complaint.

Yours sincerely,

[redacted]

Well, at this stage Ailbhe we had grown accustomed to waiting. So we were not overly disappointed that it was now almost four months on (six months from first contact) before the next correspondence arrived from the Medical Council and it contained little, if anything of consequence.

6th October 2006- "I wish to advise that I am currently awaiting observations and comments from some of the doctors concerned and as soon as they have been received I will forward a copy of same to you. If I can be of any further assistance please do not hesitate to contact me." At least we were still on their radar.

Comhairle na nDochtúirí Leighis
Medical Council

Your ref: Our ref: C35/06/JS

PRIVATE AND CONFIDENTIAL
STRICTLY ADDRESSEE ONLY

Ms. Maura Hannon,
Farranseer House,
Cornafean,
Co. Cavan.

6th October, 2006

Dear Ms. Hannon,

I refer to previous correspondence in relation to the complaint which you have made to the Fitness to Practise Committee concerning a number of doctors who were involved in Ms. Ailbhe Hannon Dunne's care.

I wish to advise that I am currently awaiting observations and comments from some of the doctors concerned and as soon as they have been received I will forward a copy of same to you.

If I can be of any further assistance please do not hesitate to contact me.

Yours sincerely,

[redacted]

4th December 2006 - A letter arrived, with written observations from six of the seven doctors they had established as those involved in your care. The letter stated that we "invite you to provide, in writing, any response you may wish to make in the matter. It would be appreciated if you could reply on or before 22nd December, in order that the committee may be in a position to consider the matter at its next meeting...I wish to advise that at present observations and comments from Dr. E have not been received and a copy will be sent to you upon receipt."

CoverLetter

Comhairle na nDochtúirí Leighis
Medical Council

Your ref: Our ref: C35/06/JS

PRIVATE AND CONFIDENTIAL
STRICTLY ADDRESSEE ONLY

Ms. Maura Hannon,
Farranseer House,
Cornafean,
Co. Cavan.

tter 8 from Medical Council

4th December, 2006

Dear Ms. Hannon,

I refer to previous correspondence concerning your complaint against Dr. [redacted] Dr. [redacted] Dr. [redacted], Dr. [redacted] and Dr. [redacted]

I now enclose a copy of Dr. [redacted] Dr. [redacted] Dr. [redacted] and Dr. [redacted] observations and comments and invite you to provide, in writing, any response you may wish to make in the matter.

It would be appreciated if you could reply on or before 22nd December, in order that the Committee may be in a position to consider the matter at its next meeting.

I wish to advise that at present observations and comments from Dr. [redacted] have not been received and a copy will be sent to you upon receipt.

Yours sincerely,

[redacted]

Well Ailbhe, at last all be it eight months into our correspondence with the Medical Council, we had a much clearer picture as to the names, duties and line of command. We were of course disappointed and felt disadvantaged at not having Dr. E's response in putting our reply together which now had to be back by the 22nd of December 2006. We felt we had not got quite the full picture as Dr. E had been the doctor we most wished to talk to as he was involved in your treatment at the most critical times, the one with the American accent.

We set into reading and reflecting on the six reports as we had just been given over two weeks within which to respond should we wish to. Although we had met with four of the doctors at the meeting on May 30th 2006 and quite a lot of what we'd heard there was reiterated in their reports, we did get a much clearer picture of (a) the line of command and individual responsibility- it became much more transparent as to who did what and when and who made the decisions (b) it cleared up the ambiguity we'd found in the letter of March 27th 2006 from the advocacy which had so riled us and frustrated our efforts at getting a clear understanding of events. The varying individual nuances and perceptions were revealing Ailbhe.

So we duly set to work reading and analysing the six reports with just over two weeks to meet the deadline set for us. I'll briefly outline what was new to us from the reports.

I'll start with team A, Dr. G and Dr. I's reports. You will have remembered them both Ailbhe. Dr. G was your primary consultant and you had got to know him and his team very well. We had much to be grateful to them for in the past and we had acknowledged that, but on this occasion you were not directly under their particular expertise. So on July 8th we established their role to be general supervisory with the relevant expertise provided by teams B and C. Now Dr. G stated in his response "I am not clear what specific issues the Hannon family now have regarding my management of Ailbhe, previously they stated they didn't have any." This was correct and precisely why we were not satisfied with the meeting offered by the patients advocate with only Dr. G and Dr. H, the latter whom up until then we'd not heard of. Dr. G goes on to say "As I understood it, the concerns of the family revolved around the expertise of the doctors who inserted the permcath and the chest tubes and whether the subsequent management of the case was appropriate....Dr. A was a senior lecturer and had previously inserted numerous permcaths for our department without any complications. I did not know Dr. E, but I understand from Dr. C that he was experienced in insertion of chest tubes and was being supervised by Dr. F. However I agree it is most unfortunate that both of these individuals returned to their native countries soon after this tragic event and were not available to discuss the case with the family...Another issue that the family have repeatedly brought up was whether manipulated of the tube at the bedside had somehow led to Ailbhe's cardiac arrest. Not being an expert in this field I had to state to the family that I was not in a position to offer an opinion."

I think I told you Ailbhe how at our meeting on May 30th 2006 we discovered that 3,000 similar cases (catheter insertion) had been carried out over the previous ten years in the hospital and your type of complication occurred only on three occasions. I wondered what the outcome had been for those three patients and I regretted not enquiring. Well Dr. G reported "This is the first case with a fatal outcome that I have come across in 29 years of practice." This makes me so sad Ailbhe. To our amazement Dr. I in quite a sensitive, humane, but surprising response stated "At the outset, I wish to record that I was unaware of the contact which Ailbhe Hannon's family have had with the hospital since her death. I would have been at all times, and remain open to attending any meeting which the hospital may arrange with Ailbhe Hannon's family. I was not aware of the inquest and was not called to give evidence at it. I do appreciate that the coroner was at the time restricted in the number of medical doctors he could call to give evidence but I wish the family to know that I would have been more than happy to attend to give evidence if contacted." He goes on to speak positively about the general standards of care on the 8th and feels that he acted appropriately in his role. "The remainder of the questions Mrs. Hannon sets out do not relate to my role in treating Ailbhe. I would emphasise that until I received the copy letter of complaint from you I was unaware that the family had ongoing questions. I wish to let the family know that I sincerely regret if they were under any impression that I was either failing or refusing to respond to any queries. I would at all times have been happy to do so."

What on earth had the patients advocate been doing Ailbhe? We'd been lead to believe that all possible efforts were being made to contact all doctors involved and get their observations. A year and three months earlier we received a letter from patients advocacy dated the 23rd of September 2005 with the usual opening apology "I am sorry it is talking so long to respond to you but I have not as yet received a report from the staff members whom I have contacted in regard your case. I am to-day sending a further reminder and hope to be able to respond to you at an early date."

I'll move on to the reports sent to the Medical Council by the medics on team B and as this team was very involved in critical expert procedures on July 8th 2002, we were very interested and we did get new insights that helped us put the jigsaw of events together. Now we were aware that Dr. A and Dr. B were involved but I had thought that Dr. H who met us at the 30th of May meeting 2006 to represent Dr. A (who was now out of the country) had had no connection to your care. In fact for some reason I thought he'd taken up duties post your death, but apparently not so. Seemingly he was senior and part of that (team B) on July 8th 2002. Dr. A writes in his report to the Medical Council on the 26th of October 2006, "She (Ailbhe) was referred to mine and Dr. H's care for urgent insertion of a tunnelled dialysis catheter so she could recommence haemodialysis." You'll remember Ailbhe at the meeting on May 30th 2006 when I asked Dr. H if he had discussed the events of July 8th 2006 with Dr A and he acknowledged that he had. When Kerill asked him, "Why did Dr. A not meet with the family?" he responded that Dr. A was now in Australia and he could not answer on his behalf. I then asked him would he have met with the family in a similar situation (at the time thinking he was new to the position since July 2002) he said that he would have. I also asked him to acknowledge that Dr. A should have met with the family and he clearly stated that yes he should have met with us. Later when I queried him as to when he himself became aware of our concerns he responded that it was when the complaint came in. Now that had to mean either February 2003 or August 2005. It was a surprise to us to discover how close to the whole situation he apparently was Ailbhe. I did feel that there was a vagueness around his engagement with us at that May meeting and I'd have to wonder why he himself being one of the top brass on the team had not gone ahead with what he said he believed Dr. A should have done, just agreed to meet us and explain.

Dr. A's report to the Medical Council also clarified the status of Dr. B. We knew and you had made no secret of the fact that you had a horror of students or trainees taking on to perform procedures. You had expressed how you did not mind them acting in an observatory role during your treatments and medical procedures but no more. That was you felt as indeed we all did one of the advantages gained from you having private health insurance that only the best qualified medics would take on your care. When I asked Dr. H at our meeting on the 30th of May 2006 if Dr B was a trainee he responded that Dr. B was a "registrar" and not a "student," yet we found out that Dr A in his report to the Medical Council states when referring to Dr. B "I was taking "a trainee," Dr. B, through the procedure. At some point in the transition of dilating up the track to accommodate the sheath my perception was that something was not quite right. I immediately took over and realised that the guide wire and dilator had migrate to be outside the right brachiocephalic vessel and in the mediastinum. Exactly how this came to be I am unsure." When I asked Dr. H if Dr. A being the senior was actively involved in the carrying out of this procedure from the start to finish he stated he could not answer for Dr. A but that Dr. B made the first puncture wound.

Dr. B in her own report to the Medical Council outlines her very active involvement from the start of the procedure stating that at that time she was a "second year specialist registrar in radiology having just successfully completed FFR, RCSI part 1 exam in radiology. "As registrars we are involved in different areas in radiology. I was scheduled for interventional radiology where I assisted in cases performed by a more senior radiologist, Dr. A."

Now it was to avoid the above type of activity that myself and Kerill were so anxious to be with you Ailbhe. That was why Kerill took the day off work and both of us spent the day in the hospital. It was so unfortunate that he was not allowed stay with you in the room where this procedure was taking place. He accompanied you to the door anxious and willing to stay with you but the medics told him it was against hospital policy. Well I don't believe that this policy is motivated from a desire to be of benefit to the patient. Dr A goes on in his report to the Medical Council, "An uncommon but recognised and serious complication did occur namely laceration to the right brachiocephalic vein. Why this occurred I am not entirely certain. Although I was taking a trainee through this everything was performed in the correct manner." I wonder Ailbhe. Certainly you, yourself, Kerill or your family would not have agreed to a trainee having such liberty in the carrying out of the procedure. So, it is understandable that we would lament not insisting on being allowed stay with you during the procedure. Dr. B herself also states in her report how she performed the procedure....I felt some resistance so I handed over to Dr. A. Dr A took over and continued with the dialation." I, as you Ailbhe would have expected that all this work would have been carried out by a senior medic, not a trainee. You had every reason to be angry when you came back, righteous anger Ailbhe. As we now have only their word for what went on I'd wonder about the level of bungling. Only hope it was not too painful or too scary for you Ailbhe.

I thought the bit of verbal gymnastics on the part of Dr. H interesting. At our meeting on the 30th of May 2006 as I already said, I asked him as to the status of Dr B, "Was she a trainee?" I asked. He hedged it by responding, "Dr B was a registrar not a student." Now, Dr. A as I've pointed out in his report to the Medical Council refers to her as a "trainee," such as "I was taking a trainee through this." Well I got out my dictionary Ailbhe to clarify the difference between trainee and student "student = one receiving instruction or technical training" "trainee = a person under going training" and "registrar = a hospital doctor between the grades."

Dr B also states "no one approached me requesting a statement or any information regarding what happened." Strange Aibhe. Then I'll conclude our analysis of team B with a quote from Dr A. "This complication however may not have been the direct cause of death. Ailbhe died of apparently electromechanical dislocation 8 hours later whilst the chest tube was manipulated. What was the cause of death at this point? I have not seen a coroner's report but only a vague mention of medical misadventure."

He claims that after the complication had occurred the treatment was expertly handled in his department and before we got his report Ailbhe we too had come to this conclusion. However we equally felt had the procedure been undertaken by a more experienced medic the complication would most likely not have occurred. We did feel that once team C identified the complication they righted it. Interestingly too Dr. A states "The following day I was notified that Ailbhe arrested some 8 hours later whilst the chest tube was manipulated on the ward. The reason for this was uncertain at the time and I suspect still remains as such. This was a tremendously sad occurrence." He says, "I did not see Ailbhe's family since the immediate post procedure meeting. I was never aware of any complaints and various meetings at the hospital, coroners and your committee." He also states in his report, "it would have been best to hold a family conference with myself in attendance some days after the event."

So say all of us. I'm just hoping you are not finding my chronology of events boring, overly detailed or utterly confusing Ailbhe. But I do feel it important to carefully and accurately untangle these events with you, lest you might feel we were remiss in not having done all in our power to have the exact circumstances relating to your tragic death exposed to the best possible investigative scrutiny. Of course we fully accept that accidents and mishaps occur in all areas of life this side of the grave. But equally I believe in the principle of personal responsibility. Indeed worthy lessons can be learned from our mistakes. Do you remember one of the captions I had on the playroom wall when you were little Ailbhe "A mistake is not a mistake if a lesson from it is learned." Surely in critical matters of life and death only absolute transparency and personal accountability should be acceptable. This principle was the catalyst that sustained and justified us in our persistent inquiries.

So, Ailbhe you'll bear with me as I launch into team C's response to the Medical Council. This is the last team and the team whose reports were eagerly awaited. You will remember how anxious we had been to meet with the medics on this team and how our efforts had been met with a wall of resistance. Apparently the governance of our hospitals are quite comfortable with this situation judging from the more recent experience of that family we spoke about earlier whose case was reported on in the Irish Independent on January 26th 2012. While the experience of the family seemed so similar to ours although it was a different hospital and different medics, on reading the report it seems nothing had changed in the intervening two years with regard to procedures in dealing with grieving families. Indeed the parents told how they too encountered "a wall of silence" and how it took seven years, a High Court action plus the Coroners Act to be amended to finally get an answer to their one question for the medics involved in the care of their son. How did this happen? I can only say to them "Well well done."

Well back to our timeline and the final stage in our analysis, that is the response of the medics on team C. Team C consisted of three medics. Dr's C, E, F all personally actively involved in your care at those most critical junctures on July 8th. The two reports from Dr's C and F clearly established this as fact. You will remember Dr E had not responded despite having been repeatedly requested to do so by the Medical Council. As we now know Dr E had been very critically involved in your care and his report was the one we most needed. He was the medic with the American accent that we spoke of as being around your bed at the time of your death and involved in the manipulation of the drain. The lack of a response from him left us at a loss as we prepared our response which had to be ready in two weeks. Anyhow the line of command in team C became very clear. Dr C was the consultant in charge of team C. The reports established that indeed he had been personally involved in your care on July 8th, despite his earlier protestations to the contrary Ailbhe and the stone-walling our efforts had met with when we tried to have him meet with us. "On that particular evening he was not the consultant on duty and indeed he was out of the country". Well not at all so Ailbhe, he was now clearly identified as being active in your care on July 8th 2006, as were his two registrars ,Dr F his senior registrar, and Dr E his junior registrar.

I'll now summarise the points of interest to us in Dr F's report to the Medical Council. So on July 8th 2006 Dr F worked as a senior registrar to Dr C. In his report he outlines the sequence of events on July 8th 2002. He points out that as his involvement was following your cardiac arrest and our concerns relate to your care prior to that there is no specific question or allegation relating to him. He does clarify the input of himself and his consultant Dr C and the junior registrar Dr E. He states while she was in radiology Dr A "requested that" Dr C's "registrar" Dr E "see the patient since he was working for Dr C------.

"He saw the patient and requested a chest x-ray to be performed then and to be performed on a daily basis while the chest drains were in. He also requested that a coagulation screen and FBC be performed. He recommended that the chest drain be placed on suction and that the output be recorded. He stated that "team C" will follow the patient with "team A, "At approximately 6pm I was in attendance with" Dr C and Dr C's "team on our ward round following conclusion of our surgical operating list" Dr C requested that a chest x-ray be performed"---Dr C also recommended that the chest drain bottles be changed to pleurovac system such as they could be placed on suction"------"At approximately 7pm"Dr E changed the chest drains to pleurovac drains during this change of chest drain equipment the patient became distressed and asked to sit forward as she found it difficult to breath"------------" I believe the family were in attendance at this point-A cardiac arrest was called at 7.20pm and a cardio-pulmonary resuscitation was commenced". At this point I was contacted by" Dr E "and I arrived within minutes as I recorded in the chart-------------. The Medical team discontinued resuscitation at 8.40pm"

The Dr C he refers to Ailbhe is of course the Dr C that we were told the previous March was out of the country. Dr F reiterates how he only heard of our requests for a meeting on May 29th 2006 and how he had been at all times willing to meet us. He states I was very surprised to hear that there was any difficulty contacting anyone of the staff involved. I first received a letter from "the patient's advocacy 29th May 2006 (letter was dated 24th May 2006) In this letter it stated "Dr G Dr H" were meeting with the patient's family on 30th May 2006. Therefore I contacted the hospital and said that I would be more than happy to attend this meeting (although I had not been invited) Amazing Ailbhe, He goes on "This was a tragic death and I was disappointed it took so long to identify the doctors involved." He also points out that he feels no specific allegation has been made relating to him personally and he hopes that he has now clarified his involvement. We did feel that yes Dr F had clarified his own involvement in his report and indeed brought much clarity and transparency on the parts played by his consultant, Dr C and his junior registrar, Dr E. Finally we felt we had pretty definitive information as to the individuals and team role in your care on July 8th 2002, information that we had been seeking for the previous three to four years. We were most interested in Dr C's report to the Medical Council, the consultant in charge of team C.

You'll remember Ailbhe how haughty and defensive I said we found his attitude at the meeting on May 30th 2006. It was our distinct impression that here was a man who resented the fact that he was sitting in front of us. Of course you'll remember the background and how the patients advocate had insisted that this Dr C would not meet with us. Then just the day before the arranged meeting I received that surprise phone call at work and when I made it absolutely clear that yes Kerill and myself would be turning up for the meeting as arranged despite our disappointment at Dr C's unwillingness to be there and how I was only back in class when that second call came informing me rather gingerly I felt that Dr C would attend next morning's meeting.

You'll recall my outrage at how I felt Dr. C tried to justify his stance by trivialising your tragic death by his remarks suggesting that he could not be expected to remember an incident like this, thought he was on holiday. I remember vividly Ailbhe how the defensive tone of his remarks plus the use of the word "incident" hit me as an attempt to normalise a tragedy that Dr A had revealed was the first such case he'd come across with a fatal outcome in his 29 years of practice in the hospital. So I think you'll well understand how Dr C's claim to justifiable amnesia riled me.

I hope I've not been repeating myself too much Ailbhe. I'll get on to Dr C's report to the Medical Council now that I have concluded the backdrop to give it context. The first thing to strike us on reading his report to the Medical Council was his complete change in tone and approach, not a trace of the hostile cavalier attitude we'd been confronted with at our meeting on May 30th 2006. Dr C divided his response to the Medical Council into two sections (1) his commentary on the involvement of his team in the management of your care and (2) the process in the hospital by which our complaint was handled. In section one he chronicles the various stages in your treatment mentioning how the insertion of a vascular access catheter in your right subclavian vein "....was unfortunately complicated....the appropriate management was instituted following recognition of this complication.....following this the patient stabilised and was transferred back to the ward." He goes onto say, "My registrar Dr E was called...." We found the next statement very revealing Ailbhe and I quote, "Although

I do not personally recall the case" Dr F "states in his report on the evening of July 8th after our theatre list we included a visit to"………"ward to review the late Ms Hannon Dunne. "APPARENTLY" I issued instructions in relation to a repeat chest x-ray, changing the infusion line from the permacath in the right subclavian to an alternative means of access and instructed that the underwater seal system be replaced by an Atrium drainage bottle which allowed for more careful monitoring of the volume of drainage and also had the option of applying negative pressure to the pleural space. Unfortunately Ms Hannon-Dunne collapsed and died rather suddenly later that evening and the post mortem indicated a 2.5cm laceration in the subclavian and brachio-cephalvic vein with a large right sided haemothorax which in the view of the pathologist had compressed the mediastinum and the opposite lung. Dr E, "my registrar was in the process of changing the underwater seal system at the bedside when the acute terminal event occurred. The patient's mother Mrs Hannon understandably associates the sudden demise of her daughter with the act of changing or interfering with the drainage system in her chest. She questions the experience of Dr E "to change such a drainage system." Dr E "like his predecessors from the hospital since 1977 was a senior resident from their highly regarded surgical training programme, who commenced work in "this hospital "on the first of July as part of his six month rotation to Dublin. Like all of his predecessors Dr E is more experienced than most Irish surgical trainees in the management of chest trauma, chest drains and conditions such as pneumothorax, haemothorax and shock. The transfer of one underwater seal system to another is a very simple matter of clamping the chest drains and quickly disconnecting from one system and reconnecting to the new system. The patient's collapse was, I am quite certain, in no way connected with the act of changing the type of underwater seal drainage system. Indeed as attested by" Dr F "there was no evidence of tension pneumothorax at the time of her collapse and allowing air in from the atmosphere to the pleural space would be the only potential mechanism associated with changing of the tubes that could have precipitated such an acute collapse. The cause of death of the late Ailbhe Hannon-Dunne was a haemopneumothorax due to laceration of the subclavian and brachiocephalic vein in the course of insertion of a vascular access device for haemodialysis. This is a recognised complication of this procedure and the vast majority of patients seal the laceration in the vein, expand the collapsed lung and do not require any additional intervention other than what was done for the late Ailbhe. Clearly had it been known that she had a 2.5cm laceration in the vein, surgical repair would have been undertaken. However as happens in the majority of patients with this problem she stabilised and her subsequent sudden collapse with cardiac arrest did not permit thoracotomy and attempted repair of the vein. The death of such a young patient from this complication is a tragic outcome and I can well understand her parents and her husband's grief and ongoing disbelief in relation to the manner of her death-I wish to extend my sympathies to them even at this late stage despite the fact that they are convinced that somehow the surgeons caused her death."

So ends section one of Dr C's response to the Medical Council and what struck us straight off, as I already said, was the interesting contrast in tone and attitude in his report to the Medical Council and how he engaged with us at our face to face meeting on May 30th 2006. You'll remember how I robustly challenged him on his dismissive attitude Ailbhe and at that meeting we noted how he reframed his answer when reporting to the Medical Council and I quote "Although I do not personally recall the case...." Strange then that his registrar and team member on the day should write in his report, "our team was deeply saddened by Ms Hannon Dunne's tragic death...." His use again of the word "apparently" in the report, "Apparently I issued instructions in relation to a repeat chest x-ray,.." Is he still trying to cast a doubt as to his involvement in your care at the critical times on July 8th? Thank goodness for the freedom of information Ailbhe. Yes Dr C you were personally involved in Ailbhe's care and at times around which we had serious concerns so there is no "apparently" about it. It's alarming that the tragic loss of a young life means so little to you. Do you not understand how uniquely precious and irreplaceable every life is.

Vera Duffy in her book "Justice for my son" outlines how over the years she did battle with the public authorities and medical profession to have them accept that her now sadly deceased son was severely brain damaged following the whooping cough vaccine. She describes how time after time her concerns were dismissed, ignored and how she met a wall of silence and a culture of denial. She seems such an extraordinarily strong woman Ailbhe to have survived all that came her way. She tells how she found in her efforts to gather the knowledge and evidence needed to establish the link between the vaccine and what happened to her son (evidence she is convinced many eminent medics and governments here in Ireland suppressed) that most of the medical professionals she encountered were more concerned with protecting each other, their medical reputations and their own bloated egos than a desire to establish the truth or act in the best interest of their patients. She also describes how despite admirable efforts that went far beyond the call of duty on the part of the coroner to get at the truth, old coroners laws stating that the coroner is not allowed to lay blame for the cause of death only where, when and how the death occurred militated against the establishment of the truth. Incidentally Ailbhe, the coroner she refers to was the coroner who dealt with your inquest and I have always said how I felt I was in the presence of an honourable, truthful man whose hands were tied as he himself pointed out to us publicly at your inquest.

This poor boy Alan would be four years your senior Ailbhe. He was born in 1973 and was a happy child until he was five months old when he was severely "brain-damaged following the whooping cough vaccine and lived until he was a skeletal, helpless 22-year-old." His mother despite, losing a second child due to a brain tumour at just gone three years in 1980 and herself having multiple sclerosis refuses to give up until she finally gets justice. This lady's courage and persistence is way beyond human understanding.

I'm just wondering Ailbhe have you met up with Alan and Renee. You'd be of the same vintage.

Moving through Dr C's report to section two, the process in the hospital by which our complaint was handled, I'd prefer if he had used the word "question" or "concerns" rather than complaint, but here goes the report. He again admits being made aware of our concerns on the 23rd of August 2005 but claims to having had "no recollection of any clinical involvement in this case." Well allowing for his amnesia surely it would be minimalist to expect that when made aware of our concerns re your tragic death he would immediately check the clinical notes and jog his memory as to when he had taken holidays and been out of the country in 2002. Interestingly he was quick off the mark to check the clinical notes when contacted by the Medical Council almost a year later. He claims to have been "very upset" about finding his name on your clinical notes when he finally checked on May 29th 2006 having being contacted by the Medical Council. His sympathy, excuses and apology in his written report to the Medical Council resonated an interesting contrast with the defensive arrogant attitude he had when meeting with Kerill and myself.

He was the consultant in charge of team C, the team that for four years now we had been seeking to have a meeting with. His "calling for a review of protocols and procedures of the patient representative's office....", has a hollow ring, pious platitudes I feel Ailbhe. It required no change in the particular office to finally have him meet us. It transpired that it was in his own best professional interest to meet us once the possibility of a Medical Council inquiry was looming as will become evident shortly Ailbhe. Do be prepared for a little surprising development before we draw down the final curtain on this fraught saga.

We quickly got our response on paper. Our concerns remained as we had expressed earlier through the patients association. We were still especially anxious to get an explanation as to the confusion and contention we had witnessed at your beside, as Dr E was handling your chest tubes immediately prior to your respiratory arrest and again we expressed our disappointment that Dr E had not seen fit to respond. Now Ailbhe they had told us at the meeting on May 30th that this contention we'd observed was merely the louder American way of communicating that we were not accustomed to and had just mistook it as contention. As you'll recall Dr E was American. Well, Kerill assured them that we could well differentiate between a loud American accent and the contestation we experienced at your bedside just prior to your collapse and sudden death. While pleased that our efforts had eventually given us a clearer picture as to who did what and having succeeded in gaining some little personal accountability on the part of some of the professionals involved in your care our expectations of getting any further semblance of justice was lower than low as we rushed off our response on December 17th 2006 to meet the deadline of December 22nd set by the Medical Council. Well Ailbhe, Christmas 2006 came and went, we missed you of course and there was no contact from the Medical Council except for the formal acknowledgement of our response in a letter dated 9th January 2007 stating that copies had been sent to Dr's C, F, A, I, B and G for their information and that all correspondence would be referred to the committee for consideration at its next meeting. They also said they would write letting us know the committee's decision. No date was given for that next meeting referred to. Then the last sentence "If" Dr E's "observations and comments are received prior to Fitness to Practice Committee's next scheduled meeting a copy will be sent to you for your response." We had thought the deadline for such responses had expired on December 22nd 2006. So it was into the waiting game again.

Letter 9

C5

Comhairle na nDochtúirí Leighis
Medical Council

Your ref: Our ref: C35/06/JS

PRIVATE AND CONFIDENTIAL
STRICTLY ADDRESSEE ONLY

Mrs. Maura Hannon,
Farranseer House,
Cornafean,
Co. Cavan.

Letter 9 from Medical Council

9th January, 2007

Dear Mrs. Hannon,

Thank you for your letter of 18th December, 2006 giving your response to the correspondence, which the Fitness to Practise Committee has received from Dr [redacted] Dr. [redacted] Dr. [redacted] and Dr. [redacted]

I wish to inform you that a copy of your letter has been sent to Dr. [redacted], Dr. [redacted] Dr. [redacted] and Dr. [redacted] for their information.

All correspondence will be referred to the Committee for consideration at its next meeting.

I will write to you thereafter letting you know the Committee's decision.

If Dr. [redacted]'s observations and comments are received prior to the Fitness to Practise Committee next scheduled meeting a copy will be sent to your for your response.

Yours sincerely,

[redacted]

Now things so rested until another letter arrived from the Medical Council dated 29th January 2007 stating "I have now been provided with additional contact details in respect of Dr E and have written again requesting him to provide his observation and comments...." We had been informed through the patients advocate as far back as

September 2005 as to where Dr E was now working. He had gone back to the hospital from whence he'd come from to Ireland and indeed Dr C had confirmed his whereabouts' at our meeting on May 30th 2006. I quote from the report on that meeting forwarded to all involved and compiled by the Patients Advocate, "Questions in relation to" Dr E Dr C "then explained that" Dr E," registrar at the time, was an American citizen and had gone back to America, he is currently on the staff of ___hospital in America. But surprise surprise Ailbhe, the Medical Council too had been correctly informed of Dr E's whereabouts by no less than Dr C in his report to them on the 3rd of July 2006 eight months earlier and I quote from his report where he acknowledges Dr E as having been his registrar on July 8th 2002 and confirms that the Patients advocate contacted him "in March 2006 in which she indicated difficulties in contacting doctors involved in the care of Ailbhe with whom Mrs Hannon requested a meeting. I informed her that Dr E "was working In____as a transplant surgeon," and you will see later Ailbhe that the contact details proved to be accurate. So the Medical Council had the correct contact information on Dr E eight months prior to sending us this letter. What was going on Ailbhe? It sure looks now like a game of cat and mouse was being played with us. Was this simply another delaying tactic? What on earth given modern communication could be the difficulty in contacting him?

Then this letter dated January 29th 2007 arrived, which we found very revealing. It proved to us that the particular doctors whom we'd been seeking a meeting with since your death almost five years earlier could apparently refuse to meet with us but once the Medical Council requested them to provide observations and comments, failure on their part to comply would under section 45 of the Medical Practitioners Act 1978 amount to professional misconduct as you will see from letter 11. Bloated egos would want to avoid such at all costs.

Comhairle na nDochtúirí Leighis
Medical Council

Your ref: Our ref: C35/06/JS

P.43
Ch.5
P. 44
Letter 10

PRIVATE AND CONFIDENTIAL
STRICTLY ADDRESSEE ONLY

Mrs. Maura Hannon,
Farranseer House,
Comafean,
Co. Cavan.

Letter 10 from Medical Council

29th January, 2007

Dear Mrs. Hannon,

I refer to previous correspondence concerning the complaint which you have made to the Fitness to Practise Committee.

I wish to advise that I have now been provided with additional contact details in respect Dr. E [redacted] and have written again requesting him to provide his observations and comments concerning your complaint. Should Dr. E [redacted] fail to provide his observations and comments prior to the Fitness to Practise Committee's next meeting, all papers will be put before the Fitness to Practise Committee for their consideration.

If you have any queries arising out of this letter please do not hesitate to contact me.

Yours sincerely,

[redacted]

Comhairle na nDochtúirí Leighis
Medical Council

Your ref: Our ref: C35/06/JS

PRIVATE AND CONFIDENTIAL
STRICTLY ADDRESSEE ONLY

Ms. Maura Hannon,
Farranseer House,
Cornafean,
Co. Cavan.

Letter

26th March, 2007

Letter 11 From Medical Council

Dear Ms. Hannon,

I refer to previous correspondence concerning the complaint which you have made to the Fitness to Practise Committee.

Your complaint was considered by the Fitness to Practise Committee at its recent meeting. The Committee, in noting that Dr.E [redacted] had failed to respond to its request to provide his observations and comments has directed that I inform him that as a registered medical practitioner about whom a complaint is received is required to comply with the Committee's request for information in the form of observations and comments to enable it to discharge its statutory duties. In this regard, the Committee previously decided that failure by a registered medical practitioner to formally respond to letters from the Fitness to Practise Committee about matters which are the subject of an application under section 45 of the Medical Practitioners Act, 1978 has been determined as amounting to professional misconduct.

Accordingly I have written again to Dr. E [redacted] advising him of the aforementioned and that the Committee further directed that he be advised that in the event of his failure to respond to its request, it may be left with no alternative but to hold an inquiry concerning him under the provisions of Part V of the Medical Practitioners Act, 1978.

I will write further in due course when a response has been received from Dr. E [redacted] If you have any queries please do not hesitate to contact me.

Yours sincerely,

[redacted]

So Ailbhe our suspicions as to the motivation behind the changed tone and attitude and the air of cooperation and willing availability expressed by Dr C in his report to the Medical Council we felt were now well and truly vindicated. Needless to say Ailbhe we wondered how this would pan out and true to form we were given plenty of time to speculate as it was all of another four months before we were again contacted by the Medical Council in a letter dated 18th July 2007.

Comhairle na nDochtúirí Leighis
Medical Council

Your ref: Our C35/06/JS

PRIVATE AND CONFIDENTIAL
STRICTLY ADDRESSEE ONLY

Ms. Maura Hannon,
Farranseer House,
Cornafean,
Co. Cavan.

Letter

18th July, 2007

Letter 12 from Medical Council

Dear Ms. Hannon,

I refer to previous correspondence concerning the complaint which you have made to the Fitness to Practise Committee.

E

I now enclose a copy of Dr. [redacted] observations and comments and invite you to provide, in writing, any response you may wish to make in the matter.

It would be appreciated if you could reply on or before 10th August 2007, in order that the Committee may be in a position to consider the matter at its next meeting.

Yours sincerely,

[redacted]

Enc:

Now interestingly Dr E's report dated the 26th June of 2007 received by the Medical Council on the 10th of July 2007 revealed the contrast in the generous time he'd been given to present his report (we'd been informed he'd been initially contacted with details of our complaint on the 8th of May 2006) and again the pressure applied to us to get our response back in less than a month.

Finally, a full five years after your tragic death Ailbhe we had succeeded in getting a written report from each individual medic on their personal involvement in your care on July 8th 2002. As we mulled over Dr E's belated report we wondered why it had taken so long, a whole year practically for the Medical Council to inform Dr E as to the possible personal consequences for him professionally should he fail to formally respond to letters from the Fitness to Practice Committee. Had this been done earlier surely it could have speeded things up for us. Again we wondered whose best interests were being served. We are I think all familiar with the defence, "Too much time has now elapsed" and Dr E's report did confirm some perturbing facts. The glaring question was as to why the delay of six hours in connecting your test tubes to suction. It had been made clear to us that Dr E was the expert in this field by both Dr's C and F all of whom made up team C. Now Dr E claims in his report to the Medical Council that he made five specific recommendations at about 1 p.m. on July 8th one of which at number 4 reads "connect the chest tubes to suction"(1p.m.) Then he goes on to state "Our team saw her at about 5p.m....we also noted that her chest drains were not connected to suction as we had originally recommended and we asked that the ward acquire a pleurovac (Altrium) suction drainage unit at? 5p.m. " We came back at about 7 p.m. when the suction drainage was available....."

7p.m. Question (1) Why were Dr E's instructions not carried out immediately at approx 1 p.m? There was a whole six hours delay and (2) Whose responsibility was it to have these instructions adhered to? He says he re-recommended to connect chest tubes to suction at approx.5 p.m. yet it appears nothing happened until 7 p.m. What does he mean when he says he came back at 7 p.m. "when the suction drainage unit was available" (3) Why was there this delay in getting the required unit? (4) Who is responsible for the delay? (5) What could have been the consequences of the six hour delay? We had already, a year earlier in our response questioned the stent insertion.

As you will remember Ailbhe how way back when we got your medical notes through F.O.I we handsomely paid independent relevant consultants to interpret them for us so as we might get a handle on what had actually happened. Well, they mentioned in their response that "stent insertion is not universally available" so we questioned the expertise and skills of team C, Dr E in particular as we'd been told that the skills necessary to manage such are not widely available. Also of course we questioned as to what the contention was about between the medics that alarmed us at your bedside as Dr E manipulated your chest drains immediately prior to your death. We noted Dr E refers to our concern here as an understandable misinterpretation "given the flurry of activity by more than 10 providers that her family witnessed at her bedside during the last hour of Ms Hannon-Dunne's life." This last hour is not the period we referred to as worrying us, it was the period before that. There were not ten people around your bedside. There was just Dr E and two other doctors observing what he was doing plus the nurse who'd been at the bottom of your bed looking up at the monitor over your bed. All was extremely calm and quiet (bar the contention immediately prior to your death). You became distressed during the process of Dr E's handling of your chest tubes and as he states suffered "a rapid respiratory arrest and became pulse less"......"and despite a lengthy attempt the patient unfortunately could not be resuscitated." The flurry of activity he refers to happened after your arrest.

Well Ailbhe yet again we complied with the Medical Council's request and met their schedule having our reply back by August 10th 2007. As I'm sure you've already concluded we had no expectation that anything more would come of the Medical Council's probing. After all it was a case of medics enquiring into medics, there was no real voice from our side. So we were most undisappointed to receive a letter dated the 7th of September 2007 confirming our expectations. These sentences say it all, "The committee decided that there was not a prima facie case for the holding of an inquiry. The committee's decision will be referred to the Medical Council at its next meeting on 19th September 2007. Under the provisions of section 45(2) of the Medical Practitioners Act, 1978, the Medical Council can either accept the Fitness to Practice Committee's decision or order the committee to hold an inquiry."

Surprise surprise this second letter (letter 14) arrived dated 20th September 2007 and as we'd expected stated "The committee's decision was accepted by the Medical Council at its meeting held on 19th September 2007."

Comhairle na nDochtúirí Leighis
Medical Council

Your ref: Our ref: C35/06/JS

PRIVATE AND CONFIDENTIAL
STRICTLY ADDRESSEE ONLY

Ms. Maura Hannon,
Farranseer House,
Cornafean,
Co. Cavan.

Letter P46 Ch5

Letter 13 from Medical Council

7th September, 2007

Dear Ms. Hannon,

I refer to previous correspondence concerning your complaint in relation to Dr [redacted] Dr. [redacted] Dr. [redacted] Dr. [redacted] Dr. [redacted] and Dr. [redacted] which was considered by the Fitness to Practise Committee at its recent meeting on 5th September, 2007.

The Committee considered all the material before it, including your correspondence, the doctor's observations and comments and having regard to the provisions of the Ethical Guide, in particular the definition of professional misconduct in the current Ethical Guide (sixth edition), which provides:-

"1.5 PROFESSIONAL MISCONDUCT

(a) Professional misconduct is conduct which doctors of experience, competence and good repute, upholding the fundamental aims of the profession, consider disgraceful or dishonourable. and / or

(b) Conduct connected with his or her profession is which the doctor concerned has seriously fallen short by omission or commission of the standards of conduct expected among doctors."

The Committee decided that there was not a prima facie case for the holding of an inquiry. The Committee's decision will be referred to the Medical Council at its next meeting on 19th September, 2007.

Under the provisions of section 45(2) of the Medical Practitioners Act, 1978, the Medical Council can either accept the Fitness to Practise Committee's decision or order the Committee to hold an inquiry.

The Committee would like to convey its sympathy to you on the death of your daughter.

I will write to you after the Council's next meeting, letting you know the final decision.

Yours sincerely,

[redacted]

Comhairle na nDochtúirí Leighis
Medical Council

Your ref: Our ref: C35/06/JS

PRIVATE AND CONFIDENTIAL
STRICTLY ADDRESSEE ONLY

Ms. Maura Hannon,
Farranseer House,
Cornafean,
Co. Cavan.

Letter 14 from Medical Council

20th September, 2007

Dear Ms. Hannon.

I refer to our letter of 7th September, 2007 informing you that the Fitness to Practise Committee, having considered your complaint, decided that there was not a prima facie case for the holding of a sworn inquiry into Dr. [redacted] Dr. [redacted] Dr. [redacted] Dr. [redacted] Dr. [redacted] and Dr. [redacted] in accordance with section 45 of the Medical Practitioners Act, 1978.

The Committee's decision was accepted by the Medical Council at its meeting held on 19th September, 2007.

The Council, as the regulatory body for medical doctors, is responsible within the terms of the Medical Practitioners Act, 1978, for maintaining professional standards. The Council depends primarily on members of the public to bring to its attention instances where the service provided may fall short of acceptable standards within the context of the Act.

While on this occasion, the Council has decided not to uphold your complaint, it nevertheless wishes to express its appreciation to you for taking the time to bring your complaint to its attention.

Yours sincerely,

[redacted]

05/09/07 NPF/JH/3

So our crusade ended. Ailbhe. How do you feel now I hear you ask? Well I feel a grave injustice was done to us by the Patients Advocacy, the hospital and the medics involved in your care on July 8th 2002 in their unwillingness to accede to our request for a meeting where our concerns could have been addressed. Instead excuses, delays and obstacles were what we experienced as you'll have seen from our chat and timeline. I am however delighted with how we persevered and I'm quite surprised that we managed to get as much information as we did via the Medical Council. I knew inside myself that we were right and I feel we were totally vindicated.

My conclusion remains yes Ailbhe a mess was made of that procedure in Radiology. It should not have happened. I believe it was righted. The fatal mess I believe was to do with Dr C team's management at your bedside as Kerill and I sat powerlessly. Was that long awaited suction drainage unit pleurovac (Atrium) faulty? Was it too late when the chest drains were eventually being changed and connected to suction? Were the medics involved at the juncture out of their depth? I may be wrong Ailbhe but these questions remain. Indeed the run around we were given by those involved when we raised our concerns does little to alleviate my anxiety. We certainly had no idea as to the mountain we'd have to climb when we started out. I know Ailbhe how you would expect accountability so I hope you are happy with the efforts we made to get same. I must mention Ailbhe that Dr C goes as Mr C being a consultant but knowing you were not one for hierarchical thinking, I thought Dr would do them all rightly. Apparently it's to do with rank but I'm sure you follow the line of command. Now, Ailbhe what about a bualadh bos for myself and Kerill.

In the future I think it's high time families be given a mandatory right of access to the relevant medics involved in the care of a family member where a tragedy such as your death Ailbhe occurs or where the family have serious concerns re medical care. Independently mediated meetings at which the relevant medics are legally obliged to attend and provide honest transparent accountability should be held. The present probone should not be tolerated. It should not be left to individual hospitals to just develop their own protocols nor should it be just in the gift of the medical profession. Citizens in any civilised republic should have such a right. It's not about getting at anyone but human life is very precious and irreplaceable. Of course mishaps and mistakes will happen but it's only when they are dealt with openly and honestly that improvements will be made and a more equal trusting relationship evolve between patient medic and hospital.

I was glad to learn from the article in the Irish Independent (26th January 2012) about baby Pierce that the Coroners Act has been amended. I'm glad we petitioned for change there after your death Ailbhe. I only hope the change goes far enough. I understand too that the Medical Council now has some non medics on its board. I don't know what proportion or how much teeth they have. Anyway I don't think the Medical Council could adequately provide what I'd be recommending. I'd be concerned about an institutional bias Ailbhe. Institutions being as they are! Start a campaign I hear you say.

Interestingly Ailbhe, I listened to an interview on RTE this morning, with a lady who spoke of her experience of trying to get answers from medics involved in the care of her late husband. He was a relatively healthy man in his forties who became ill suddenly. Sadly he died unexpectedly. She had concerns re his diagnosis and treatment. She just wanted the truth and like ourselves was not motivated by vengeance. But she felt uneasy and needed clarity. She felt that if mistakes had been made they needed to be identified and rectified in the interest of future patients. She herself works as a therapist and had always promoted and followed the 'win win' approach. Her efforts to get at the truth of what had happened met with lies and non-co-operation. She found she had to change tact and become a 'shark' in her pursuit of the truth. Reluctantly she took the litigation route. Eventually eight years on, the consultant admitted liability having dragged her to court. She got no apology bar an apology she got from the judge. It all seemed more than a little familiar Ailbhe.

I think people like her should get an award for their courage and endurance. Her son who was with her on the show is involved in the theatre. His play called 'Have I No Mouth' is to be staged in the theatre in Dublin shortly. The play is to do with their personal experience of the grieving process and although mum has no previous acting experience she will take part in the play.

Page 1 of 3

[redacted] I DR. A Team B.

[redacted]

From: [redacted]
Sent: 26 October 2006 07:35
To: [redacted]
Subject: Re: Team B. DR. A's Report to the Medical Council

[redacted]

RE: Ailbe Hannon - Report to the fitness to practice commitee

I met Ailbe hannon in mid 2002. I was the Interventional Radiology Fellow employed through the Royal College of Surgeon's Iireland and based at [redacted] hospital. An advanced training position which i occupied for 2 years.

Ailbe was an unfortunate young lady who i believe had glomerulonephritis since approximately 15 years of age and a susequent failed renal transplant. She was referred to mine and [redacted] care for urgent insertion of a tunnelled dialysis catheter so she could recommence haemodialysis. I met the family and Ailbe immediately prior to insertion of the catheter and discussed the procedurewith Ailbe including risks. I cannot recall if the actual consent form was obtained through my unit or the nephrology department.

The procedure was performed in the standard fashion with both ultrasound and fluroscopic guidance. A right internal jugular access was used as per standard.
I was taking a trainee through the procedure who continually rotate through the various areas of the radiology department including intervention. Again as per standard in a tertiary referral training centre. At some point in the transition of dilating up the track to accommodate the sheath, my perception was that something was not quite right. I immediately took over and realised that the guide wire and dilator had migrate to be outside the right brachiocephalic vessel and in the mediastinum. Exactly how this came to be i am unsure. I pulled the dilator back to the point of exit in the right brachiocephalic vein and advanced the wire to the right atrium. The catheter was then placed in the location it needed to be in the manner intended. I was aware that we had a tear in the brachiocephalic vein. Before we could sutur the exit point of the catheter, Ailbe's blood pressure began to drop. I therefore, asked that an arrest be called, as it was likely that we would soon need staff to resuscitat and may need thoracic surgery. I also asked that thoracic surgery be called.
I believed Ailbe to be pre arrest and that she was beginning to compress her SVC due to tension in her right thoracic cavity, due to haemothorax. This is unusual but was obviously the case from the image attached and almost certainly was facilitated by her profound growth retardation (due to transplant medication in her mid teens). I placed a chest tube in her right pleural space as her blood pressure plummeted and she lost consciousness. As soon as the chest tube was in Ailbe's blood pressure normalised and she woke up. The arrest team and cardiothoracic turned up. Ailbe stabilised and was transufused a small amount of blood.

I discussed this complication with both the patient and Ailbe's family afterwards. ?

The following day i was notified that Ailbe arrested some 8 hours later, whilst the chest tube was manipulated on the ward. The reason for this was uncertain at the time and i suspect still remains as such. This was a tremoendously sad occurrence.

I did not see Ailbe's family since the immediate post procedure meeting.
I was never aware of the complaints and various meetings at the hospital, coroners and your committee. ?
Obviously, i have been unable to furnish you o[redacted] with a report for the earlier committee deliberation as i had never been informed of it.

In regards to fitness to practice,

Firstly, this is an unfortunate set of events.
An uncommon but recognised and serious complication did occur, namely laceration to the right brachiocephalic vein. Why this occurred I am not entirely certain. Although, i was taking a trainee through this, everything was performed in the correct manner and that trainee had performed a number of these procedures. This was direct supervision with myself scrubbed and assisting and directing. Obviously, we have to train people or the very nature of any specialty would no longer exist in a short period of time.

26/10/2006

Page 2 of 3

[redacted] 2

is complication however, may not have been the direct cause of death. The usual treatment for this is chest be, resuscitation and to sit the patient up. The vein usually heals itself and surgery rarely needs to be p rmed. Ailbe died of apparently electromechanical dissosciation 8 hours later whilst the chest tube was ma ipulated. What was the cause of death at this point? I have not seen the coroners report but only a vague mention of medical misadventure.
After the complication had occurred, the treatment of Ailbe's condition was handled expertly. The complication was diagnosed straight away, the catheter was placed were it should be to allow urgent dialysis, The large haemothorax was drained in amatter of minutes. The arrest team was called pre arrest, resuscitation was begun, blodd products replaced. Cardiothoracic team were straight to the patient and treatment plan put in place. Both these teams deserve to be commended.
There is obviously ongoing pain for Ailbe's family, and some of this is due to me not seeing the mother after the death. This is a difficult issue and obviously it would have been best if this had occurred. This is also made a little more complicated by us being involved late in Ailbe's care for a relatively technical purpose of siting a dialysis catheter. The family were no longer at the hospital when i arrived the following day and [redacted] DR G. [redacted] informed me he was currently in discussions with the family. Although, i had seen the family after the complication, it would have been best to hold a family conference with myself in attendance some days after the event.

In conclusion, i do not believe we have any wrong doing here. There are an unfortunate set of events [redacted]. The right brachiocephalic laceration is an uncommon but recognised complication. The events immediately after the complication were handled expertly.

Would you also provision me with the coroners report ?.

Sincerely yours

[redacted]

----- Original Message -----

[redacted] I Team-A @ DRG

[redacted]

Team A

November 1, 2006 DR G-s/ Response to the Medical Council

THE MEDICAL COUNCIL RECEIVED 03 NOV 2006 PROFESSIONAL [illegible]

[redacted]

Team A DR. G.

I am not clear what specific issues the Hannon family now have regarding my management of Ailbhe Hannon.

Previously they had stated they didn't have any, and in fact the father thanked me for my care of Ailbhe over the years at the end of the Coroner's inquest!

By way of background, Ailbhe was diagnosed with allograft nephropathy in 2001 and was begun initially on haemodialysis therapy in January 2002 via an internal jugular permcath. Subsequently, she was placed on Continuous Ampulatory Peritoneal Dialysis (CAPD). In June of that year she began to complain of severe pain in her renal allograft. Because of lack of response to medical treatment, consideration was being given to removal of the graft. Her clinical situation was further complicated by the development of severe oesophagitis, gastritis, duodenitis and a restless leg syndrome, which was progressing in severity despite daily peritoneal dialysis. For these reasons, the patient was admitted to [redacted] Hospital to re-evaluate her clinical situation and begin a trial of daily haemodialysis in an attempt to control her symptoms which were causing the patient much distress.

On July 8th 2002 Ailbhe was brought down to the X-ray department for insertion of a permcath under x-ray guidance. I should state that literally hundreds of these procedures are performed in the [redacted] X-ray department each year and in my experience, this is the first case with a fatal outcome that I have come across in 29years of practice as a Renal Specialist. On the other hand a pneumo thorax or haemo thorax, while rare, are recognised complications of this procedure.

Beaumont Hospital is the principal teaching hospital for the Royal College of Surgeons in Ireland

[redacted] 2

I had begun my renal out patient clinic that day, when I was informed by the Renal Registrar, Dr [redacted], that Ailbhe had suffered a haemo-pneumo thorax while in the x-ray department. I was also told that while initially she had gone into shock; that after a chest tube was inserted and she was given blood products, her blood pressure had stabilised and she was alert.

I was responsible for a large out patient clinic that day and was already short staffed but I decided to send Dr [redacted] the X-ray department to assess the situation first hand and to let me know if there were any further concerns. I was informed by him that her situation was now stable but on being transferred back to the ward she was to be placed in the high dependency area so that she could be closely monitored, on the recommendations of Radiology and Surgery. I was also informed that the surgical team [redacted] DR C S team) who had inserted the chest tubes would closely monitor her and advise re further management as required.

Around 5pm when my clinic was finished, I went up to the floor where Ailbhe was, to be told that the patient was clinically stable, alert and talking to the family who I recognised were at her bedside. I subsequently left the hospital, while Dr [redacted] together with Nursing and [redacted] team agreed to continue to monitor the patient closely. Around 8pm that evening I was informed by Dr [redacted] that Ailbhe had suffered a cardiac-respiratory arrest while the chest tube was being adjusted by the Surgical team. Subsequently, I was informed that she had passed away.

As I understood it, the concerns of the family revolved around the expertise of the doctors who inserted the permcath and the chest tubes, and whether the subsequent management of the case was appropriate. Dr [redacted] was a Senior Lecturer in [redacted] radiology department and had previously inserted numerous permcaths for our department without any DR C complications. I did not know Dr [redacted] but I understand from [redacted] that he was experienced in insertion of chest tubes and was being supervised by an SPR, [redacted]. However, I agree it is most unfortunate that both of these individuals returned to their native countries soon after this tragic event, and were not available to discuss the case with the family.

Another issue that the family have repeatedly brought up was whether manipulation of the chest tube at the bedside had somehow lead to Ailbhe's cardiac arrest. Not being an expert in this field I had to state to the family that I was not in a position to offer an opinion!

With regard to the management of the haemo thorax, this was undertaken by the Surgical team who were the experts in this field. While I have little experience in this area, the 3-4 cases I have previously observed who developed a similar problem, after catheter insertion for dialysis access, were all successfully managed in a similar manner to that undertaken in the case of

[redacted] 3

Ailbhe Hannon. I think it also noteworthy to point out that Ms Hannon was clinically stable for a number of hours after the chest tubes were initially inserted and she had been closely monitored throughout both by the Surgical, Medical and Nursing staff.

With regard to the cause of death, as explained by the Pathologist at the inquest this was most likely due to a large haemothorax secondary to a 2cm laceration to the right brachio cephalic vein.

I hope this information which incidentally has previously been shared with Mrs Hannon is of help.

Yours sincerely

[redacted]

Team A
DR G's Registrar. [redacted] I
DR. I's Report to M.C.

1

[redacted]

12th October, 2006

Your Reference: C35/06/23066/JS

[redacted]

Team A. DR I's Response to the Medical Council

RECEIVED
13 OCT 2006
PROFESSIONAL STANDARDS

Re: Ailbhe Hannon, Deceased

[redacted]

This letter is to set out my observations and comments and response to the letter of complaint which you have received from the family of the late Ailbhe Hannon, dated 24th April 2006.

I remember Ailbhe and wish to express my very sincere sympathies to her family on her death.

At the outset, I wish to record that I was unaware of the contact which Ailbhe Hannon's family have had with the hospital since her death. I would have been at all times, and remain, open to attending any meeting which [redacted] Hospital may arrange with Ailbhe Hannon's family. I see from the letter which is attached to the letter of complaint, being a letter from the hospital to Mrs Maura Hannon dated 27th March 2006, that [redacted] and [redacted] are happy to meet with the family. If the family so wish, I can attend any such meeting should it be organised.

2 [redacted] 2

2

I was not aware of the Inquest and was not called to give evidence at it. I do appreciate that the Coroner was, at the time, restricted in the number of medical doctors he could call to give evidence but I wish the family to know that I would have been more than happy to attend to give evidence if contacted at any stage.

Included in the documentation which the family have sent to you is a report which I prepared and which appears to have been attached to the letter to Mrs Hannon from the hospital of 27th March 2006. That report is undated and runs to four pages. I wish to clarify that although there is a handwritten entry at the top of the report which reads "report received March 29th 2006" that report is one which I prepared following the death of Ailbhe Hannon, and at the request of [redacted] My recall is that I gave it to [redacted] within a month of the death of Ailbhe Hannon. This report along with the hospital records, both of which you have, I believe fully document my role and actions on the 8th of July 2002, the date of Ailbhe Hannon's death.

I ask that the report prepared by me be read in parallel with this letter and with the medical records.

On 8th July 2002, I was working in [redacted] Hospital as Nephrology Registrar to DR.G. [redacted] I had commenced that position on 1st July 2002, after completing a two year Senior House Officer Programme in [redacted] Hospital. During my Senior House Officer Programme I had worked with [redacted] from 1st March 2001 - 30th June 2001. DR. G.

DR. G.

I was one of two Nephrology Registrars working with [redacted]. The team also consisted of a Senior House Officer and an Intern. The workload was divided between the team. The Intern and I were looking after the ward to which Ailbhe Hannon was admitted.

From my report she was admitted for transplant nephrectomy and management of her restless legs syndrome. The decision was made by [redacted] that haemodialysis would be the more suitable form of renal replacement therapy. This was because the dialysis achieved via this method would be more effective at treating her restless legs syndrome and it would be appropriate post transplant nephrectomy.

On the day of the procedure, 8th of July 2002, Ailbhe was informed of the procedure. The copies of the documents from the chart include a consent form witnessed by my intern. I consented her for the procedure as well. While informing her of the risk factors I included the risk of major haemorrhage. This consent form is not in the photocopied sheets. After being fully informed she signed the consent form. I had no further contact

[redacted] 3

3

with the patient until I was called, as can be seen from my report prepared for [redacted], at approximately 1 p.m., when I was contacted by the medical Registrar on call. I immediately attended to Ailbhe Hannon and escorted her back to the ward after ascertaining what had occurred and being informed that the newly inserted permcath which was already attached to intravenous fluids, was fit for use.

Please see the report prepared by me following the death and the hospital chart for the sequence of events during the afternoon and evening.

On arrival to the ward she was maintained on I.V. fluids. I fully informed her family members of the events that had occurred and they remained at her bedside.

At approximately 4pm I contacted the surgical team regarding continual blood loss via the chest tube. It had drained approximately 1.5 litres of serosanginous fluid. They reviewed her and stated she was stable. They suggested red cell concentrate and fresh frozen plasma.

A portable check C.X.R. was performed and indicated confluent white shadowing of the right hemi thorax. Ailbhe received fluids and blood. Her blood pressure remained stable while on the fluids.

At 6.30pm the surgical team returned and reassessed the situation. They suggested that we no longer use the permcath and stated they would change the chest tube drain to one with suction.

At 7.20pm during manipulation of the chest tube Ailbhe became apnoeic and bradycardic. An arrest call was placed. A number of medical staff where on the ward at this time including myself and full A.C.L.S. protocol was commenced immediately.

The arrest team arrived to the ward and included the anaesthetist on call, medical Registrar on call, medical S.H.O. on call and medical intern on call. Present on the ward at the time were my intern and myself. The surgical team present at the time consisted of [redacted] and [redacted] arrived within minutes, as documented in his medical note. The Cardiology Registrar on call also attended the arrest. I played an active role in the resuscitation attempts along with the team members present.

The anaesthetist performed intubation. An E.C.G. and physical examination confirmed pulseless electrical activity. Venous access was achieved via a right-sided femoral vascath. She received emergency medications including adrenaline and atropine. There was no spontaneous pulse. She received further medications including calcium [redacted] 4 4

gluconate and sodium bicarbonate. At one point her E.C.G. indicated Ventricular Fibrillation with no palpable pulse. Shocks were administered with no return to sinus rhythm.

The Cardiology Registrar performed a portable echocardiogram, which indicated no pericardial effusion or spontaneous heart movement. Portable C.X.R. was performed which was similar to the earlier film. We continued the chest compressions and ventilations. There was no palpable pulse at any stage. The E.C.G. finally showed asystole.

Unfortunately, prolonged resuscitation attempts were not successful. Death was pronounced at 8.40 p.m. As Mrs Hannon has recorded on page 10 of her background letter, all of us treating Ailbhe were very upset and emotional but made every effort to be professional in our approach to her treatment and in speaking to her family. I informed the family of Ailbhe's death in the presence of a staff nurse. I cannot remember if it was the staff nurse looking after Ailbhe or the Sister on the ward. There was no other doctor present at the time.

The family have raised a number of detailed questions and I am going to answer these, to the best of my ability. Some of them are not relevant to me and are directed to separate treatment of Ailbhe Hannon, and so I do not repeat them below but I will answer those that do relate to me.

1. **Was the standard of care provided by [redacted] Hospital adequate?**

   I believe that my role in caring for Ailbhe Hannon was highly acceptable and appropriate. I have reviewed the chart again, and gone over in my own mind the events on the day and I sincerely believe there is nothing more I could have done to avoid the very sad outcome.

2. **Were doctors who performed the listed relevant procedures adequately trained, experienced and supervised during these procedures?**

   My training is outlined above and I believe I was certainly well trained, supervised and experienced during all my dealings with Ms Hannon.

3. **The hospital notes show little observation having been made for especially - interval between (July 8th) 14.00 and 17.25 apart from some reference to nursing notes. Who was responsible for this paucity of notes? This was a crucial period in Ailbhe's after care.**

[redacted] 5

5

Having reviewed the hospital chart, the medical notes I wrote at the time reflect all important events and interventions by me on that day. I would add that medical notes do not reflect the minute by minute care that patients receive, but report any new findings, investigations or changes in management plans. On reviewing the medical notes made by me I feel they are clear and reflect the observations and management plan.

4. **Mrs Maura Hannon asks "surely Dr [redacted] must know who performed the procedure that Dr [redacted] was supposed to have performed".**

I recall [redacted] being a surgeon from America who was on a programme which rotated through [redacted] Hospital at the time. My recollection of the events is that [redacted] was present, and treated Ailbhe Hannon as documented. I believe there is no falsification of documents. [redacted] was part of the surgical team whom I recall being present and was involved to the best of my recollection in the manipulation of the chest tube. He was present at the time of her respiratory arrest on the ward and took an active role in her resuscitation attempts.

The remainder of the questions which Mrs Hannon sets out do not relate to my role in treating Ailbhe. I would emphasise that until I received the copy letter of complaint from you, I was unaware that the family had ongoing questions. I wish to let the family know that I sincerely regret if they were under any impression that I was either failing or refusing to respond to any queries. As stated above, I would at all times have been happy to do so.

I wish sincerely to state how sorry I was at the sad death of Ailbhe Hannon, despite all our efforts to resuscitate her. May she rest in peace.

Yours sincerely,

[redacted]

DR-B, Team B

[redacted]

July 21, 2006: Team B DR. B's Report to the Medical Council

Observations and comments on case of Ailbhe Hannon, DOB 19/06/1977.

To whom it may concern,

First of all I would like to express to Ailbhe's family through the council my condolences on their sad loss. DR-B
My name is [redacted] I am a radiologist. I was involved in the interventional radiology procedure carried out on Ailbhe on 08/07/02. At that time I was a second year specialist registrar in radiology having just successfully completed FFR.RCSI Part 1 exam in radiology. As registrars we are involved in different areas in radiology. I was scheduled for interventional radiology where I assisted in cases performed by a more senior radiologist, Dr [redacted] A
The procedure was performed as follows: the right internal jugular vein was identified on ultrasound imaging in the interventional room to assess anatomy and patency of the vein. The site of the vein for puncture was marked. Ailbhe was given sedation and analgesics (100micrograms Fentanyl and 2mg Medazolam).
Dr [redacted] and I both scrubbed for the procedure. The right side of the neck was prepared and [redacted] anaesthetic was administered. I inserted the micropuncture needle into the right internal jugular vein and confirmed its position in the vein by aspirating venous blood. I then passed a 0.018 inch short wire through the needle and into the right atrium. I confirmed the position with fluoroscopy.
I then placed an exchange catheter over the wire.
I removed the 0.018 inch wire as well as the central portion of the exchange dilator. I placed the 0.035 inch wire to begin track dilation. I felt some resistance so I handed over to Dr [redacted]. Dr [redacted] took over and continued with the dilation. He proceeded to insert the catheter.
The catheter was in good position. After reversal of Ailbhe's sedation her blood pressure dropped and she was drowsy. Dr [redacted] noticed a right-sided haemothorax under fluoroscopy. He acted very quickly and called an arrest. He proceeded to insert a chest drain into the right pleural space to relieve the haemothorax. Not much fluid was coming out through the chest drain so he proceeded quickly to inserting a second chest drain. At that time the arrest team had arrived. Ailbhe had now come to and the arrest team did not need to intervene. Appropriate bloods were taken in case she needed to be transfused later. Ailbhe returned to the high dependency unit with the clinical team. I had no further dealings with the care of Ailbhe. She was stable and alert the last time I saw her. I was saddened and upset to find out the next day what had happened.
Dr [redacted] subsequently informed me that he had written a statement and showed it to me. Afterwards no-one approached me requesting a statement or any information regarding what had happened.

[redacted]

The procedure that was carried out that day was a common procedure in radiology in [redacted] The procedure was carried out in a standard way. Image guidance using ultrasound and fluoroscopy was used from the beginning of the procedure. Dr [redacted] was present and actively involved throughout the whole procedure. Steps were carried out methodically to ensure correct placement of the needles and wires whilst inserting the catheter.

It is common to experience resistance whilst dilating the tract because it is in effect stretching the tissues to aid insertion of the catheter. I handed over because I wanted someone more experienced to verify. The procedure was performed and the haemothorax was rapidly responded to by Dr [redacted] who had the situation under control before the arrest team arrived.

Again let me express my condolences to Ailbhe's husband, mother and family.

Yours Sincerely

[redacted]

DR. C- Team C

[redacted]

3 July 2006

[redacted]

RECEIVED
11 JUL 2006
THE MEDICAL COUNCIL

Re: Complaint by Ms Maura Hannon.

Team C DR. C's Report to Medical Council
3rd July 2006.

Dear [redacted]

Further to your correspondence of the 8th of June I have prepared my response to the allegations contained in Mrs Hannon's letter. I have divided my response into two sections firstly commentary on the involvement of my team in the management of the late Ms Ailbhe Hannon-Dunne and secondly the process in [redacted] Hospital by which Mrs Maura Hannon's complaint was handled.

DR-G's

Ailbhe Hannon-Dunne was a long term patient of [redacted] at [redacted] Hospital who had had a failed renal transplant on July 8th 2002. She was referred to the radiologists for insertion of a vascular access catheter in her right subclavian vein. The insertion of the catheter by Dr. [redacted] an Australian Radiologist who was a Lecturer in the Department of Radiology was unfortunately complicated by the development of a right sided haemopneuomthorax. The appropriate management was instituted following recognition of this complication and IV access was established and chest drains were placed in the right chest cavity. Following this the patient stabilized and was transferred back to the ward. Because my surgical service at [redacted] Hospital deals with conditions of the thorax such as pneumothorax and thoracic trauma

Z

[redacted]

my Registrar Dr. [redacted] was called to the assistance of the Radiologist during the event in the x-ray department. He subsequently lent assistance in relation to resuscitation, organization of chest drains and continued assessment of the patient back in the renal ward. He also informed my senior registrar at the time [redacted] Dr. D.
[redacted]

Although I do not personally recall the case [redacted] states in his report on the evening of July the 8th after our theatre list we included a visit to St. [redacted] ward to review the late Ms Hannon Dunne. Apparently I issued instructions in relation to a repeat chest x-ray, changing the infusion line from the permacath in the right subclavian to an alternative means of access and instructed that the underwater seal system be replaced by an Atrium drainage bottle which allowed for more careful monitoring of the volume of drainage and also had the option of applying negative pressure to the pleural space. Unfortunately Ms Hannon-Dunne collapsed and died rather suddenly later that evening and the post mortem indicated a 2.5cm laceration in the subclavian and brachio-cephalic vein with a large right sided haemothorax which in the view of the pathologist had compressed the mediastinum and the opposite lung. Dr. [redacted] my registrar, was in the process of changing the underwater seal system at the bedside when the acute terminal event occurred. The patient's Mother Mrs Hannon understandably associates the sudden demise of her daughter with the act of changing or interfering with the drainage system in her chest. She questions the experience of Dr. [redacted] to change such a drainage system.

Dr [redacted] like his predecessors from the [redacted] Hospital since 1977 was a senior resident from their highly regarded surgical training programme, who commenced work in [redacted] on the first of July as part of his six month rotation to Dublin. Like all of his predecessors Dr [redacted]s more experienced than most Irish surgical trainees in the management of chest trauma, chest drains and conditions such as pneumothorax, haemothorax and shock. The transfer of one underwater seal system to another is a very simple matter of clamping the chest drains and quickly disconnecting from one system and reconnecting to the new system. The patient's collapse was, I am quite certain, in no way connected with the act of changing the type of underwater seal drainage system. Indeed as attested by [redacted] there was no evidence of tension pneumothorax at the time of her collapse and allowing air in from the atmosphere to the pleural space would be the only potential mechanism associated with changing of the tubes that could have precipitated such an acute collapse.

[redacted] 3

The cause of death of the late Ailbhe Hannon-Dunne was a haemopneumothorax due to laceration of the subclavian and brachiocephalic vein in the course of insertion of a vascular access device for haemodialysis. This is a recognised complication of this procedure and the vast majority of patients seal the laceration in the vein, expand the collapsed lung and do not require any additional intervention other that what was done for the late Ailbhe. Clearly had it been known that she had a 2.5cm laceration in the vein surgical repair would have been undertaken. However as happens in the majority of patients with this problem she stabilized and her subsequent sudden collapse with cardiac arrest did not permit thoracotomy and attempted repair of the vein. The death of such a young patient from this complication is a tragic outcome and I can well understand her parents and her husband's grief and ongoing disbelief in relation to the manner of her death. I wish to extend my sympathies to them even at this late stage despite the fact that they are convinced that somehow the surgeons caused her death.

I wish now to turn to the process in [redacted] Hospital by which Mrs Maura Hannon's complaint was handled. As I have directly informed Mrs Hannon at a meeting in [redacted] on the 29th of May it is my own practice that when a patient dies under my care and there are questions in relation to that death I always invite the relatives to come to see me and discuss the matter at an interval of about four to six weeks after the death. Over twenty years of practice I have found this process to be therapeutic both for the families and also for myself and my surgical team. You will note that in my account above of the clinical scenario I indicated that I 'apparently' visited the patient on the evening of the 8th of July.

When I received a letter from the patient representative office on the 23rd August 2005 a copy of which you have on your file I had no recollection of any clinical involvement of this case. Indeed I routinely am on holidays in the first two weeks in July and therefore I indicated to [redacted] in that office that I could not be of assistance because I was not in the country. It appears from Ms Hannon's letter to the Medical Council that she has misinterpreted my correspondence to [redacted] and concluded that other Doctors were not in the country who had clearly signed the clinical notes. This of course is not the case. I next had contact from [redacted] patient representative in March in which she indicated difficulties in contacting the doctors involved in the care of Ailbhe with whom Mrs Hannon requested a meeting. I informed her that Dr. [redacted] was working in [redacted] as a transplant surgeon. I indicated in writing that I was unable to assist since I was certain I was not in the country at the time. At no stage in these early months was I shown the clinical notes of Ailbhe Hannon-Dunne. Had I personally reviewed the chart of course I would have seen notes indicating that I saw the patient late on Monday evening July the 8th and I also would have been able to confirm that both Dr. [redacted] and [redacted] were involved in her clinical care.

E DR D

P.41
[redacted] 4 Ch.5

I regret to say that the first sight I had of the relevant clinical notes was on the night of the 29th of May 2006 the night before I agreed to meet with Mrs Hannon and the late Ailbhe's husband Mr Dunne. I was quite shocked to see the clinical notes indicating my attendance in [redacted]s ward on July the 8th. Needless to say I was very upset about this and indicated same to [redacted] in the patient representative office. She then confessed that there were extreme difficulties with medical record availability and her detailed log of the events from the time of receipt of Mrs Hannon's letter of complaint indicate ongoing difficulties with access to the medical record. Furthermore our medical administrator [redacted] had been involved on several occasions in meetings with [redacted]. These facts can be verified from [redacted] herself and indeed from [redacted]

Despite only receiving the complete information at the eleventh hour I agreed to meet with Mrs Hannon as part of a [redacted] group, which included [redacted] representing Dr.[redacted] and [redacted] on the 30th of May 2006. It was quite understandable that Mrs Hannon and Mr Dunne would feel deeply aggrieved not only about the circumstances of Ailbhe's death but also at the manner in which the progression of their requests for information had been stalled repeatedly. I fully understand that it was difficult for them to accept the veracity of what both myself and [redacted] were saying. Reference to the record of who were senior registrars in surgery in the Hospital at the time could have readily deduced the owner of the signature. Despite this [redacted] was not informed about his involvement until the 26th of May 2006. Had I seen the record myself I would have immediately identified both Dr. [redacted] writing and also [redacted] and could have progressed matters a lot more expeditiously. I am sorry for the Hannon family that their understandable right to information and to reports and accounts of events has been denied over a ten month period. I am sorry that the family had to seek redress through the fitness to practice committee of the medical council. I am calling for a review of protocols and procedures of the patient representatives office at [redacted] so that any Doctors in the future enjoined in a complaint no matter how peripheral will have full access to all of the clinical notes in a timely manner.

In summary therefore whilst I can in retrospect stand over the clinical management from the surgical view-point of Ms Hannon's clinical problem I believe that the Hospital and its representatives have fallen well short of an acceptable standard in dealing with the complaint as submitted by the patients Mother and husband. I wish to take this opportunity again to apologize to Mrs Hannon and Mr Dunne for the additional distress caused to them by the lengthy process over the past ten months.

[redacted] 5

would also like to express my sympathies again to both of them in their sad loss. I trust this report is satisfactory and if I can be of further assistance please get in touch with me.

Best wishes,

Yours sincerely,

[redacted]

[redacted] DR. P Team C

[redacted]

[redacted]

RECEIVED
23 JUN 2006
THE MEDICAL COUNCIL

Dict: 15 June 2006 Team C DR. D's Report 6th June 2006
Typd: 19 June 2006

[redacted]

Thank you for your letter on 8th June 2006 regarding a letter from Miss Maura Hannon in relation to the sad death of her daughter Albha Hannon-Dunne on April 7 2002. I have enclosed a copy of the report which I wrote for the Patient Representative Body at [redacted] Hospital recently. Their letter to me was the first I had heard of any controversy and conjecture and I was very surprised to hear that there was any difficulty contacting anyone of the staff involved. I first received a letter from [redacted] (Patient Representative Manager, [redacted] Hospital) on 29th May 2006 (letter was dated 24th May 2006). In this letter it stated that [redacted] and [redacted] (Nephrology and Radiology respectively) were meeting with the patient's family on 30th May 2006. Therefore I contacted the hospital and said that I would be more than happy to attend this meeting (although I had not been invited).

The minutes of that meeting were very clear in that Mrs. Hannon said she had no problems with the aspect of her daughter's care following her cardiac arrest which was the time at which I was involved. Her problems relate to her daughter's care prior to that. I was not directly involved at this time. As you will see from my notes, I was called by Dr. [redacted] following the patient's cardiac arrest and I believe that all aspects to my involvement were han[redacted] both professionally and responsibly. I also note that, although your letter of 8th June suggests that the letter from Mrs. Hannon relates to me specifically, I am neither mentioned in name in that letter nor was any involvement by me alluded to. Nevertheless, I have been more than willing to participate in any of these proceedings in order to help any clarification process. This was why I attended the meeting with the family on 30th May 2006.

Please let me know if I can be of any assistance in this matter at any other time. This was a tragic death and I was disappointed it took so long to identify the doctors involved. This was something that I thought would be somewhat remedied by my presence at the meeting of 30th May 2006 since it was indicated to me that neither [redacted] nor Dr. [redacted] were going to be present. I must say that I am unaware of any allegation tha[redacted] specificall[redacted]elating to me and I would be grateful if you would indicate to me at some point if there is some alleged professional misconduct query directly specifically against me. In the meantime, I hope that this report clarifies my involvement.

I would be grateful to receive correspondence to the above hospital address.

Yours sincerely,

[redacted]

[redacted]

[redacted]

(DR. D.) Team C

I

06 June 2006

Team C DR. D' Report 6th June 2006.

MEDICAL REPORT

RE: Circumstances of Mrs. Ailbhe Hannon-Dunne's Unfortunate death 8TH JULY 2002

Mrs. Hannon-Dunne was a patient of [redacted]. I remember her case very well. She had renal failure and, if I recall, had had a previous transplant. She was then on peritoneal dialysis and had placement of a permacath in order that she have venous dialysis on 8th July 2002 by Dr. [redacted] in the Department of Radiology, [redacted]Hospital. It is recorded in the notes that during this procedure she developed a right-sided pneumothorax in associated with a haemothorax. Therefore a cardiac arrest was called. The patient responded immediately to the measures that were instituted including a reversal of sedation, intravenous fluid, and placement of two chest drains (20 French apical, 28 French basal). The patient then stabilised and was transferred to the ward.

While she was in radiology Dr. [redacted] requested that [redacted] Registrar (Dr. [redacted]) see the patient since he was working for [redacted] who looks after the thoracic surgery in the hospital. He saw the patient and requested a chest x-ray to be performed then and to be performed on a daily basis while the chest drains were in. He also requested that a coagulation screen and FBC be performed. He recommended that the chest drain be placed on suction and that the output be recorded. He stated that the surgical team will follow the patient with the medical team.

At approximately 6pm I was in attendance with [redacted] and [redacted] team on our ward round following conclusion of our surgical operating list. [redacted] requested that a chest x-ray be performed and that a full blood count be performed to check the patient's haemoglobin. [redacted] also recommended that the chest drain bottles be changed to Pleurovac systems such that they could be placed on suction. [redacted] recommended stopping the intravenous fluids and blood that were being given via the [redacted] view of the fact that a haemopneumothorax had occurred. The fluids and blood were to be given via peripheral lines instead. This intravenous access was placed in the right arm by Dr. [redacted]Registrar).

At approximately 7pm Dr. [redacted] changed the chest drains to Pleuorovac drains. At that point the patient's blood pressure was 122/89 with saturations of 99% on 35% of oxygen. The patient's blood pressure had remained stable over the preceding hour. During this change of chest drain equipment, the patient became distressed and asked to sit forward as she found it difficult to breathe. Her oxygen saturations dropped to 73% and therefore a rebreathable mask was applied. [redacted] was called to assist as the patient became unresponsive. I believe that the family were in attendance at this point. A cardiac arrest was called at 19.20pm and cardio-pulmonary resuscitation was commenced. Dr. E [redacted]intubated the patient. At this point I was contacted by Dr. [redacted]nd I arrived within minutes as I recorded in the chart.

[redacted]

[redacted]

I found the patient intubated with a central trachea and breath sounds bilaterally. The chest drains were disconnected temporarily from the underwater seal and I did not find any evidence of a tension pneumothorax or haemothorax since the drains appeared to be functioning normally. The patient was in electromechanical disassociation with no response to fluid (1.5L colloid, 2L crystalloid, 4 units of fresh frozen plasma, 4 units of red blood cells). There was also no response to the various measures that were attempted by the medical team (Cardiac Arrest Team, Anaesthetic Registrar on-call, Dr. [redacted], Cardiology Registrar on-call). These included intravenous adrenalin, calcium fluoride, atropine, sodium bicarbonate, magnesium sulphate, and DC shock. All of these were given on multiple occasions.

The Cardiology Registrar had been requested to be present by me. I requested that he perform an Echocardiogram in order that we establish that there was no pericardial effusion or blood. This Echocardiogram did not demonstrate any of such abnormalities. The haemoglobin taken at the time of arrest was reported to be at 9g/dl and her femoral vein was full when a right femoral line was inserted. In other words, there was no evidence of circulatory shut down or hypopolaemia in terms of the use of these parameters. Therefore, I was satisfied that the arrest was not due to hypopolaemia and to that, in my opinion, a post-mortem should be performed in the event of death. I discussed this with [redacted] on the telephone and we agreed that there was no surgical intervention that we could do at this point that would make any difference to her outcome. I recorded these events in the notes at 8.30pm.

The medical team discontinued resuscitation at 20.40pm. Dr. [redacted] ([redacted] Registrar) offered to inform the patient's family. I offered Dr. [redacted], whom I know well, that I would also attend as I was one of the other senior doctors present during the resuscitation attempt. Dr. [redacted] said that he thought it would be most appropriate if he informed the family of this difficult situation himself as he knew the family very well since he had been involved in the patient's care for some time. I was quite happy with his ability to handle this in a professional manner and therefore I had no objection to this. I am sure that it was made clear that we would be happy to discuss this situation with the family at any stage should they have any questions. This was a most unfortunate problem and I would like to express my condolences to the family again on their tragic loss.

I received a letter from [redacted] Patient Representative Manager, [redacted] Hospital on 29th May 2006. The letter was dated 24th May 2006. In the letter it states that the family were requesting clarification in relation to aspects of her treatment and therefore a meeting with the family had been arranged for 30th May with [redacted] and [redacted] (Consultant Radiologist). In the letter it states that the patient's family feel that the main problem with Ailbhe's care related to the intervention by the surgical team who attended her following her procedure. It also states that the Medical Council had contacted the hospital requesting the names of staff who were involved in Ailbhe's care during this time. This was the first I had heard of any issues relating to this unfortunate case. I had no correspondence from the hospital and I was completely unaware that there were any issues related to it. I received no communication, either verbal or otherwise, from any of the doctors or indeed the patient representative body of the hospital. Therefore, I was shocked and distressed to hear that the family had been seeking meetings with members of the medical and surgical teams who were involved in the patient's care since it is definitely not my practice not to talk to relatives when such adverse events had happened. If I had my way, this would have been avoided by a meeting with all of the medical and surgical staff and family.

[redacted]

4

[redacted]

Team C – DR. D's Report 6th June 2006.

On 29th May 2006, I contacted [redacted] who was my consultant at the time of the patient's event (I was working as his Senior Registrar at the time). I discussed the case and my recollection of it with [redacted] I was given a short sequence of notes relating to my specific input. I offered to go along to the meeting and [redacted] welcomed this. I hoped that this would clarify my involvement and role in the event of resuscitation of the patient.

At the meeting the family made it clear that they were very happy with the patient's management and how the teams reacted after the patient's cardiac arrest. I requested this be put on record in the minutes of that meeting. It appears that the main complaint from the family relates to Dr. [redacted] Junior Registrar) in that they appear to believe that in manipulating the patient's chest drains or changing them to Pleurovac drain bottles that he in some way caused the patient to have a cardiac arrest. I made it clear that I could not clarify for them what indeed had caused the cardiac arrest.

I did express that I found Dr. [redacted] to be an excellent doctor who was very experienced in trauma (gun shot wounds etc). He would have been very experienced in dealing with chest drains etc and I did not think that he had performed any inappropriate steps in relation to the drains and their management. When I was asked by the patient's husband for evidence of Dr. [redacted] qualification to handle these problems, I stated that I was unaware of how I could provide such evidence. I believe that one of the family's main contention is that there was no meeting with Dr. [redacted] and Dr. [redacted] whom they would have liked to have meet. Unfortunately, both of these doctors have now returned to their native countries (Australia and America respectively). I am sure that these points were communicated to both of these doctors that they would be of some assistance in the enquiries.

As the meeting drew to a close, the family stated that in their opinion it was Dr. [redacted] that had been responsible for Ailbhe's death. It had been made very clear to them that the complications had occurred in the radiology department and that the appropriate management had been instituted. I pointed out that when the cardiac arrest occurred, that I considered all of the possibilities that were possible under those circumstances including a tension pneumothorax, a tension haemothorax, pericardio fluid build up, hyperkalaemia or air embolus. All of these points we attempted to exclude as a team by disconnecting the chest drains to demonstrate that they were not blocked, sending in blood for laboratory evaluation and requesting an Echocardiogram. I am at a loss to come up with a circumstance in which this sad death could have been avoided. Since Ailbhe was stabilised in the Radiology Department and remained stable when we saw her on the ward round, I do not believe that surgery or any other intervention other than that instituted would have been indicated at that time. I do note, however, from the report of the post mortem that, since there was blood in the chest cavity that the cause of death, in the opinion of Dr. [redacted] (Consultant Pathologist), was due to haemothorax secondary to a traumatic tear in the right brachiocephalic vein commencing at the junction of the right subclavian and right internal jugular veins.

This concludes my medical report and again I would like to express my condolences to the family on their tragic loss.

[redacted]

[redacted]

[redacted] 11:42:07 a.m. 07-09-2007 1 /2

[redacted]

Dr Segev- DR. E

Team C.

26 June 2007

[redacted]

26th June 2007

Re: Ms. Ailbhe Hannon-Dunne RIP

Team C DR. E Report

Dear [redacted]

I am writing to you in response to questions of the management of the late Ms Ailbhe Hannon-Dunne on the 8th of July, 2002. This response is based on my recollection of the events, my detailed notes in the chart, and the notes of [redacted] who was my senior registrar and supervisor at the time. I am currently an attending surgeon in renal and liver transplantation at the [redacted]

At about 1 PM our thoracic surgery team was called to the radiology suite to see a 25 year-old woman with end-stage renal disease and a failed kidney transplant who, during placement of a right sided subclavian vein catheter, had become hypotensive and hypoxic with a mediastinal shift and haemothorax seen on fluoroscopy. These were classic signs of a tension pneumothorax. I responded immediately, as I had seen this condition numerous times during my training in thoracic surgery, transplant surgery, critical care, and chest trauma. In fact, I had written a book chapter earlier that year on Vascular Access and the management of its complications. Two chest tubes were placed, one apical and one basal. The patient's clinical status improved and, by fluoroscopy, her mediastium regained a midline position and her haemothorax had resolved. At that time, I documented the following recommendations: (1) obtain a formal chest x-ray to confirm fluoroscopic findings; (2) make sure the patient was not coagulopathic; (3) check haemoglobin and transfuse if needed; (4) connect the chest tubes to suction; and (5) record chest tube output. I also informed [redacted] of the events and of my recommendations, which he confirmed. DR. D.

Since the patient had stabilized, she was returned to the ward. Our team saw her at about 5 PM during our evening rounds and found her to be stable but still somewhat hypotensive. Her chest tubes had drained about 1.5 liters and she was receiving blood as well as FFP for her coagulopathy. Apparently she was receiving her infusions through the right subclavian catheter, and we recommended that an alternate means of access be used. Her hypotension did resolve after resuscitation. At that time we recommended continued resuscitation, serial x-rays, and serial labs. We also noted that her chest drains were not connected to suction as we had

11:42:39 a.m. 07-09-2007 2/2

[redacted] [redacted] [redacted]

originally recommended, and we asked that the ward acquire a pleurovac (Atrium) suction drainage unit.

We came back again at about 7 PM when the suction drainage unit was available. A chest x-ray obtained in the interim showed increased fluid in her right chest, so it was imperative to convert her chest tubes to suction drainage in order to apply negative pressure to the pleural space and properly drain the fluid. I proceeded to convert her chest tubes to the suction drainage unit in the standard fashion. This was a simple procedure that I had performed hundreds of times which basically involved placing a clamp on the tube, disconnecting the tube from the first drainage unit, connecting the tube to the second drainage unit, and unclamping the tube. During this process, the patient suffered a rapid respiratory arrest and became pulseless. I immediately initiated advanced cardiac life support (ACLS) protocol in the manner that I had been extensively trained. I rapidly intubated the patient, confirmed that there was no evidence of tension pneumothorax, confirmed appropriate placement of the endotracheal tube, placed a large bore infusion line in her right femoral vein, and administered vigorous resuscitation, bicarbonate, epinepherine, and atropine. A chest x-ray confirmed significant improvement of her haemothorax with no evidence of tension pneumothorax. At this time the cardiac arrest team also arrived and continued ACLS protocol. The patient's cardiac rhythm converted briefly to ventricular fibrillation which responded briefly to cardioversion, but otherwise the patient remained in pulseless electrical activity. Unfortunately, despite a lengthy attempt, the patient unfortunately could not be resuscitated.

Our team was deeply saddened by Ms. Hannon-Dunne's tragic death, and still to this day I extend my most sincere sympathies to her family. Ironically, those maneuvers which were performed by our team in an effort to save the patient's life have been misinterpreted by her family as those which caused her demise. This misinterpretation is of course understandable given the flurry of activity by more than 10 providers that her family witnessed at her bedside during the last hour of Ms. Hannon-Dunne's life. However, there is no doubt that the post-mortem showed a laceration in the right subclavian and brachiocephalic veins, a known complication of subclavian vein catheter insertion and one which is usually self-limiting. The post-mortem also demonstrated a large haemothorax, which indeed was the condition that we were trying to relieve at the time of her respiratory arrest.

Please feel free to contact me if additional questions arise.

Sincerely,

[redacted]

Chapter 6

The Big Question

Since your death Ailbhe, I've given much consideration to that question you asked me the week before your death, the Big Question, "What happens when you die mammy?"With the benefit of hindsight I can see how superficial my response was. I just outlined the peripheral traditional rituals around death, the removal, the funeral, but I didn't delve into the reality of death. I've sometimes regretted this. But of course you'll understand Ailbhe that at that time I thought we'd have plenty of time and opportunity in the future to reflect on this topic. I felt by the law of averages that it would be your prerogative to see me off to this great unknown, the afterlife, if such a place or state exists. Well after your death this question stuck in my psyche, so much that I considered doing a post-grad on it. I had my title decided on, a question, "Is death the final exit or the great entrance?" That did not work out so I thought Ailbhe, the two of us could explore this a little. Perhaps we'll end up with more questions than answers but it doesn't matter. If we knew everything, life could be boring. We will be in good company, Plato first explored this big question and oxymoron, "Life after death," in the 4th century B.C. Now there are those who go about their daily business happily believing that this life is all there is, so for them there is no question. If they are correct, it is the same for everyone after death -nothing to look forward to, nothing to fear. All I'll say is that if this is the scenario it was great to have had you for 25 years and nothing will take the memories away from me, "For death he taketh all away but these he cannot take."

"What if you get Alzheimer's?" I hear you say Ailbhe.

I believe it still could never erase the memory of you.

Well let's leave that group and move to another cohort, those who claim to be absolutely sure of there being an afterlife. Indeed, listening to the vivid absolutist descriptions of some, one would think they'd already been there and sussed out the place.

They'd nearly tell you the colour of the wallpaper. Now, most of this latter group would claim a strong religious affiliation while the former group would be largely non-mainstream religious or not subscribe to any religion. So what if at the start we were to set both these groups aside. Let's remain sceptical on both counts adopting the ancient Greek stance of one who neither believes nor disbelieves, but one who keeps searching for the truth. Let's adopt the mindset of a doubting agnostic.

We'll start with a look at what science has to offer. I find the ongoing study on the paranormal by Dr Raymond Moody very interesting. He is a highly-educated academic, a medical doctor with a PhD in Philosophy plus an MA and BA who has extensively researched the near death experiences of people who were pronounced dead, resuscitated and who came back. These were all people of sound mind, mixed race, gender, age, some religious, some non-religious. He himself had no religious upbringing. He approaches our question from a scientific basis trying through sound logic and balanced reasoning to come to a conclusion re the existence of life after death. Had you lived longer I'd likely have directed you to his research. Moody found that while no two accounts of near death experience were identical, there were striking similarities among various accounts. Some too came back reporting that they had no memory of anything.

The actual experiences reported fell mainly into the following elements; inexpressive, no words could express what they wanted to say; a feeling of peace and quiet often came when they were pronounced dead; noise-unusual noise, some found it pleasant, while others found it very annoying; dark tunnel- a sensation of being pulled along rapidly through a dark tunnel; out of body, usually after the tunnel, with a sense of leaving their body and looking at themselves from a physical point outside it.

Many were able to describe medical activity in such detail that the attending doctors interviewed later concurred that some kind of actual witnessing of events on the part of the comatose patient had occurred. Out of body experience and the tunnel experience was usually followed by meeting others (spiritual beings). Beings who ease them through their transition and into death or to tell them that it wasn't their time to die. The Being of Light was the most common experience and the one that had the greatest effect on the individuals. The light first appeared as a dim light and then became rapidly brighter until it reached a great brilliance. Some described the light as Jesus, God, and an angel by those with religious leanings Others described pets, animals, dead relatives. The light communicated with the individual, sometimes in a language that they had never heard before, often asking them if they were ready to die. The questions evolved in a non-judgemental way and their aim was to gather information that could help the person proceed along a path of truth and self-realisation. The Light was often described as funny, pleasant and secure.

Some said they experienced what they called the review, a moment when their entire life was displayed before them in panoramic intensity. The review was very quick, in chronological order, incredibly vivid and real, highly-charged, emotional and even multi-dimensional so that the individual could understand the thoughts and emotions of everyone in the review. The review was often described as aiming to help the person understand themselves better. The person sometimes spoke of approaching a border or limit beyond which they would not return, like, water, grey mist, a door, fence across a field, a line or imagined line. Some reported that they resisted coming back. They wanted to stay. Some reported a return trip through the tunnel and back to their physical bodies. When they did return they had moods and feelings that lingered a long time. Many were transformed and became "better" people.

The people Moody studied were well-balanced, functioning people. Yet because they were afraid of not being believed, thought to be delusional, they largely kept the experience to themselves. Moody claims that the effect on lives was profound and noticeable. Many said they had broadened their lives and had become more reflective. They no longer feared death though many felt they had a lot of personal growth to attend to. While there were no rewards or punishments the light made it clear that their life was a learning process. Moody is anxious to emphasize that his findings cannot be taken as absolute proof of an afterlife, rather evidence of what likely happens at death.

Some feel that these near death experiences are merely hallucinations caused by fear or lack of oxygen to the brain, a physiological phenomenon rather than a spiritual one. So, Moody has now interestingly gone on to study what he calls, "shared death experiences," the study of the experiences of healthy people sitting at the bedside of a dying loved one. These people are not ill, so should they have these experiences, it would present a new framework in which to explore this big question.

I've already talked to you Ailbhe about the experience I had as I sat at your bedside on July 8th 2002, so I look forward to following Moody's further study. Following publication of his work, Moody became embroiled in a battle with religious people and new age people. Both believed that the near death experience was proof of life after death and wanted him to publicly agree, but as he felt this was as yet a work-in-progress he could not accommodate their requests so apparently he was not flavour of the month with either party. His greatest adversaries, he says, were the fundamentalist Christians whose main complaint was that people of all religions and even none would report seeing beings of light and would sometimes describe these beings as God. They claimed that only the godly like them could see God. All others were seeing the devil, they claimed, and by studying near death experiences he was "letting the devil out of his box." Therefore, they asserted, the study of near death experience was the work of Satan.

In my quest for information on this big question of yours Ailbhe, I consulted a variety of opinions and beliefs using books, talking to people of different persuasions and of course the internet but my research is far from comprehensive. From this side of the grave, dealing with a topic as mystifying as death and the afterlife, can only be a work-in-progress for us humans.

Indeed, I found my research journey very interesting and revelatory as to how all the belief systems have developed and evolved through centuries thanks to the combined works and reflections of science, religion, philosophy and the creative artists leading us hopefully to a possible future time when as John O'Donohue suggested we will have a much clearer understanding and connection between the visible and invisible.

I was also quite dismayed by the arrogant claims by some that they had exclusive access to absolute truth on this topic, a topic as elusive and mysterious as death and the afterlife and how some had no difficulty in equating a loving, fatherly God with meeting out the most vindictive monstrous suffering to people, even little children after death if they'd been found not to have measured up. So in a way I felt kinda relieved that we had not delved too much into this before your death lest this cohort disturb you. Seriously Ailbhe, if I thought these barbaric pontifications were even remote possibilities, I'd never have given birth to children. Better I'd suggest for humanity to become extinct than bring innocent people into a situation where this most monstrous suffering could become their ultimate lot. Then knowing you Ailbhe, I think you would not have been in the least perturbed. All this mindset would cost you, would be a little human sympathy tempered with your hearty laugh.

Anyhow let's move on Ailbhe. Some sort of vague timeline might be useful so I'll go back to what claims, according to my research, to be the oldest of the received world religions which taught monotheism. It has quite a long name, called Zoroastrianism and is thought by many to have probably had more influence on mankind directly or indirectly than any other single faith. It also seems it was the first to teach the doctrine of an individual judgement, heaven, hell, the future resurrection of the body, the general last judgement and life everlasting for the reunited soul and body. It is believed by many scholars that Zorastrian beliefs and practices founded by Zarathustra, may go back to 600 B.C. Its theology had massive influence on Judaism, Christianity and other later religions in their beliefs about God, Satan, the soul, heaven, hell, Virgin birth of the Saviour, Resurrection, final judgement and so on. Its founder lived in Persia (Iran) and legends say that his birth was predicted and that attempts were made by evil forces to kill him as a child. Prior to this, the country had followed a polytheistic religion. Zarathustra was attacked for his teaching of a monotheistic religion but finally won the support of the king.

Zoroastrianism became the state religion of various Persian empires until the 7th century CE when Muslims and Arabs invaded Persia. The Zorastrians were persecuted, forced to convert, slaughtered and compelled to pay heavy taxes, so many left and fled to India. Apparently there are presently around 18,000 Zorastrians and they are now called Parsees. Their general philosophy on which this general final judgement was based before the soul was assigned its destiny, heaven or hell was (1) good thoughts (2) good words (3) good deeds. I found the book by Mary Boyce, "Zorastrians Their Religious Beliefs and Practices" very useful.

So Ailbhe, we have discovered that a belief in an afterlife and what happens when we die goes back a long way. In the early days of Judaism their particular belief was that those who died went to Sheol, a place of shades. Everyone went there when they lost their breath and body. There were no rewards or punishment, only a type of existence that was closer to non-existence. Now the Hebrew concept of everlasting life changed enormously when the prophets and others began to speak about the resurrection of the dead around 55 B.C., but the idea was not apparently universally accepted. In the days of Jesus some Jews did not believe it (the Sadducces) and I heard one theologian remark, "That is why they are sad you see." In researching Judaism apart from using Google, I sourced information from George Robinson's, "Essential Judaism (pocket book 2000)," Rabbi Amy Scheinerman's homepage, The Torah and The Old Testament.

Most traditional Jewish movements now accept the concept of a resurrection of the dead. Heaven and hell and judgement are accepted concepts of the afterlife. Heaven known as (Gan Eden) the Garden of Eden is a place of great joy and peace, sitting at golden banquet tables enjoying lavish banquets, celebrating the Sabbath, enjoying sunshine and sexual intercourse. Other sages hold a spiritual view, suggesting there will be neither eating nor drinking nor procreation of children or business transactions and that there will be no envy, hatred or rivalry, but only the righteous sitting enthroned with crowns on their heads, reunited with their families. The wicked will be cut off from their people.

Gehinnom or Sheol is the post-mortem destination of the unrighteous Jews and gentiles. The souls in Gehinnom according to some references are punished for up to a maximum of 12 months. After the appropriate period of purification the righteous continue to the Garden of Eden. The wicked, following the full year of punishment, are either annihilated (after 12 months), their bodies consumed and their souls burned while the wind scatters what's left under the feet of the righteous (Rosh Hashanah 17a) or they continue to be punished. Apparently this belief is the basis for the Jewish practice of mourning and asking blessings for deceased loved ones for only 11 months as one would not want to imply that the departed loved one needed the full 12 months for purification.

Ancient Egypt had quite a prescriptive belief about death and the afterlife. I'll try and do it justice. They believed that arriving at ones reward in the afterlife was a demanding ordeal requiring a sin-free heart along with the ability to recite the spells, passwords and formulae of the Book of the Dead. To explain about the sin-free heart- when the body died parts of its soul known as (ka) (body double) and the (ba) personality would go to the Kingdom of the Dead while the soul dwelt in the fields of Aaru. In the hall of the two truths the deceased's heart was weighted against the shufeather of truth and justice taken from the headdress of the goddess Maat. If the heart was lighter than the feather it could pass on but if it were heavier they would be devoured by the demon Ammit. Egyptians also believed that being properly mummified was the only way to have an afterlife. So only if the corpse had been properly embalmed and entombed in a mastaba could the dead live again in the fields of Yalu and accompany the sun on its daily ride. This is all such a long time ago but then Ailbhe we can't really know where we are going if we don't know where we are coming from and I have been surprised at how much these ancient beliefs colour much of today's customs and rituals around death. In a way, the more things change, the more they remain the same.

I think I'm correct in saying that today all mainstream religions teach a belief in an afterlife but that's about as far as the agreement goes. They all have their individual teachings and interpretations. So we'll have a look now at what modern day believers propose. I'll start with what the Christian churches teach on death and the afterlife. Even among Christians there are sharp differences. So let's look at various Christian denominations starting with the Roman Catholic Church. I have used the Catechism of the Catholic Church, Addis, Arnolds Catholic dictionary, Catholicism for Dummies, Vatican Council documents and personal experience as my main sources.

According to the Catechism of the Catholic Church, paragraph 1030,"All who die in God's grace and friendship but still imperfectly purified are indeed assured of their eternal salvation but after death they undergo purification so as to achieve this holiness necessary to enter the joy of heaven." The second Vatican Council on page 63 states that the truth has been divinely revealed, that sins are followed by punishments. God's holiness and justice inflict them. Sins must be expiated. This may be done on this earth through the sorrows, miseries and trails of this life and above all through death, otherwise the expiation must be made in the next life through fire and torments or purifying punishments. The process of purification occurs in a place referred to by the Roman

Catholic Church as purgatory. Purgatory is not supposed to be a place of punishment but of purification. The nature of this purification according to differing catholic theologians ranges from an extreme awareness of loss to an excruciating painful purifying fire. The Catholic dictionary (Addis and Arnolds) points out that there is a bright as well as a dark side to purgatory. The souls there are certain of their salvation, they are willing sufferers and no words according to St. Catherine of Genoa can express the joy they have as they increase in union with God.

Only baptised infants who die before the age of accountability and Catholic saints who lived holy lives are excused from "the purifying fires."

The Catechism of the Catholic Church defines heaven. "By Heaven is meant the state of supreme and definitive happiness. Those who die in the grace of God and have no need of further purification are gathered around Jesus and Mary, the angels and the saints. They thus form the church of Heaven where they see God face to face. (1.Corinthians 13:12) They live in a communion of love with the most blessed trinity and they intercede for us."

Then page 83 (212) 1033 1035 1050 1057 of the Catechism defines hell. Hell consists in the eternal damnation of those who die in mortal sin through their own free choice. The principal suffering of hell is eternal separation from God in whom alone we can have life and happiness for which we were created and for which we long. Christ proclaimed this reality with the words, "Depart from me, you cursed, into eternal fire" (Matthew 25:41).

The particular judgement is defined, "It is the judgement of immediate retribution which each one after death will receive from God in his immortal soul in accord with his faith and his works. This retribution consists in entrance into the happiness of Heaven immediately or after an appropriate purification, or entry into eternal damnation in Hell."

It continues, "Then the final or universal judgement consists in a sentence of happiness or eternal damnation, which the Lord Jesus will issue in regard to the 'just and unjust' (Act 24:15) when he returns as the judge of the living and the dead. After the last judgement, the resurrected body will share in the retribution which the soul received at the particular judgement," and "This judgement will come at the end of the world and only God knows the day and hour."

Then there is the hope of the new heaven and the new earth, the Catechism goes on to state, "After the final judgement the universe itself freed from its bondage to decay, will share in the glory of Christ with the beginning of "the new Heavens" and a new earth (2 Peter 3:13). Thus, the fullness of the kingdom of God will come about, that is to say, the definitive realisation of the salvific plan of God to "unite all things in Christ, things in Heaven and things on earth.(Ephesians 1:10). God will then be all in all (Corinthians 15:28) in eternal life."

Well are you still with me Ailbhe? Not much left to the imagination. Why as John O'Donohue asks, do religious people still so often want "to unriddle and control the unknown?" Certainly in their answers to these great questions the lawyer decided. Are these beliefs not merely a projection of our own literalist brand of God? Perhaps it's the fact that these dogmas are the outcome of a near exclusive male reflection that has left their conclusions so bereft of the qualities of compassion, common humanity and creativity? When Socrates was granted a wish he asked not for knowledge but for an understanding heart.

I think back Ailbhe to how I, like many others were rushed to church to be baptised without my mother, as she'd just given birth and would not be physically able. That was the custom at the time and I often wondered why? Well when I researched the origin & concept of Limbo, I discovered it evolved following the considerable energy and enquiry that the Roman Catholic Church invested in determining the destination of babies who die unbaptised while having not yet reached the age of accountability, I now fully understand the rush. According to the Catholic dictionary the fate of such babies much exercised the mind and study of the Catholic Church back in the Middle Ages and they came up with the name "Limbo" as their destination. Limbo the Latin word *Limbus* or "(fringe)" was used for the place on the fringe or outskirts of hell in which the just who died before Christ were detained till the resurrection from the dead. It likewise signifies a place (also supposed to be beneath the earth and on the outskirts of hell) inhabited by infants who die in original sin (Limbus infantium). It is down in my Catholic dictionary as an article of faith that those who die without baptism and in whose case that want of baptism has not been supplied in some other way cannot enter heaven, Council of Florence in the decree of Union (Denzinger-Bannwart, 693).

No wonder children were rushed off to church for baptism with this sentence hanging over them. Apparently there were a few theologians who found this belief repugnant and thought that God might be pleased to supply the want of baptism in infants by other means. St Bernard and some other suggested that perhaps the faith of the parents might save such infants. A theologian named Knoll believed that God might commission angels to confer baptism on infants to prevent them from otherwise perishing without it. But the theologians of the Augustinian order had a very different opinion- that the infants in question were punished both by exclusion from heaven and positive pain, though much less pain than is inflicted on those who died in actual mortal sin. This is the opinion of St. Augustine (Sern 294, Pl, XXXV111 1337) where he said that unbaptised infants were consigned to eternal fire, though their damnation will be lightest of all (De Peccat Merits et Remiss 1:20) No, I didn't read this in some horror novel. I read this in Addis and Arnold's Catholic dictionary revised by Mgr.P.E. Hallett. What monstrous beliefs! Were these so-called eminent Fathers of the Church saints or sadists? Thankfully the Roman Catholic Church has moved on and bid a fond farewell to Limbo. It was alive and well in my youthful days along with the awful related practice of the Catholic Church's refusal to allow these unbaptised babies to be buried in the church graveyards; consecrated ground was not for them. So the grieving parents had to bury these little bodies in fields or gardens and I think the custom was to get it done quietly and as secretly as possible very early in the morning.

Remember the poetry competition (we spoke about it earlier) you entered while in primary school, you were in about 5th class? I went with you to the celebration arranged by Heather Brett and Cavan Arts. I'm glad to say they are still going strong and now produce a lovely publication – an anthology of young people's work, poetry and art edited by Heather and supported by the Arts Council. Many school children have poems published this way. I think I told you how Aidín had the poem she wrote following your death published. Well I came across this poem published in the 2002 September edition just two months after your death. It is titled "The Minaun Babies" and was written by Tricia Kellet, aged 18, N.U.I Galway. It brought back the cruel reality of Limbo and it goes;

The Minaun Babies

Early morning on misty Minaun as I trekked out to visit the babies. On the edge of the cliff jutting out into the broad and boisterous ocean they lie, their graves unmarked, their names unknown. An unwelcome wave of death and sorrow ebbs into a sea of grief.

On the remote part of this island is where these evil stillborns must be buried ordered the priest in the 1950's. As the grieving young mother was prevented from a farewell, the clergy stole away her heart, her innocence and threw her only son in a pit, wiped his hands as he walked away. No prayers, no condolences, no remorse. A monument of white rocks was built on that cliff face decades later, and blessed at the dawn of a new millennium. "My mother died that day when my older brother was left somewhere over there," Celine told me. Like so many before me, I stay silent and think for a while, say a prayer by the angel for the angels, turn and walk away. I will forget as the church forgot, but mourning Minaun will never forget her babies.

Tricia Kellett
N.U.I Galway
Published in voices from the Hollow
September 2002

Thankfully Ailbhe when your baby brother Aodhghán died just an hour after his birth we met with no such restrictions and as you know he is buried in Coronea Cemetry same as yourself. I presume a nurse or someone in the hospital privately baptised him as I think that was the policy, so then of course his situation was different. Mind you, I don't remember any formal retraction by the Roman Catholic Church with regard to its position on Limbo.

Interestingly, as recent as April 2007 the advisory body known as the International Theological Commission released a document originally commissioned by Pope John Paul II entitled, "The hope of Salvation for Infants who die without being baptised." It said, "The theory of Limbo remains a possible theological opinion. Benedict authorised publication of this document dismissing the earlier media report that "The Pope closed Limbo."

I sense a noticeable shift to a more humane stance which evolved in the 2006 publication of Catechism of the Catholic Church as it suggests possible different ways of getting the benefits of baptism such as Baptism of Desire while still holding to the concept of original sin. It responded to the question "Why does the church baptise infants?" and said, "The church baptises infants because they are born with original sin. They need to be freed from the power of the Evil One and brought into the Realm of Freedom which belongs to the children of God". 258 Catechism of the Catholic church 1250.

To the question "Is Baptism necessary for Salvation?" it said, "Baptism is necessary for salvation for all those to whom the Gospel has been proclaimed and who have had the possibility of asking for this sacrament." (1257) Finally to the question, "Is it possible to be saved without Baptism?" the response was, "Since Christ died for the salvation of all, those can be saved without Baptism who die for the faith (Baptism of blood). Catechumens and all those who even without knowing Christ and the church, still (under the impulse of grace) sincerely seek God and strive to do his will can also be saved without Baptism (Baptism of Desire) The church in her liturgy entrusts children who die without Baptism to the mercy of God. Catechism of the Catholic Church 1258-1261, 1281-1283.

"Is this not true for all Ailbhe, clergy themselves included? These modern responses are still quite opaque and nuanced but does that last sentence, "The church in her Liturgy entrusts children who die without Baptism to the mercy of

God" give the opt-out clause for the need for Limbo or is there still a question? In recent times Ailbhe, I never hear of stillborn children being refused admission to consecrated ground and I think some clergy have at the behest of the laity blessed some of these fields where these babies were buried, and memorials have been erected in some places. Still the recent response I've just quoted from, the modern catechism, has I find a terrible cold, clinical air. As far as I'm aware the other Christian churches never taught the doctrine of Limbo nor did they have the tradition of not allowing burial of unbaptised babies in church grounds.

This rule in the Catholic Church of not allowing unbaptised babies to be buried in consecrated ground was also meted out to people who died by suicide. Now Ailbhe, you'll remember our good neighbour Phylis Faris, well she gave me a present of a book written by Richard Holloway Anglican bishop of Edinburgh - a city now well-known to us. He was a regular broadcaster on television and radio and she knew I had found his open and questioning approach liberating. In this book "Anger Sex and Death" published in 1992 he voices his outrage at this practice and I quote from his book because it puts words on how I feel, as we chat about this, "The refusal to give Christian burial to a suicide or to allow a suicide to rest in consecrated ground was the worst example of this mysterious coldness of heart that can afflict spiritual people. Laertes words to the priest who denied his sister Ophelia proper burial should be stamped on the bottom of every Christian practitioner's licence. "Churlish priest a ministering angel shall my sister be when thou liest howling."

Well Ailbhe, I totally agree but I'd put the Roman Catholic notion of Limbo ahead of this on a scale of harshness. Holloway writes, "The agents of ultimate salvation were the clergy who issued final passports." He also notes, "The enormous power that was made to reside in those men" whom he refers to as largely "hectoring moralizers inflamed by their own self righteousness."

John O'Donohue too asks what is it in religion that can so harden people and advises strongly that we claim back our power and never give that power away to anyone or anything outside ourselves. That's what I admire about your generation Ailbhe, how you have claimed back your power and pushed out the boundaries. Then I suppose my generation, your mentors, can too claim a bow for good parenting.

I'm quite surprised at the time we've spent discussing this Ailbhe. As I said while all Christian churches teach the existence of an afterlife that's as far as the agreement goes. The Protestant Churches do not teach purgatory nor do the Eastern Orthodox Church, I'm reliably informed. Some of the arguments they put forward are; (1) Purgatory is not explicably found in the Bible, (2) Purgatory implies that the righteousness of Christ does not cleanse us from all sin, "We cannot add to or subtract from what Christ has done," they claim, (3) Purgatory implies that there is something we must do in order to be cleansed of sin. It implies that justification is not by faith.

Orthodox Christians believe that when a person dies the soul is temporarily separated from the body, though it may linger for a short time on earth, it is ultimately escorted either to paradise (Abraham's bosom) or to the darkness of Hades following the temporal judgement. Mormons believe that all who have died without knowledge of (the) Gospel and who would have received it if they had been permitted to tarry shall be heirs of the celestial kingdom of God.

Remember our friend Allison who stayed in the flat? She was a Jehovah's Witness. Well Jehovah's Witnesses and Christadelphians have taught that the dead are unconscious (or even non-existent) while awaiting their destiny on Judgement Day. They with Seventh Day Adventists teach that sinners are destroyed rather than tortured.

Though the Hebrew bible according to the Catholic dictionary contains few direct and clear announcements of a life beyond the grave, it goes on to define hell "as the place and state in which the devils and such human beings as die in enmity with God suffer eternal torment." While it states that it is certain from scripture and tradition that the torments of hell are inflicted in a definite place, it is uncertain where that place is. According to the common opinion of fathers and theologians, it is in the centre of the earth, but many other theories have been propounded and St Thomas himself thought it "more probable" that hell is under the earth. Various passages in the New Testament are referred to as proving the existence of hell-MT.X V III 8, XXV 41 Sgg- MK. IX.48. The new testament the dictionary tells us has a new name for hell, viz Gehenna which occurs it says repeatedly in St Matthew (v22, 29, 30, x28 XV III.9 XX1111533) three times in St Mark (IX.4345,47), once in St Luke (XII.5) and once in St James (111.6) Jesus' words are quoted as making reasonable doubt impossible, "depart from me ye cursed, into eternal fire prepared for the devil and his angels.... the fire which will never be quenched." The dictionary goes on to state, "It is certain that the devils and disembodied spirits of the damned suffer from material fire... at present all theologians... nay all Christians are agreed that the fire of hell is corporeal and material." It goes on to say ,"Though the matter has not been settled as yet by any decree of the church."

It continues, "To those who ask how material fire can affect spirits no certain answer can be given." But St. Thomas had a go at a possible scenario. "St. Thomas thinks that God gives to the fire as the instrument of his justice a permanent power of constraining the spirit and impeding its action so as to cause intense suffering." Christ's own words are used in the dictionary as proof as to the eternity of hell's punishment and its everlasting nature and that there is absolutely no hope of escape. Those in hell "are doomed to endure the society of other reprobates like themselves and they know that all hope is over.... after the Resurrection the body is subjected to torment." It rejects the view of origin in ("De Principis" 1.6 PG, X1 169) the possibility of universal salvation and the more recent Catechism of the Catholic Church seems to concur – page 83, 212, 1033-1035, 1056, 1057, "Hell consists in the eternal damnation of those who die in mortal sin through their own free choice..."

St Thomas Aquinas and Jonathan Edwards, again according to the dictionary wrote that "the saved in Heaven will delight in the suffering of the dammed." While the essential happiness of Heaven has been given in the article on the Beatific Vision on the Beautitudes (the sight of God face to face) because God is incorporeal, it is with the eyes of the soul not bodily eyes that God is seen. "Some will see more perfectly than others" and it says, "It will be according to the diversity of their merits."

That stuff belongs way back in the dark ages I hear you say. Well, this Catholic dictionary (15th edition) was published in Easter 1948, the year after my birth and I don't feel in the least bit ancient Ailbhe. I hear you respond, all head and no heart- the head got too big. I suppose in fairness the compilers of that period did not have the advantage of the more recent psychological and scientific awareness, but I do feel for vulnerable people who vested their trust in such absolutist barbaric depictions. I'll quote again Bishop Holloway who referred to these people as, "hectoring moralizer inflamed by their own self righteousness" and I think he hits the right note when he suggests "that on a topic as uncertain and elusive as death there can be no excuse for magisterially determining another's position. Christians have felt in this and other matters that they had a right to dictate the conduct and preferences of others. In the face of the great mystery of death surely we should operate with enormous reserve and sensitivity. When we speak at all we should only speak to affirm and console."

He sees Christianity "as a Gospel of Grace shared out of joy rather than religious superiority." Isn't it amazing Ailbhe how harsh and cold so much of the Christian and some other religious language and depictions are? One writer, (can't remember the nam)e remarked that they turned what is purported as the Good News of the Gospels into lethal weapons when pontificating on death. These depictions totally disconnected from the heart, only act to keep people emotionally and creatively crippled through fear and obedience. These groups promote their assumed easy certitude and stale ideology. Some of it made me feel sick, so thankfully you were not over-exposed to this thinking and indeed your generation to your credit knocked a lot of this on the head and liberated yourselves from such.

Yourself and Kerill had some good Muslim friends so I've had a look at how they might respond to your question. Well Muslims believe that Islam is the complete and universal version of a primordial faith that was revealed at many times and places before, including through the prophets Abraham, Moses and Jesus. They maintain however that previous messages have been partially changed or corrupted over time but consider the Quran to be both unaltered and the final revelation from God, and Muhammad the last prophet in a series of prophets, as taught in the Quran, restored and uncorrupted. They claim that whoever seeks a religion other than Islam, it will not be accepted from him and he will be one of the losers in the hereafter (Quran 3:85). So those who die while not believing that "there is no true God but God and Muhammad as His messenger (prophet) of God or are not Muslim will lose Paradise forever and will be sent to Hellfire, as God has said." I got my information mainly from "The Everything Understanding Islam Book." written by Christine Huda Dodge and True Religion God written by Abuameenah Philips Bila.

Islam teaches that at death the angel of death comes to remove the soul from the body. The souls of good people are lifted out gently while the souls of the wicked people "are yanked" out with terrifying force. After the soul is lifted from the body, the angel carries it up to the gates of heaven. There the person will become aware of whether he or she is destined for heaven or hell. Then God orders the soul to be returned to earth, it rests in the grave until the day of resurrection. Muhammad taught that the soul rests in the company of angels who question the person about his or her beliefs. They ask three questions. (1) Who is your Lord? (2) Who was your Prophet? (3) What was your way of life? If the soul responds adequately to the three questions then the angels give it pleasant company and the grave begins to seem spacious and comfortable. If the person shows a rejection of God in the answers then the space of the grave begins to seem tight and suffocating. The angels will torment such souls until the day of judgement. This is known as the punishment of the grave. Muslims also believe that the entire world will come to an end on an appointed day when everything will be annihilated. The Quran is clear that both men and women will dwell in Paradise - a place of peace with rivers and fruits, sweet smell, goblets of gold and the shade of God himself.

But the greatest bliss is the good pleasure of God that is supreme (Quran 9:72). The Quran indicates that some people will be higher (more respected) and closer to God than others. Just as those who believe and do good deeds are rewarded for their efforts, those who reject God and rebel against his laws will face punishment in the hereafter. Hell is described as a fierce fire that will consume and punish those within it. But beyond the pain and torment of the fire, the ultimate punishment is the shame and disgrace before God. Just as Paradise contains levels within it, the fire of Hell contains levels with varying degrees of heat and intensity. People will be placed there depending on the extent of their disbelief and sins. The Quran indicates that the hypocrites will be at "the lowest depths of the fire" (Quran 4:15). Muslims reject the belief that the souls of the departed may dwell among human beings, interact with them, harm them, benefit them or communicate with them. Islam teaches that the dead stay in the grave until the day of resurrection.

I feel we need to take a break Ailbhe What about a poem? Judgement, By R.S Stephenson springs to mind;

Judgement

Pray, don't find fault with the man who limps or stumbles along the road,
Unless you have worn the shoes he wears- or struggled beneath his load.
There may be tracks in his shoes that hurt, though hidden away from view.
For the burden he bears- placed upon your back might cause you to stumble too.
Don't be harsh with the man who sins, or pelt with words or stones,
Unless you are sure - yes doubly sure, that you have no sins,
Know perhaps that if the tempters voice should whisper as soft to you
As it did to him when he went astray it could cause you to stagger too.
Don't sneer at the man who's down today unless you have felt the blow
That cause his fall, or felt the shame that only the fallen know.
You may be strong- but still the blows that were his if dealt in the self same way
Might cause you to stagger too.

Ailbhe who said poetry does not tell it shows? How right! We have looked at the beliefs as taught by three main monotheism religions, Judaism, Christianity and Islam. So why not have a look at some of the other ethical systems and their teachings on the afterlife? Hindu and Buddhism would be two of the largest and best known.

Do you remember Ailbhe our visit to that lady outside Bawnboy years ago? You'd have been about 12 years old. It was after you had your kidney removed, the kidney which apparently never functioned and became diseased and caused your kidney problem. Well I'd heard about the therapeutic effect of reflexology from Granny as Mags had taken her for a treatment in Dublin and she spoke commendably about its positive relaxing effects. Mags herself had studied it and we had personal experience of its diagnostic credibility from your confirmation day when she was the first to spot that your headaches and problems emanated from your kidney, through doing your feet. I had heard the recently arrived Buddhists to Owendoon House, Jampa Ling outside Bawnboy had a reflexologist, so I rang and got an appointment for you, thinking it would help you after your surgery. So off the two of us went taking in a visit to nearby Derryvella to say hello to Gran and Granddad of course. I have since visited the lovely old house that the Buddhists now own on quite a few occasions. They have an open, welcoming atmosphere and regime. The public are free to join them in meditation, prayers and friendship. I've found a great peace and inclusivity there. If I remember correctly I think the reflexology was a positive experience for you Ailbhe.

Well I found The Tibetan Book of Living and Dying which I used in my research quite fascinating. Like Hindu, the Buddhist teachings tell us that until we reach a degree of self-awareness and enlightenment, our suffering may go on for thousands of lives until our true potential or Buddha nature are freed from our ignorance and merge with the deathless enlightened mind. Until we reach this there can be no end to the rounds of life and death. Those who achieve realisation can choose to return in life after life to help others if they wish. The kind of birth we will have in the next life is determined by the nature of our actions in this one, the effects of our actions depending entirely upon the intention or motivation behind them, and not upon their scale. So Buddhism advises us to develop a good heart that longs for other beings to find lasting happiness and do acts that help secure that happiness, nourish and practice kindness. The Dalai Lama has said, "There is no need for temples, no need for complicated philosophy. Our own brain our own heart is our temple, my philosophy is kindness." With regard to reincarnation Voltaire said, "After all it is no more surprising to be born twice than it is to be born once." "In the Buddhist approach life and death are seen as one whole, where death is the beginning of another chapter of life. Death is a mirror in which the entire meaning of life is reflected."

The Tibetan Buddhists divide our entire existence into four continuously interlinked realities (1) Life (2) Dying and death (3) After death (4) Rebirth, known to Buddhists as the four bardos. The bardos, they believe, are powerful opportunities for liberation with the greatest moment being the moment of death. The source of their teaching is the enlightened mind, the completely awake, and the teachings are transmitted by a long line of masters that stretch back over many centuries to the Primordial Budda. If through meditation we have come to realise the fact that our bodies and all phenomena are illusionary and free ourselves from attachments to it without fear, leave it behind willingly, knowing it now for what it is, we will be able "to die when we die" and so achieve ultimate freedom. So what happens in death is that there is a gap or space, fertile with vast possibilities, where the only thing that can matter is how our mind is, the naked, revealed mind. So consciousness at its subtlest level continues without the body and as we no longer have a body, there is no reason to fear any experience. "How can any harm come to nobody." The difficulty arises if we go on grasping at physical solidity. People who accomplish complete detachment will go through the physical process of dying but will not have to go through the subsequent bardo states, having reached Enlightenment "Ultimate Liberation."

I hope I've got this right Ailbhe. I found it quite fascinating how they spoke of the newly liberated soul moving towards a bright light at the passage end of a dark tunnel. Of how often the presence of others is sensed in the passageway and how some perceive been welcomed across into the light by friends or relatives who have already crossed over, beings who loved us in our life or sometimes a spiritual figure, angel, Buddha, Jesus, Mary, Mohammad or one's own ancestors, whatever epitomised love, truth, beauty and justice for the dying person.

Well, if my research is accurate Ailbhe, Buddhism goes back to the 6th Century B.C. I went back even further back to the ancient practice of Shamanism to see what their belief was. Here we depend on anthropologic evidence, a discipline close to Kerill's heart, as if I remember correctly he studied anthropology in his primary degree course. The paleoanthropologist Hank Wesselman tells us that shamanism is the first spiritual practice of human kind and dates back tens of thousands of years. So much of what we know of early shamanism comes from human excavation. The word shaman means "the one who sees in the dark." While religion tends to be based on belief, shamanic spiritual practices are based on personal, direct experiences so although shamanism may contain elements of ritual it is not really a religion.

Shamanism views the world as being made up of two distinct parts, a world of things seen, the visible world, and a world of things hidden, the unseen or invisible world but no distinction is drawn between them. The shaman is the visionary (male or female) who learns through practice to enter the unseen world or parallel reality, the spirit world. Shamans develop relationships with these spirits and they claim that they can help heal emotional, physical, mental and spiritual illness and access information from the spirit world. Some may be able to guide the souls of the dead to where they are supposed to go in the afterlife, so a shaman mediates between the visible world of form and matter and the invisible world of energy and spirits. I found the modern book "Awakening to the spirit world\; The Shamanic Path of Direct Revelation" by Sandra Ingerman & Hank Wesselman most informative and interesting.

But what is the nature of the afterlife according to shamanism? Shamans see death not as an ending but as a natural rite of passage, into a transcendental level of reality. They claim that we in the west have tried to make death invisible, while they believe in honouring the cycle of life and death, claiming that just as the body knows how to be born in the same way it knows how to die. Normally they say, we return to spirit naturally but on rare occasions some will not make the journey to the spirit world naturally and where there is resistance we can become earth-bound. If this occurs assistance is needed on the journey. Help can then come from our spirit guides. Shamanism sees death as a transition beginning with a sense of wellbeing, peace and surprise at finding oneself out of one's body and being able to see and hear everything that is going on in the immediate vicinity of the deceased physical body. They speak of going through different stages, bardo, dream-like worlds, middle worlds where we are met by celestial beings (our own spirit guides) for our life review and our return back home to the original source. I thought how wise of Sandra Ingerman, herself a teacher of shamanism through international workshops and also a psychotherapist and author to draw our attention to what she calls the shadow side of shamanism. She stresses how crucial it is to self-reflect and acknowledge the darker shadow side. She wisely points out that in any practice that works with the principle of power, there will be those who will abuse the power and use it to manipulate others. She speaks as a woman of the importance of being aware of and integrating the influence of ego and emotions on our lives. So I feel obliged to quote this short section, "The Feminine principle of the visionary steers us away from seeing the practice as a series of techniques and methods to seeing shamanism as a way of life in which we honour and respect the spirit that lives in all things. This way considers how you live to be more important to what you do. This includes the principle of experiencing power with versus power over." Spot on I hear you say Ailbhe. "Now is it accurate to conclude from our findings so far that the more paternalistic religions we've met when speaking on death and the afterlife were those using the most vivid, horrific, fearful depictions and language when pontificating on what awaits those of us who don't measure up when we pass over 'fires of hell' 'damnation' 'everlasting torment' 'people burned dragged along in chains' 'constantly tormented' 'given putrid liquid to drink and thorny bitter plants to eat. Have the powers that be fallen into the trap Sandra Ingerman warns of, failing to honestly accept and monitor how emotions, ego and desire for power and control can influence their own lives and colour their judgements.

Let's fast forward Ailbhe from what is claimed to be the oldest of belief systems-(shamanism) to a system that claims to be based on quite recent revelations. Now you might remember this family who came to live outside Cavan. Our paths crossed and they had occasion to visit us here in Farranseer. They enlightened us as to their beliefs. They were members of the "Bahai Faith" which claims to be based on a relatively modern revelation to Bahaullah, a Persian. They claimed it was the most recent in the succession of spiritual messengers, Zoroaster, Krishna, Buddha, Abraham, Moses, Jesus, Bahaullah (hope I did not leave anyone out) preaching one God, one human race. Bahaullah taught that all the world's religions represent stages in the Revelation of Gods will and purpose for humanity. The earth he claimed is but one country and mankind its citizens. "Universal Civilization," "Global unification," "Accept Oneness" would appear to be their motto Ailbhe.

But back to your question. They believe that after its separation from the physical body the soul enters into a spiritual realm of existence in which it draws ever closer to God. Its progress depends on the preparation it made on this earthly plane in response to the teachings of God's messenger so they believe that the soul lives on after the body and embarks on a spiritual journey towards God through many worlds or planes of existence. If the soul fails to develop, one remains distant from God. This condition of remoteness from God can in some sense be understood as hell. But heaven and gell are not regarded as literal places but rather descriptions of one's spiritual progress towards God.

This concept of "Oneness" and "Interconnectness" suggested in both the ancient spirituality of Shamanism and the much more recent Bahai faith has a special significance for me since my experience of being present at your cousin DJ's funeral following a tragic accident. DJ as you know was an accomplished guitarist. He was also a most dedicated fan of U2. In fact tickets he'd bought for their concert arrived in the post around the time of his funeral. As the Catholic Church has restrictions on the particular genre of music and input during the funeral service in the church, the band in which he played guitar in his spare time assembled at his graveside and backed their lead singer's rendition of U2's song "One." Until that experience I would most likely have ignored this type of music, not being a U2 fan but I found those lyrics at the time so powerfully appropriate and poignant.

Who was it Ailbhe who said, "A poem is the cry of the occasion?" Well this song "One" was very much the cry of that occasion. A nice elderly priest remarked as he left the graveside having listened to the song, "Aren't the words and message of that song as Christian as anything we have, in our church?" Sadly, an obsession of religious leaders with protecting their traditions and control has often left a staleness and lack of creativity and personal authenticity in church services. Again lines from one of your own poems come to mind Ailbhe, "Something unvoiced connects us to a reality unchanged by time."

In the interest of balance Ailbhe, let's have a look at those who reject the whole notion of an afterlife. While practically all agree that once we are born, death at some stage is inevitable and inescapable for all. Oh, I think I mentioned my Jehovah Witness friend telling me she believes some people will not die, those alive at the time when Jehovah decides to end this world order, and are living when he comes to judge the living and the dead and establish his kingdom here on earth. But what of those who claim that complete annihilation is what happens when we die. One friend claims we live on through our children, that only the memory of our lives and the fruits of our input and actions, be that good bad or I expect a mixture of both endure.

Some well-known scientists and philosophers have publicly declared their total disbelief in any possibility of an afterlife. Richard Dawkins is one, and in his book "The God Delusion" he quotes the following declaration by Bertrand Russel's 1925 Essay. "What I believe" which is "I believe that when I die I shall rot, and nothing of my ego will survive. I am not young and I love life. But I should scorn to shiver with terror at the thought of annihilation. Happiness is nonetheless true happiness because it must come to an end, nor do thought and love lose their value because they are not everlasting. Many a man has borne himself proudly on the scaffold surely the same pride should teach us to think truly about man's place in the world. Even if the open windows of science at first make us shiver after the cosy indoor warmth of traditional humanizing myths, in the end the fresh air brings vigour, and the great spaces have splendour of their own."

Dawkins himself questions the sincerity of the professed belief in an afterlife of many Christians and Muslims. He asks if their belief is genuine why they don't all behave like the Abbot of Amplefort who when Cardinal Hume told him that he was dying responded by saying he was delighted for him, "Congratulations That's brilliant news. I wish I was coming with you." So, while Dawkins accepts the Abbot as a sincere believer he questions why this would not be the normal reaction for all believers in an afterlife. When a religious believer is told by a doctor that she is dying he asks why "doesn't she beam with excited anticipation as if she had just won a holiday in the Seychelles I can't wait? Why don't faithful visitors at her bedside shower her with messages for those that have gone before? Do give my love to Uncle Robert when you see him...."

Jesse Bering, a psychologist is the director of the Institute of Cognition and Culture at Queens University Belfast and writes for Scientific American under the catchy title "Bering in Mind." I have read his book "The God Instinct: The Psychology of Souls, Destiny, and the Meaning of Life." He contends that the whole God and afterlife belief is just our "overactive Theory of Mind" and that it is "a phantom cast out upon the world by our species own peculiar evolved theory of mind." Bering does however have the diffidence to concede that such cannot be proven either way and that science speaks to the improbable not the impossible. Science like religion does not speak with one voice. The eminent neurosurgeon Dr. Eben Alexander in his book titled Proof of Heaven tells how personal experience trumped convincing him, an ardent scientist, that there is life beyond death.

So Ailbhe, what if we got back our yesterdays and were able to rewind our time back to that day in July 2002 when you posed the BIG QUESTION, "Mammy what happens when we die?" What would my response be post-research and my personal experiences of death? Well I'd certainly take your question much more seriously and without a doubt Ailbhe, as I said at the start of our research I'd point you in the direction of the late John O'Donohue's writings on death. John, the highly-respected Irish poet, philosopher and author who much inspired by our ancient Celtic tradition and imagination portrays dying, death and the afterlife in a way that has genuine resonance for me. So, you with your own Celtic leanings and psyche would definitely connect with it.

I feel that he puts words on my experience. In his books Anam Chara, Eternal Echoes, Divine Beauty and his books of poetry and BlessingsEchoes and Benedictus, I find his exploration of death and dying described in a most genuine, humane way as he shares some of his personal experiences of assisting the dying during his early life as a former priest coupled with his own meetings with family loss, that of his father and uncle. John's philosophy on death so succinctly depicts what it was like for me having had the privilege of being so closely involved with you at the time of your dying, that his books are now some of my best friends. I would present you with the C.D, "Anam Chara-Wisdom from the Celtic World" (John O'Donohue)(Sounds True) and would especially recommend discs seven and eight where John explores death under the title, "Death the Horizon in the Well." John speaks of God as "the greatest circle of all" and "the largest embrace in the Universe" which holds visible an invisible temporal and eternal as one. He uses the Celtic imagery of the circle. The Celtic mind was not comfortable with the liner he reminds us.

The dead then John suggests, "Return to the nest of their identity within the great circle of God." If we live life to the full and not harm anyone, which you did Ailbhe, we will have nothing to worry about when death comes and our death will not seem like a destructive negative event. He suggests when the soul leaves the body it is free, no longer under the burden and control of space and time. Death will become the moment of release into the deepest treasures of our own nature, our full entry into the temple of our soul. That release can bring us to a completely new divine belonging where there will be no more separation or shadow or tears he suggests. I admire his wisdom in noting the danger of neon vision when we come to address the mystery of death and his favouring the perception of candlelight as the best approach. The candlelight will allow the darkness to keep its secrets and will not force "our tormented transparencies upon the mystery."

The glimpse he feels is enough. Now, the dead John believes, are all around us. We have, he feels, falsely spatialised the eternal world. He believes the eternal world to be a different state of being rather than a specific place. There is nowhere else for the soul to go so it goes nowhere. The dead remain here with us in the air we move through, all the time in invisible form. We can, he claims, sense their presence even though we cannot see them in human form. That's such a lovely consoling thought Ailbhe and a most believable thought for me from experiences we've had since your death. Yes, I've sensed your presence.

I love the story he tells of being at the graveside of a young boy as he was being buried in Connemara, a boy about about the same age as yourself Ailbhe. As his coffin was lowered into the grave a terrible wail of grief rose from the brothers and sisters. The mother put her arms around them and said in Irish, "Ná bígí ag caoineadh. Níl tada dhó thíos ansin ach amhaín an clúdach a bhí air." Translated as, "Let ye not be crying there is nothing of him down there only the covering that was on him in this life." That's pretty much how I've always felt when I visit your grave Ailbhe. Indeed lines from Patrick Kavanagh's poem, "In Memory of my Mother" often come to my mind as I stand at your grave."I do not think of you lying in the wet clay of a Monaghan graveyard." (Cavan graveyard of course in your case Ailbhe). "I see you walking among the poplar......"

And while I'd never associate you as "piling up the sticks against the moonlight" I'd have no difficulty in visualising you walking along Grafton Street "through the shops and stalls and markets free in the oriental street of thought." "O you are not lying in the wet clay...." "And yes you smile up at us eternally."

The similarity between the 20th century writer John O'Donohue's depiction of death and afterlife and that of the ancient shamanic view going back thousands of years is striking. Both have an awareness of the seen and unseen worlds, the interconnectedness that at the time of death the "veil" between visible and invisible worlds part enabling the dying person to enter into world of spirit. Perhaps Ailbhe it's true to say that the "truth is one but different sages call it by different names."

In truth Ailbhe of course in response to your question I'd have to tell you none of us at this point in time know exactly what happens after we die. It's in the realm of hopeful speculation and exploration that we all tread but I find it difficult to accept that life does not have a non-material element and I believe there is a lot more to truth than mere facts.

Science looks at matter and we can only say so far in science. I'm equally put off too by some belief systems and religions who in their quest for certainty and supremacy define the afterlife in a dogmatic, materialistic way killing off the notion of mystery and transcendence. Try as we may none of us can control the unknown.

As John O'Donohue reminds us death is not an experience any of us can have and no one we know has come back to clarify exactly what happens, therefore as he says we cannot see the other half of the circle which death opens. He suggests that as there is "no public access to the divine individuality is the only gateway to spiritual potential and blessing." So perhaps Ailbhe, life after death is a special individual experience for each of us with some general similarities just as our lives this side of the grave held their own individual uniqueness with some common components.

The only place to find certainty I believe is within oneself. Have I already quoted words of wisdom from Buddha Ailbhe? "Believe nothing just because a so called wise person said it. Believe nothing just because a belief is generally held. Believe nothing just because it is in the ancient books. Believe nothing just because it is supposed to be of divine origin. Believe nothing just because someone else believes it. Believe only what you yourself test and judge to be true."- Buddha.

An elderly song writer was asked in the course of a recent radio interview what he believed awaited him when he died. He replied that no one could know that but that it could be "nothing" or "anything." While there is now no single infallible answer to your question Ailbhe, there is no reason that we can't analyse and speculate using our intelligence, reason and reflection to seek some clarity.

One of the more humane memories I have of my own years in primary school was of one fine summer's day when the teacher took us out to the yard for English lesson. I was I'd say in about fourth class. We all sat in a circle on the grass as the teacher took a stick and made three circles on the ground with it, one small circle surrounded by a bigger one and a third much larger surrounding the first two as he recited the following poem (written I think by Carl Sandberg)

The white man drew a small circle in the sand and
told the red man this is what the Indian knows
and drawing a big circle around the small one said
This is what the white man knows.
The Indian took the stick and swept an immense
ring around both circles saying
This is where the white man and the Indian know nothing.

In their book "The Celestine Prophecy" James Redfield and Carol Adrienne suggest that "as we all evolve towards the best completion of our spiritual missions, the technological means of survival will be fully automated as humans focus instead on synchronistic growth. Such growth will move humans into ever-higher energy states, ultimately transforming our bodies into spiritual form and uniting this dimension of existence with the afterlife dimension, ending the cycle of birth and Death."

I look forward Ailbhe to following Raymond Moody's research on shared near death experiences. Some of those extreme, dogmatic, pre-packaged ideas we've met on our journey of enquiry reveal such closed thinking surely the antithesis of Christian philosophy and yet some present day fundamentalists and visionaries continue to hold these barbaric notions with regard to the afterlife, finding them quite compatible with the loving all powerful father called God that they promote. Who'd want to know much less wish to spend eternity with such a monster? There is little or no acceptance of the uncertainty and mystery but this neurotic need for certainty and being absolutely right. Some wise person concluded, "The clinical theist and the clinical atheist are sisters under the skin."

Poetry, being where language reaches its greatest suggestion, avoiding certainty by accepting the mystery remains for me the most appropriate and effective genre with which to approach the Big Question Ailbhe. I find Rainer Maria Rilke's advice apt. "Have patience with everything unresolved in your heart and try to love the questions themselves, as if they were locked rooms or books written in a very foreign language. Don't search for the answers which could not be given to you now because you would not be able to live them. And the point is to live everything live the questions now. Perhaps someday far in the future you will gradually without even noticing it live your way into the answer."

My friend John O'Donohue tells us that "the poem is shaped to enter and inhabit forgotten or not yet discovered alcoves in the reader's heart." I am so grateful to John for the great legacy he has left us, his spiritual insights and his reflective study in his poetry and books and CDs. Perhaps his drawing on the wisdoms of the ancient Celtic thought and imagination in his writings gives his work a more intimate resonance with us due to our Celtic origins. I regret Ailbhe that you (as far as I know) did not have the opportunity to sample his insights on death and the afterlife.

Father Tony Flannery. a well-known Redemptorist priest, writer and preacher suggests that while in the church, "We do well on the ritual, we have a problem with our efforts to explain what might be going on, to shed light on the mystery." Well Father Tony had a somewhat similar experience to myself

Ailbhe, when his 90 year old mother whom he and his sister were attending to lay dying or as Father Tony depicts her situation, "She was in a sense gazing into eternity into that mist that surrounds our death, and trying to lift the veil." Now he says that both he and his sister had agreed to give their dying mother honest answers no matter how awkward her questions might be and to resist the temptation to cover the reality or give simple answers. So when in one of her more lucid moments she posed the question, "Tell me, do you believe in the next life?" and when he responded "I think so," she continued "What will it be like"? As he knew his mother was dying, time was not on her side so her question had a relevance and an immediacy that gave it the urgency he detected in her voice. He delayed his response, sensing her eyes "boring into" him.

"You should know," she said, "after all you are a priest."

Tony replied, "I don't, I believe that it will be good, that it will surpass all our expectations. But beyond that I know nothing."

He says how the long silence that followed from her left him anxiously searching her face for signs of fear and much to his relief he could only find "wonderment."

Then came her response, "It's such a puzzle, someday I must sit down and try to work it all out."

So Tony reflected, "Ninety years in this world and the puzzle remained."

She went into eternity he tells us a few days later, still with that sense of "wonderment," still not knowing what was ahead of her, but as far as he could see without fear and ready to embrace what awaited her as she had embraced life and believed it would embrace her and welcome her. Tony suggests maybe that is as much as any of us can do in the face of death. "Maybe it is enough." Thanks Tony for sharing that personal experience with us. I hope I did it justice.

Because your question came from a perspective of your youth and relative good health Ailbhe, I failed to sense any urgency. I thought you'd have many years and opportunities to probe such big questions so you'll understand if my response seemed superficial and deflective. Down through the ages we've seen thinkers, philosophers, writers, both religious and non-religious reflect on and explore this big question. Socrates openly analysed it for the Greeks.

Did you read Mairtín O Caidhn's humorous "Cré na Cille?" If not you've missed a good laugh.

Father Tony Flannery in his essay "The Promise is Life not Death" published in his book "Fragments of Reality" tells of being on a mission in Lisdoonvara when this gentleman crossed his path and persisted in enlightening him on religious matters and presented him with typed A4 pages with "each instalment getting more lurid than the previous one." The final one "predicting that the large majority over 95% of people were destined for hell." He backed up his arguments using various quotations, most frequently quoted was St. Alphonsus. "Heavenly Head Wreckers" Pat Ingoldsby called these people in one of his poems, anyhow Tony tells how he got the perfect antidote to his "hell promoting gentleman" the next week when he went to the Chekov play adapted by Brian Friel "Uncle Vanga." Aidín, Assumpta and myself attended the Chekov play "The Three Sisters" a while back and found it excellent. Now the play Uncle Vanga is about a dysfunctional family. At the end only Vanga and his niece Sonya remain on stage. Vanga curls up like a ball on the sofa telling Sonya how unhappy he is and asking what can they do now as their whole world has fallen apart. Sonya sits with him putting her arm around his shoulder telling him, "What we must do is endure, keep on living and keep on working and when our time comes to die we will face that too. We will say to God that we have done our best. And a great wave of mercy and compassion will sweep over us, the sky will be like diamonds for us, and we will be at peace. We will look back on our lives, with all the misery and unhappiness and we will smile." That Father Tony says "is a message worth preaching."

The first of the five most common regrets that the palliative care nurse Bronnie Ware documented based on her personal experience of accompanying dying patients was, I wish I'd had the courage to live a life true to myself not the life others expected of me. It gives me great comfort Ailbhe that just like Sonya in that Chekov play

"Uncle Vanga" you too played the hand you were dealt to the best of your ability. Using equine speak, you too completed your course. You were true to yourself as you fully embraced the life you were given and I have no doubt that great wave of mercy and compassion that Sonya spoke of swept over you and that "the stars shine in the sky like diamonds for you" and you are now at home at peace. One of the best analogies I came across on death recently (I'm afraid I can't remember the author) was likening death to "a child running into its mother's arms." We'll leave the last word to the writers, just some lines I came on randomly here and there that resonated with me Ailbhe.

"You would know the secret of death. But how shall you find it unless you seek it in the heart of life? The owl whose night-bound eyes are blind unto the day cannot unveil the mystery of light. If you would indeed behold the spirit of death, open your heart wide unto the body of life. For life and death are one, even as the river and the sea are one. In the depth of your hopes and desires lies your silent knowledge of the beyond, and like seeds dreaming beneath the snow your heart dreams of spring. Trust the dreams, for in them is hidden the gate to eternity. Your fear of death is but the trembling of the shepherd when he stands before the king who's hand is to be laid upon him in honour. Is the shepherd not joyful beneath his trembling, that he shall wear the mark of the king? Yet is he not more mindful of his trembling? For what is it to die but to stand naked in the wind and to melt into the sun? And what is it to cease breathing but to free the breath from its restless tides, that it may rise and expand and seek God unencumbered? Only when you drink from the river of silence shall you indeed sing. And when you have reached the mountain top, then you shall begin to climb. And when the earth shall claim your limbs, then shall you truly dance."
Kahlil Gibran in "The Prophet."

"Eternal life is eternal memory, therefore, it becomes possible to imagine a realm beyond endings where all that has unfolded is not cancelled or lost, but where the spirit-depths of it are already arriving HOME."
John O'Donohue

'Life and death are both verbs. Life is not a noun, neither is death. Life is a process. Death is a process."
OSHO

Yes Ailbhe something unvoiced connects us.
A reality unchanged by time.'

Ailbhe, death is not a final goodbye, but see you later.
Slan Go Fóill Ailbhe (goodbye for now).

Bibliography

I am deeply grateful to the O'Donohue estate, Bantam Press, The Random House Group for their permission allowing me to use poems and extracts from the works of John O'Donohue.

Poems The Blessing of a child entering the World taken from Benedictus published by Bantam Press

Entering Death taken from Benedictus

For a parent on the death of a child taken from Benedictus

November Questions in memory of my uncle the late Pete O'Donohue Taken from Echoes of Memory published by Transworld

Coffin taken from Echoes of Memory

Extracts from Anam Cara, Divine Beauty

Wisdom from the Celtic World published by Bantam Press

My gratitude to Mark Patrick Hederman abbot of Glenstal Abbey Co Limerick for his generosity inspiration and encouragement.

Resources I found Stimulating

Unveiling India by Aness Jung (Penguin Books)

May you be the mother of a hundred Sons
by Elizabeth Bumiller

Justice for my Son
by Vera Duffy with Martin Duffy
Gill & Macmillan

Poems so fresh and so new
Yahoo Pat Ingoldsby
Willow Publications Dublin

Underground Cathedrals
by Mark Patrick Hederman OSB
The Columba Press

Paranormal My Life in pursuit of the Afterlife
by Raymond Moody (Rider)

Going Home
Colm Keane
Capel Island

Anger Sex and Doubt
by Bishop Richard Holloway
SPCK

The God Delusion
by Richard Dawkins
Black Swan

Zoroastrians Their Religious Beliefs and Practices
By Mary Boyce

A Catholic Dictionary
by William E.ADDIS and Thomas Arnold M.A.
fifteenth edition Fifth impression
London Virtue & Co Ltd 1955

Catholicism for Dummies
by Rev-John Trigilio Jr.PHD THD
and Rev Kenneth Brighenti PHD
Wiley Publishing, Inc-

Catechism of the Catholic Church (2006)
Veritas

The Bible

The Everything understanding Islam Book
a complete guide to Muslims beliefs and practices and culture
by Christine Huda Dodge

The True Religion GOD
by Abu Ameenah Bilal Philips

The Quran

The Tibetan Book of Living and Dying
by SOGYAL RINPOCHE (Rider)

The Celestial Prophecy
by James Redfield and Carol ADRIENNE
Bantam Books

Fragments of Reality
by Father Tony Flannery
The Columba Press.

The God instinct The psychology of Souls

Destiny and the meaning of Life
by Jesse Bering
Nicholas Brealey Publishing

Proof of Heaven
by Dr. Eben Alexander
-a neurosurgeon's journey into the afterlife.
Pilatus

Awakening to the Spiril World
The Shamanic Path of Direct Revelation
by Sandra Ingerman and Hank Wesselman
Sounds True

The Prophet
by Kahlil Gibran
Penguin Books

The Art of Living and Dying OSHO
Watkins Publication

Thanks to Nicola and Elaine (Bridge Street Centre) for their typing skills and encouraging comments.

I'm grateful to the Publishers "Original Writing" for their professional guidance.

A sincere thanks to everyone mentioned by name in the book my apologies if I've left anyone out but you'll know who you are. Míle Buiochas "Ar Scáth a chéile a mhaireann na daoine"

Denouement

O God-A cataclysm of terminal ABSENCE.
The house SHOCKED, your chair LISTENING
OUT----but O—NO-----NOUGHT, only a chronic
echoless void in reply. How piteous I barter decease,
then the Gyres ----to WARCRY----to PETITIONS----
then LACHRYMOSE AMEN----Now though still
basking in awe of your marvel I allow this knot
unravel. Though my heart still holds you prism
I abrogate you to HEAVEN
-----------------my heart lamenting-------------------
DEATH-----------the gulf to our UNION
DEATH-----------the gateway to our COMMUNION

Written by Aidín Hannon

Denouement = unravelling the knot
Gyres = handcuffs
Lachrymose = tearfully